Nomenclature of
The Vedas

Nomenclature of
The Vedas

Swamini Atmaprajnananda Saraswati

PRINTWORLD
Publishers of Indian Traditions

Cataloging in Publication Data — DK
[Courtesy: D.K. Agencies (P) Ltd. <docinfo@dkagencies.com>]

Atmaprajnananda Saraswati, Swamini, 1955-
Nomenclature of the Vedas / Swamini Atmaprajnananda Saraswati. — 1st ed.
p. cm.
Includes bibliographical references (p.).
ISBN 13: 9788124606445

1. Vedas — Criticism, interpretation, etc. I. Title.

DDC 294.5921046 23

ISBN 13: 978-81-246-0644-5 ISBN 10: 81-246-0644-7
First published in India in 2012

Published and printed by:
D.K. Printworld (P) Ltd.
Regd. Office : '*Vedaśrī*', F-395, Sudarshan Park
(Metro Station: Ramesh Nagar)
New Delhi – 110 015
Phones : (011) 2545 3975; 2546 6019; *Fax* : (011) 2546 5926
E-mail : indology@dkprintworld.com
Web : www.dkprintworld.com

Dedicated to

Pujya Swami Dayananda Saraswati

who gave me a new lease of life in 1996,
and another lease of life in 2008

Preface

I AM an Advaitin. After studying Advaita Vedānta for eight years in the traditional *guru-śiṣya paramparā* and *gurukula-vāsa*, I was exposed to the Vedas at university level in 2003, while doing my Masters in Sanskrit. This book has evolved out of my own needs. With no access to consummate Vedic scholars, I wanted to gain some insight into the Vedic corpus, its language and literature, the *ṛṣi*s and the *chanda*s, the Vedic deities and religion. I explored a number of books, but did not come across a cogent and easily comprehensible text that would explain the nomenclature of the Vedic corpus required for a basic understanding, without being overtly scholarly. I came to feel that there might be many others, like myself, i.e. university students and general non-Vedic scholars who would appreciate such an attempt. Therefore, I decided to arrange my notes into chapters, so that the basic understanding that I had gained in this endeavour, could be transformed into a book. The interest and effort kept increasing, and the book became more voluminous. The whole book was complete to be published in 2009, when my last laptop crashed. About seventy pages in A4, I had to redo from memory.

There is nothing original in what is contained in the pages that follow — this book is an arrangement of what I have studied during the last few years. It is not possible to acknowledge the debt I owe to several Vedic scholars on the subject, from each of whom I have borrowed something quintessential.

As my research slowly progressed over years, I was faced with two different presentations of the Vedas. One was the traditionalists starting from Veda Vyāsa, followed by Kumārila, Śaṅkara, the latest being Sri Chandrasekharendra Saraswati. They present the Vedas as coeval with the universe and being eternal.

The other group was the Western scholars and historians whose research included other oriental scriptures. There are both advantages and disadvantages in referring to the Western scholars. The Western Vedic scholars have studied various aspects of the Vedic corpus out of their interest in comparative literature, language, religion and culture. The advantage is that their scholarship allows them to relate to the Vedic concepts and terms, and compare them with Avesta, and to provide conceptual clarity and placement with reference to the language, literature, terms, religious practice within a wider context. The disadvantage is that, most of these studies are academic in their presentation, and do not deal with the subject with a sensitivity that is natural to us. Most of the Western scholars place the date of the Vedas between 4000-2500 BCE. These scholars also consider religious texts as mythology, and their followings as sectarian.

Thus, I had to choose between the traditionalists and the Western scholars and arrive at my own understanding. Traditionalists claimed that the Western scholars translate the Vedas for their ulterior motives, while the Western scholars and historians derided the traditionalists as sentimental and sectarian. I have chosen both sometimes.

From the Western scholars I learnt that there are 1,875 *sāmans* in the *Sāmaveda,* out of which 1,504 are from *R̥gveda,* 272 are repetitions, and only 99 of them are independent of *R̥gveda;* and that 20 per cent of the content in *Atharvaveda* is from *R̥gveda* with variations in reading, and that three *ṛcā* in the Āprīsūktam of Vasiṣṭha and Viśvāmitra are identical, and that many *sūktam* of the *Ṛgveda* are available in other Vedas with some changes.

I have attempted to tread carefully the tight rope between the Western and the Indian scholars. While covering some of the areas, I have reserved the details for the endnotes.

There are 29 tables in all (five of which are at the end of relevant chapters depicting the nomenclature of the five Vedas) within the text listing out details, 25 images, and there is a list of Sāyaṇa's total work in Chapter 7. These are besides (19+27=) 46 pages devoted to the listing of 10 *maṇḍala*s of *Ṛgveda*[1] and 20 *kāṇḍa*s of *Atharvaveda*. In the chapter, 'Commentaries on the Vedas', the traditional commentators, the Western translators and the modern commentators are presented chronologically for better understanding. This is again supplemented by a table. I have tried to maintain objectivity in the presentation, while equally respecting the tradition of *śraddhā*. I have presented the objectivity of the Western researchers to present to the readers how they perceive us, our tradition.

I have also furnished elaborate notes on the legend of Śunaḥśepa, birth of Vasiṣṭha, list of *saptarṣis*, Yama-Yamī-Saṁvāda, story of Śyāvāśva becoming a Seer, contribution of Dara Shikoh, the Vrātyas, since I had my own doubts about these legends and when I cleared them, I wanted to share my views with my readers. The 25-pages of glossary are almost a chapter, which again I did not feel like editing, and hope it will be useful to the readers.

I am still on the learning curve with reference to the *Nomenclature of the Vedas*. Anyone attempting to have a glimpse of the Vedas will sympathise with Maharṣi Veda Vyāsa as to why he gave the responsibility of maintaining and propagating the four Vedas to four of his select disciples, after appreciating the limitations of the human mind.

I see a lot of criticism on the internet against the Western

Vedic scholars. However, very little has so far been done by our Indian Vedic scholars regarding translation of the Vedas in any of the Indian languages including English, much less the commentaries on them. We still refer to the Sacred Books of the East, Whitney and Griffith, notwithstanding the fact that we have a treasure-trove of Vedic literature easily available to us, penned by the great scholars, such as Swami Dayananda, S.D. Satavalekar, Sri Aurobindo, Kapali Sastry, Jayadev Sharma, Ramgopal Trivedi, Bhagadevacharya, Durgamohan Bhattacharya, Devi Chand, Satyabrata Sāmaśrami, Romesh Chandra Dutt, Siddheswar Shastri Chitrav, Shriram Sharma, Braj Behari Chaubey and Kunja Bihari Upadhyaya.

I have deliberately refrained from giving too many footnotes to prevent the text from appearing like a research work, although it is one (there are 174 footnotes). I sincerely want the university students of the Vedic Literature, the non-Vedic scholars, and the general readers to use this work and appreciate it. I am also very hopeful that this work would be useful in creating interest among the people at large in the Vedas, the original source of our invaluable literary, philosophical and social culture.

28 January, 2012 **Atmaprajnananda Saraswati**
Vasanta Pañcamī

1. This part is heavily drawn from R.L. Kashyap's Book on *Ṛgveda*.

Acknowledgements

My grateful thanks to,

- Br. Arvind Pare of Swami Dayananda Library, Rishikesh, and Br. Venkatesh of Arsha Vidya Gurukulam, Anaikatti Library, for providing me the freedom to use these two invaluable libraries,
- Dr. Martha Doherty, Swami Parabrahmananda Saraswati, Swami Shivabrahmananda Saraswati, and Smt. Nilofer Giri for offering enormous encouragement and appreciation for the effort,
- Sri Sanjay Rout for providing the Diacritical Software,
- Sri Bibhuti Mohapatra, for his endless support and assistance,
- Sri Akshay Kumar for immediately providing a new laptop in September 2009, when two of my laptops crashed one after the other within fifteen days, erasing all my work of ten years,
- Smt. Payal Parija, for her consistent support during my years of studies and research,
- All the traditional and Western commentators, and Vedic scholars and researchers, on whose vast work, this tiny attempt stands.

My special gratitude to Sri Susheel Kumar Mittal, Director, D.K. Printworld, for accepting the manuscript and agreeing to publish it. Truly, by doing so, he has singlehandedly reciprocated on behalf of all those (individuals and the community) for whom I have done whatever I could.

My reverential gratitude to Vedamātā, who continues to reveal herself to me as stated in *R̥V* X.71.4.

Lastly, my *bhūmiṣṭha praṇām*s to Devī Saraswatī for the flashes of ideas and inspiration that kept coming, and keep coming.

28 January, 2012 **Atmaprajnananda Saraswati**
Vasanta Pañcamī

Note on Transliteration

In this book, Devanāgarī characters are transliterated according to the scheme adopted by the international Congress of Orientalists at Athens in 1912, and since then generally acknowledged to be the only rational and satisfactory one. In it, the inconsistency, irregularity and redundancy of English spelling are ruled out. The letters f, q, w, x and z are not called to use. One fixed value is given to each letter. Hence, a, e, i and g always represent अ, ए, इ, and ग respectively, and never ए, इ, ऐ and ज् or other values which they have in English. The letters t and d are always used for त् and द् only. One tialde (˜), one accent, four macrons (¯) and 10 dots (2 above, 8 below) are used to represent adequately and correctly all Sanskrit letters. The letter c alone represents च्. Since the natural function of h will be to make the aghoṣa into ghoṣa (e.g. kh, ch, ṭh, th, ph, gh, jh, ḍh, dh, bh), it would be an anomaly for a scientific scheme to use it in combinations like ch and sh for giving च् and ष् values; hence ch here is छ and sh स् ह्. The vowel ऋ is represented bt r̥ because ri is legitimate for रि only, is out of place, and the singular r̥ is an altogether objectionable distortion. The tialde (˜) over n represents ञ् ñ. Accent mark over s gives श् ś; dots above m and n give anusvāra. (ं), ṁ and ङ्, ṅ, respectively. Dots below h and r give visarga (:) ḥ, and ॠ r̥, respectively. Dots below s, n, t and d give their corresponding cerebrals ष्, ण्, ट्, and ड्, ṣ, ṇ, ṭ and ḍ; and macrons (¯) over a, i, u and r give आ, ई, ऊ, and ॠ ā, ī, ū, r̥̄ respectively. Macrons (¯) are not used to lengthen the quantity of e and o, because they always have the long quantity in Sanskrit. Sanskrit words are capitalised only where special distinctiveness is called for, as in the opening of a sentence, title of books, etc. The scheme of transliteration in full is as follows:

अ a,	आ ā,
इ i,	ई ī,
उ u,	ऊ ū,
ऋ r̥,	ॠ ṝ,
ए e,	ओ o,
ऐ ai,	औ ou,
ं ṁ,	: ḥ,
क् k,	ख् kh,
ग् g,	घ् gh,
ङ् ṅ,	च् c,
छ् ch,	ज् j,
झ् jh,	ञ् ñ,
ट् ṭ,	ठ् ṭh,
ड् ḍ,	ढ् ḍh,
ण् ṇ,	त् t,
थ् th,	द् d,
ध् dh,	न् n,
प् p,	फ् ph,
ब् b,	भ् bh,
म् m,	य् y,
र् r,	ल् l,
व् v,	श् ś,
ष् ṣ,	स् s,
ह् h.	

Contents

CHAPTER 2: ṚGVEDA

CHAPTER 5 : SĀMAVEDA

CHAPTER 6 : ATHARVAVEDA

CHAPTER 7 : COMMENTARIES ON THE VEDAS

Illustrations

Map & Chart

Tables

Images

Abbreviations

Anu.anu.	*Anuvakānukramaṇī of Śaunaka*
Aṣ.	*Aṣṭādhyāyī*
AV	*Atharvaveda*
Bṛ.De.	*Bṛhaddevatā*
Bṛ.Up.	*Bṛhadāraṇyaka Upaniṣad*
Bh.Gī	*Bhagavad-Gītā*
Br.Sū.	*Brahmasūtra*
BSSB	*Brahmasūtra Śāṅkara Bhāṣya*
Ca.Vy.	*Caraṇavyūha*
Ch.Up.	*Chāndogya Upaniṣad*
Ga.Dh.	*Gautama Dharmasūtra*
Go.Br.	*Gopatha-Brāhmaṇa*
Ja.Br.	*Jaiminīya-Brāhmaṇa*
Ja.Sū.	*Jaiminisūtra*
KYV	*Kṛṣṇa-Yajurveda*
KYS	*Kṛṣṇa-Yajurveda-Saṁhitā*
Ma.Bh.	*Mahābhāṣya*
Ma.Bh.Pa.Ah.	*Mahābhāṣya-Paspaśāhnikam*
Ma.Bhā.	*Mahābhārata*
Ma.Sm.	*Manusmṛti*
Mah. Up.	*Mahānārāyaṇa Upaniṣad*

Muk.Up.	*Muktikā Upaniṣad*
Muṇ.Up.	*Muṇḍaka Upaniṣad*
Ni.	*Niruktam*
Ny.Sū.	*Nyāya-Sūtra*
Pū.Mī.Sū.	*Pūrva Mīmāṁsā Sūtra*
R̥VBB	*R̥gveda-Bhāṣya-Bhūmikā*
R̥V.Bh.	*R̥gveda-Bhāṣyam*
R̥VS	*R̥gveda-Saṁhitā*
R̥VS.Bh.	*R̥gveda-Sāyaṇa-Bhāṣyam*
SV	*Sāmaveda*
Śā. Bhā.	*Śābara-Bhāṣyam*
Sā.Bh.	*Sāyaṇa-Bhāṣyam*
Śrī.Bhā.	*Śrī Bhāṣyam*
Śa.Br.	*Śatapatha-Brāhmaṇa*
ŚYV	*Śukla-Yajurveda*
ŚYV.Mā.Saṁ.	*Śukla-Yajurveda-Mādhyandina-Saṁhitā*
Tai.Ār.	*Taittirīya-Āraṇyaka*
Tai.Br.	*Taittirīya-Brāhmaṇa*
Tai.Br.Bh.	*Taittirīya-Brāhmaṇa-Bhāṣyam*
Tai.Saṁ.	*Taittirīya-Saṁhitā*
Ve.Sā.	*Vedāntasāra*
Vi.Pu.	*Viṣṇu Purāṇa*
YV	*Yajurveda*

1

Nomenclature of the Vedas

Introduction

THE Vedas are the first literary documents in the history of humankind that are still in existence. They transcend far beyond their identity as holy scriptures. The *Ṛgveda*, the oldest among the four Vedas, is the fountainhead of the Āryan culture. This valuable treasure of the ancient world has been preserved in the form of manuscripts in India, and handed down over centuries from generation to generation.

The Vedas are also the primary source of Hindu *dharma*. According to the *Gautama-Dharmasūtra*, 'The Veda is the source of *dharma* and the tradition and practices of those who know it.'[1] It contains hymns, incantations, and rituals from ancient India. The Sanskrit word *veda* is derived from the root √*vid* – *jñāne* — meaning 'to know'. Etymologically, the word *veda* means 'knowledge', but it has come to mean 'revealed and sacred knowledge'. According to Manu, the Vedas are the source of *dharma*.[2]

yaḥ kaścit kasyacit dharmo manunā parikīrtitaḥ ।
sa sarvo'bhihito vede sarvajñānamayo hi saḥ ॥

Veda does not denote any one single literary work, it is rather a large extent of literature that came into being in course of time, and was transmitted by oral tradition from generation

1. *vedo dharmamūlaṁ, tadvidāṁ ca smṛtiśīle* — *Ga.Dh.* I.1.2.

2. *Ma.Sm.* II.7.

to generation. Thus, the appellate Śruti was ascribed to the Vedas. Manu has further said:

śrutistu vedo vijñeyo dharmaśāstraṁ tu vai smṛtiḥ ।
te sarvārtheṣvamīmāṁsye tābhyāṁ dharmo hi nirvabhau ॥[3]

Definition of the Vedas

pratyakṣeṇa-anumityā vā yastūpāyo na budhyate ।
enaṁ vidanti vedena tasmād vedasya vedatā ॥[4] —Sāyaṇācārya

Sāyaṇācārya (CE 1315-1387) the most celebrated commentator on Vedic texts, has defined the Vedas as, *iṣṭaprāptyaniṣṭa-parihārayor-alaukikam-upāyaṁ yo grantho vedayati sa vedaḥ*,[5] meaning, 'that which contains the esoteric ways to achieve the desired objects, and to avoid the undesired, is called the Veda'. Thus, Veda is a source of knowledge of esoteric measure, which cannot be known through any other *pramāṇa*, i.e. *pratyakṣya* or *anumāna*.

Apauruṣeyatvam of the Vedas

Apauruṣeyatvam is a central concept in the Mīmāṁsā and Vedānta Schools. Orthodox Indian thoughts maintain that the Vedas are revealed literature, i.e. they are not authored by any human being. Thus, the Vedas are said to be impersonal (*apauruṣeya*), and hence unquestionable. They are referred to as Śruti (that which is heard), and is accepted to be what was envisioned by the Vedic seers (*ṛṣis*).

Pūrva-Mīmāṁsā treats the Veda as a Dharmaśāstra, since its first *sūtra* says, *athāto dharma-jijñāsā*. Jaimini's *Pū.Mī.Sū.* I.1.5 states that 'words were self-sufficient in authority'.

The Mīmāṁsā explanation is like this — since the Veda deals with *dharma*, and *dharma* is outside the field of sense-

3. *Ma.Sm.* II.10.
4. *ṚVBB.*
5. *Tai.Br.Bh.*

experience/inference, so any text that deals with *dharma* will necessarily have to deal with objects outside the range of sense-experience/inference. Since all human experience lies solely within the range of senses, any person can speak of objects lying within his/her own field of sense-experience only. If a person claims to have composed a text that deals with *dharma*, it is highly suspect, as it will undoubtedly contain certain errors in the discussion of *dharma*. The primary way to ensure that the text is devoid of any error regarding *dharma* is to ensure that it is not a product of human authorship. Thus, the Mīmāṁsakas claim that the Veda is not a human product at all, so this secures the Veda against all objections concerning knowledge of *dharma*. Since there is no means of knowing *dharma* other than an unauthored text that deals with *dharma*, the Veda reigns supreme in all dhārmic matters.

It is to be understood that Jaimini's *Pū.Mī.Sū.* does not prove the *apauruṣeyatvam* — the 'unauthoredness' of the Veda, instead, it is a claim of the Mīmāṁsakas. Since it cannot be proved that the Vedas are authored, the assumption remains that the Veda is an unauthored text.

I found a small article titled 'The Vedas and the Genetic Fallacy' recently, by Arvind Sharma of McGill University. The same is reproduced below *in toto*,

> The Vedas, according to the Hindu tradition as represented by the philosophical schools of Mīmāṁsā and Vedānta as *apauruṣeya* and *nitya* — that is to say, 'the Veda is not a human production, because no man is mentioned as its author. Not only is the Veda not a human production; it is not also a composition of god. There is no need to postulate a god as the author of the Veda, for the Veda is eternal.'[6]

6. T.M.P. Mahadevan, *Outlines of Hinduism* (Bombay: Chetana Limited, 1971, pp. 132-33; M. Hiriyanna, *Essentials of Indian Philosophy* (London: George Allen & Unwin, 1948), pp. 139-40.

> Modern Hindus are somewhat embarrassed by this doctrine, as it seems a bit of stretch.[7]
>
> It is however possible to reassess this doctrine as a Hindu version of rejection of the genetic fallacy. What is the genetic fallacy? It is the fallacy involved in claiming that you can determine the truth of a statement. But the truth of a statement really stands on its own, irrespective of the author. Even if a liar tells us that 'It is raining'; the truth of the statement has to be determined by empirically determining whether it is raining or not; and not by appealing to the trustworthiness, or otherwise of the speaker. The character of the speaker affects the credibility of the statement, not the truth. In the sense, authorship is irrelevant when it comes to assessing the true value of a statement. By claiming that the Vedas have no author, the Mīmāṁsā and Vedānta[8] tradition could be seen as rejecting the genetic fallacy with a vengeance.

Kumārila Bhaṭṭa is credited with the logical formulation of the Mīmāṁsic belief that the Vedas are unauthored (*apauruṣeya*). His defence in particular against the medieval Buddhist position on Vedic rituals, is noteworthy. Every extant school held some scripture to be correct. In order to show that the Vedas were the only correct scriptures, Kumārila ingeniously said that 'the absence of an author (*apauruṣeya*) would safeguard the Vedas against all reproach'. There was 'no way to prove any of the contents of Buddhist scriptures directly as wrong in spirit — unless one challenges the legitimacy and eternal nature of the scripture itself'. It is well known that the Pāli canon was composed after the Buddha's *parinirvāṇa*. Further, even if they were the Buddha's words, they were not eternal or unauthored like the Vedas. Some believe that

---

7. T.M.P. Mahadevan, *Outlines of Hinduism*, p. 140. Also see G.C. Pande, *ekam sad bahudhā vadanti* (Varanasi: Sampurnananda Sanskrit University), p. 40.
8. Śaṅkara's view about *apauruṣeyatvam* and *nityatvam* is given in the next paragraph.

this contributed to the decline of Buddhism in India. Record of this is found from Yi Jing's travelogue.

Kumārila's work strongly influenced other schools of Indian philosophy, most notably Advaita Vedānta, especially since Vedānta adopts Pūrva-Mīmāṁsā's epistemological arguments almost *verbatim*, with the exception that while Mīmāṁsā considers the Upaniṣads subservient to the Vedas, the Vedānta School does not think so.

Apauruṣeyatvam of the Vedas is stated in the Vedas itself in *R̥V* X.90.9[9] (Puruṣa-sūktam), which is repeated in *ŚYV* XXXI.7 (Puruṣa-sūktam), *AV* X.7.20[10] (Sarvādhāra-varṇana-sūktam).

VIEW OF VYĀSA, THE UTTARA-MĪMĀṀSĀKĀRA

The earliest reference is by Uttara-Mīmāṁsākāra Bādarāyaṇa Vyāsa who has declared the Vedas to be *apauruṣeya* in his *sūtra śāstrayonitvāt,*[11] which is deciphered as *śāstrasya yoniḥ*[12] meaning — *Brahman* is the source of the *śāstra,* i.e. the Vedas, hence it is *apauruṣeya.*[13]

VIEW OF ŚAṄKARA

Śaṅkara attributes the authorship of the Vedas to omniscient *Īśvara* in his *BSSB*, while commenting on the same *sūtra, Br.Sū.* I.1.3. Elsewhere, he redefines the word *apauruṣeya* to make it signify not that the Veda has no author and is timeless; but that it is produced or, more properly, resuscitated at the beginning of each *kalpa*, by one that cannot interfere either

---

9. *tasmād-yajñāt sarvahutaḥ, r̥caḥ sāmāni jajñire* |
   chandāṁsi jajñire tasmāt, yajus-tasmād-ajāyata || — *R̥V* X.90.9.
10. *yasmād-r̥co apātakṣan, yajur-yasmād apākaṣan* |
   sāmāni yasya lomāni, atharvāṅgiraso mukham. . . || — *AV* X.7.20.
11. *Br.Sū.* I.1.3.
12. *ṣaṣṭhi tatpuruṣaḥ,* hence *apauruṣeya.*
13. The other meaning is *śāstra yoni yasya* (*bahuvrīhi*) meaning, through which (*śāstra*), it (*Brahman*) can be known.

with its content or with the order of its words. In the case of works like the *Raghuvaṁśa,* the author composes it just as he likes. On the other hand, in case of the Vedas, the first promulgator of the Veda in every cycle who is *Īśvara,* repeats it anew, but precisely as it was in the other cycles (*pravāha-nityam*). That is, the Veda is self-existent in this view also; only it is not the self-same Veda that always is, but a series of what may be described as re-issues of a timeless (*pravāha-nityam*) edition which goes back to the beginningless time. This view is not different in substance from the Mīmāṁsā view, excepting that it finds a place for *Īśvara* in the doctrine. (Mīmāṁsā does not accept *Īśvara*).

Nityatvam or Eternity of the Vedas

The subject of *nityatvam* of the Vedas is accepted by all the *āstika* (Pūrva-Mīmāṁsā,[14] Uttara-Mīmāṁsā,[15] Sāṁkhya,[16] Vaiśeṣika,[17] and Nyāya[18]) schools. Jaimini has established the eternity of the Vedas by his six *sūtra*s starting with — *nityastu syād-darśanasya parārthatvāt.*[19] The Mīmāṁsā School asserts that since the Vedas are composed of words (*śabda*), and the words are composed of phonemes, the phonemes being eternal, the Vedas are also eternal. To this, if asked whether all words and sentences are eternal, the Mīmāṁsakas reply that the rules behind the combination of phonemes are fixed and pre-determined for the Vedas, unlike other words and sentences. Kumārila's establishes his arguments logically as under,

> Ontology of words → Epistemology of sentences → Unauthoredness of the Veda.

14. *Ja.Sū.* I.1.5.
15. *Br.Sū.* I.1.3.
16. *Sāṁkhya* II.58-60.
17. *Vaiśeṣika* II.2.21-37.
18. *Nyāya* I.1.7.54-57 & II.2.13-17.
19. *Ja.Sū.* I.1.18.

The Vedānta School accepts this line of argument. This is evident in *Brahmasūtra* I.3.29 – *ata eva ca nityatvam*. The Nyāya School holds, *anādi-nidhana nityā vāgutsṛṣṭa svayaṁbhuvā, ado vedamayī divyā yataḥ sarvā pravṛttayaḥ.*

Apauruṣeyatvam directly implies flawlessness of the Veda, but *nityatvam* does so indirectly and through *apauruṣeyatvam.*

An argument is adduced by Yāska in this context. He argues that the knowledge residing in human beings being impermanent,[20] the *mantra* in the Vedas is justified in giving directions about ritualistic action. This is tantamount to the statement that the Veda as the repository of eternal knowledge consists of eternal words, and is necessary for human guidance.

The Subject Matter of the Vedas

Unknown End	Known Means (Charity), Unknown End (Heaven)	Unknown Means (*Somayāga*), Unknown End (Heaven)
Known End	Known Means, Known End (not the area of Veda, it's the area of Science)	Unknown Means (*Putra-kāmeṣṭi, Kārīri*), Known End (Child, Rains)
	Known Means	**Unknown Means**

Swami Dayananda Saraswati (b.1930-) founder of Ārsha Vidyā tradition gives the above model in explaining the subject matter of the Veda.

(i) **Unknown means, known end** — The Veda contains *putra-kāmeṣṭi,* which is otherwise unknown, and the result is the birth of a child(ren), which is known/ visible. *Putra-kāmeṣṭi* is a very expensive ritual, which only a king or a very rich man can perform. Perhaps the Veda designed it as such.

20. *puruṣavidyā-anityatvāt karmasampattir-mantro-vede* || — *Ni.* I.1.3.

It also tells about the know-how of *kārīri*, that brings about rains, which is visible. *Kārīri* unlike *putra-kāmeṣṭi* is an inexpensive ritual. It is performed even now, and it works.

(ii) **Known means, unknown end** — The Veda tells about *pūrta-karmas*[21] that will lead a person to heaven hereafter. Here the charitable action is known, however the promise of heaven is unknown (heaven is a *śrutānta*, not *dṛṣṭānta*).

(iii) **Unknown means, unknown end** — The Veda tells about various *somayāga*/s that will result in going to heaven and better births hereafter. Here the know-how of *somayāga* is unknown except through the Veda, and heaven or better life hereafter is also unknown (It is a matter of *śraddhā*, at the best).

(iv) **Known means, known end** — This is not the area/ subject-matter of the Veda; it is the area within which science operates. Hence, people's frantic attempt to prove the Veda as scientific, is their lack of understanding.

The Vedas as Pramāṇa

Various Indian philosophical systems have taken different positions on the Vedas as authority — *pramāṇa*. Philosophical systems that accept the Vedas are known as *āstika* or orthodox schools; these include Nyāya, Vaiśeṣika, Sāṁkhya, Yoga, Pūrva-Mīmāṁsā and Uttara-Mīmāṁsā. The term *āstika* or *nāstika* here is not based on acceptance or non-acceptance of god. It is based on whether the school accepts the Vedas as *pramāṇa* or not. Thus, of these six systems, although Sāṁkhya[22]

21. Altruistic deeds, acts of outreaching activities.

22. In Sāṁkhya's 25-principle model of *Sṛṣṭitattva*, *Īśvara* is not there.

and Pūrva-Mīmāṁsā[23] do not accept the existence of *Īśvara*, nevertheless, they are considered as *āstika* systems.

In fact, the systems that are directly based upon the Vedas are Pūrva-Mīmāṁsā and Uttara-Mīmāṁsā. These two schools accept the Vedas as *svataḥ-pramāṇa*[24] (self-evident means of knowledge). The other four schools (Nyāya, Vaiśeṣika, Sāṁkhya, Yoga) are not directly based on the Vedas, but do accept its testimony, and try to show how their systems are harmonious with the Vedas.

The philosophical systems that do not accept the authority of the Vedas are — Buddhism, Jainism, the Cārvākas[25] (Cāruvākas). They are termed *nāstika* or heterodox schools.

Interestingly, many non-brāhmaṇa Hindus in south India do not accept the authority of the Vedas. Certain south Indian brāhmaṇa communities such as the Iyengars consider *Tamil Divya Prabandham* or the writings of the twelve Āḷvār saints as equivalent to the Vedas. In most Iyengar temples in the southern India, the *Divya Prabandham* is recited daily along with the traditional Vedic chanting.

There are many stories in the Vedic literature regarding the vastness of the Vedas. One such story in the *Taittirīya Brāhmaṇa* of *Kṛṣṇa-Yajurveda* goes thus — Sage Bharadvāja devoted his entire life to the study of the Vedas, but could not finish it. So he prayed to Brahmā to extend his life for another 100 years for the pursuit and completion of the Vedic studies. Brahmā granted his desired boon. The sage engrossed himself once again in the studies, but the end of the studies was nowhere in sight. Thereupon a spontaneous utterance

23. Pūrva-Mīmāṁsā contends that performance of *karma* (rituals) creates its result, there is no need or scope of intervention by an external principle (*Īśvara*).
24. Although each of the six *pramāṇas* are *svataḥ-pramāṇa*, the expression is used only for *śruti-pramāṇa*.
25. A movement that existed between 600 BCE–CE 1400.

came from the heart of Sage Bharadvāja, *anantā vai vedāḥ* meaning, 'Infinite indeed are the Vedas'. This story reaffirms the fact that the Vedas are not confined to some particular text; rather it is a vast literature.

Compilation of the Vedas

According to the *Viṣṇu Purāṇa,* the Vedas, when revealed to the seers, comprised 100,000 verses, and had four divisions.[26] With the passage of time, these divisions got mixed up, and many portions of the Vedas fell into obscurity. Therefore, in the beginning of Dvāpara-Yuga, Kr̥ṣṇa Dvaipāyana resuscitated the Vedic study, and classified the work into four Saṁhitās and gave them to four seers as follows — *R̥gveda* to Paila, *Yajurveda* to Vaiśampāyana, *Sāmaveda* to Jaimini, and *Atharvaveda* to Sumantu. As he classified the Vedas, he became renowned by the name Veda Vyāsa, i.e. the classifier of the Vedas.

Maharṣi Veda Vyāsa

Modern scholars consider that the Vedic corpus was compiled over a millennium, and was arranged around 500 BCE in four great compilations.[27]

Without getting into any debate, the credit of bringing out the Vedas to the educated masses worldwide indeed goes to the Western scholars. Western scholarship along with many Indian *puṇḍit*s opened up the Vedas not only for Westerners, but also for the Indians. Today Vedic Research is gaining importance although still a neglected branch of Indology.

26. *ādau veda-catuṣpādaḥ śatasāhasra sammitaḥ* |
tato daśaguṇa kr̥tsno yajñaā sarvakāmadhuk || — *Viṣṇu Purāṇa* III.4

27. See 'Written form of the Vedas' in Chapter 7 of this text.

Comparative Study of the Four Vedas

Of the four Vedas, the *R̥gveda* is a metrical work, containing only *mantras* — verses, composed mostly in simple metres of three or four lines of eight (*anuṣṭubh*), eleven (*triṣṭubh*) and twelve (*jagatī*) syllables. There are many complicated metres also. The principles of classical Sanskrit metres do not apply to the Vedic metres in many cases.

The *Yajurveda* is essentially a prose work, its occasional metrical passages being stanzas quoted from the *R̥gveda*, often with variations in reading. For example, the R̥gvedic passage — *dyumnaṁ citraśravastamam* (*R̥V* III.59.6) becomes in the *Yajurveda*: *satyaṁ citraśravastamam* (*YV* III.4.2.5). In size, the *Śukla-Yajurveda* (2,085 *mantras*) is about 1/5th of the *R̥gveda* (10,552 *mantras*). *Kr̥ṣṇa-Yajurveda* has 700 hymns from *R̥gveda Saṁhitā*. Sacrificial *mantras* and prayers are interspersed with explanatory passages in the *Kr̥ṣṇa-Yajurveda* (that is why the title *Kr̥ṣṇa* — mixed up), while the *Śukla-Yajurveda* contains only sacrificial *mantras* (hence the title *Śukla*).

The *Sāmaveda* (1,875 *sāmans*) is less than 1/5th the size of the *R̥gveda* (10,552 *mantras*), with a considerable part borrowed from it. It is meant to be sung, not chanted. There are 1,875 (1504+272+99) *sāmans* in the *Sāmaveda* (*Rāṇāyanīya-Śākhā*), out of which 1,504 are from *R̥gveda*, 272 are repetitions, and only 99 of them are independent of *R̥gveda*.

When we come to *Atharvaveda* the subject matter is different. While in the *R̥gveda* the greater portion of *mantras* is of use in sacrifices, and in the *Yajurveda* and the *Sāmaveda* the entire purpose is sacrificial, the *Atharvaveda* has practically no connection with sacrifices, except in its last portions. It is also mainly a metrical work, though the second half contains some passages in prose. In this Veda, we meet with the magical charms and spells to drive away diseases, to injure the enemy, to bring prosperity and long life to the king, to achieve domestic harmony and peace, and for other similar purposes.

In size, it (5,977 *mantras*) is around 56 per cent the size of the *Ṛgveda* (10,552 *mantras*). About a fifth (20 per cent) of its material is from the *Ṛgveda,* with variations in reading.

Division of the Vedas: Karma-Kāṇḍa and Jñāna-Kāṇḍa

The Vedic literature, as stated before, comprises *Ṛgveda, Yajurveda, Sāmaveda* and *Atharvaveda*. Each of these again has four divisions, viz. the Saṁhitās, the Brāhmaṇas, the Āraṇyakas and the Upaniṣads. According to Vedic etymologist Yāska, there are only two divisions of the Vedas, i.e. the Saṁhitās and the Brāhmaṇas (the Āraṇyakas forming only a part of the Brāhmaṇas). Āpastamba, one of the most renowned lawgivers of ancient India, also holds the same view as *mantra-brāhmaṇayor-veda-nāmadheyam*. The Upaniṣads are mostly different chapters of the Āraṇyakas, although some Upaniṣads are in the Brāhmaṇa[28] portions, and one Upaniṣad in the Saṁhitā.[29]

Based on the subject matter (*viṣaya*), the purpose (*prayojanam*), and eligibility of the student (*adhikārī*), the Vedic corpus is divided into two parts called *karma-kāṇḍa* and *jñāna-kāṇḍa*. Two distinct and different[30] philosophical systems developed out of this division — Pūrva-Mīmāṁsā on the *karma-kāṇḍa* and Uttara-Mīmāṁsā on the *jñāna-kāṇḍa*. Sage Jaimini wrote an analytical text on the *karma-kāṇḍa* portion of the Vedas

---

28. *Praśna, Muṇḍaka, Māṇḍūkya* Upaniṣads belong to *Gopatha Brāhmaṇa* of the Paippalāda-Śākhā of the *Atharvaveda.*
29. *Īśāvāsyopaniṣad* is the 40th Chapter of the *ŚYV Saṁhitā.*
30. By stating *āmnāyasya kriyārthatvāt, ānarthakyam atad-arthānām,* = *āmnāyasya* (*vedasya*) *kriyārthatvāt* (being committed to *kriyā*-actions, rituals) *ānarthakyam* (*aprayojanam* = meaningless, *niṣphalam* = useless) *a-tad-arthānām* (that which does not tell anything about the do's and dont's). *Ja. Sū.* I.2.1 Jaimini dismissed the Upaniṣad portion of the Vedas.

named *Pūrvamīmāṁsā-Sūtra* or *Jaimini-Sūtra*. Subsequently,[31] Bādarāyaṇa, Vyāsa wrote *Brahma-Sūtra*, also known as *Uttaramīmāṁsā-Sūtra*. The subject of *karma-kāṇḍa* is performance of rituals (obligatory as well as optional). The *jñāna-kāṇḍa* presents the reality of *Īśvara*, the *jīva*, the *jagat*, and the equation between them. This division is rather loose, since many Upaniṣads are placed in the Saṁhitā and Brāhmaṇa portions, as stated earlier.

Division of the Vedas: Saṁhitās, Brāhmaṇas, Āraṇyakas and Upaniṣads

SAṀHITĀS

The Saṁhitās (collection) are collection of sacred hymns (*sūktas*) in different metres[32] and are mostly addressed to various deities. As the Saṁhitās are predominantly in verse or metres, they are also known as *chandas*. There are four Saṁhitās, viz. *Ṛgveda Saṁhitā*, *Yajurveda Saṁhitā*, *Sāmaveda Saṁhitā* and *Atharvaveda Saṁhitā*, each of which is again available in several recensions (*śākhās*).

Ṛgveda contains hymns for invoking various deities. *Yajus* means sacrificial formulae, and *Yajurveda* consists of about 2,000 formulae (*ŚYV* 2,086 in exact) in prose for varied rituals. When ritualistic practice developed, people wanted to sing rather than just recite the hymns. This was the origin of *Sāmaveda*. All but 99 of *Sāmaveda*'s[33] 1,875 verses are borrowed from *Ṛgveda*. *Atharvaveda* contains charms and spells chanted to avert calamities, and to destroy the enemies. There are around 6,000

---

31. Jaimini has been referred in the *Brahma-Sūtra* 11 times (I.2.28, I.2.31, I.3.31, I.4.18, III.2.40, III.4.2, III.4.18, III.4.40, IV.3.12, IV.4.5, IV.4.11).
32. *Gāyatrī, Bṛhatī, Jagatī, Anuṣṭubh,* etc.
33. Rāṇāyanīya-Śākhā.

(5,977 in exact) formulae in *Atharvaveda,*[34] mostly spells against diseases, enemies and evil spirits.

Various Śākhās of the Saṁhitās

Based on various authorities who expounded the Vedic *mantra*s through the oral tradition, there was a large number of Vedic recensions (*śākhā*s), of which only a few are now extant. In each of the four Vedas, there are different recensions — *pāṭha*s and *pāṭhabheda*s or *pāṭhāntaras*. Each *pāṭhāntara,* or each version is called a *śākhā* or recension. The various *śākhā*s are the branches of the Vedic tree. The branches belong to one of the four Vedas — *R̥k, Yajus, Sāma* and *Atharva.*

Each *śākhā* consists of the Saṁhitā, the Brāhmaṇa, and Āraṇyaka. There may be more *sūkta*s in some *pāṭha*s than in others. There may also be differences in the order of the *mantra*s. When one speaks of *veda-adhyayana,* it refers to Saṁhitā only. One may bring out the Saṁhitā of *R̥gveda* and still call it *R̥gveda.* The Saṁhitā is indeed the very basis of a *śākhā,* its life-breath. The word *saṁhitā* means 'systematised and collected together'. Kr̥ṣṇa Dvaipāyana divided the corpus of Vedas into four, and subdivided them into *śākhā*s.

Number of Śākhās

There are differences of opinion as regards the number of the *śākhā*s.

i. 1,180 — The *Viṣṇu Purāṇa* mentions the number of *śākhā*s to be 1,180, out of which, the *Sāmaveda* had the largest number of *śākhā*s, i.e. 1,000. In *R̥gveda* there were 21, in the *Yajus* 109 (*Śukla-Yajurveda* 15, and *Kr̥ṣṇa-Yajurveda* 94), and in the *Atharvaveda* 50.

ii. 1,133 — The enumeration of recensions varies in *Caraṇavyūha,* an index text of the Vedas authored by

34. Śaunaka-Śākhā.

Sage Śaunaka. As per *Caraṇavyūha* there were 1,133 *śākhās* — *Ṛgveda* 21, *Yajurveda* 101 (*Śukla-Yajurveda* 15, and *Kṛṣṇa-Yajurveda* 86), *Sāmaveda* 1,000, and *Atharvaveda* 11.

iii. 1,131 — Patañjali, the great commentator had mentioned 21 recensions of *Ṛgveda*, 101 recensions of *Yajurveda* (*Śukla-Yajurveda* 15, and *Kṛṣṇa-Yajurveda* 86), 1,000 recensions of *Sāmaveda*, and 9 recensions of the *Atharvaveda* as follows:

catvāro vedāḥ sāṅgā-sarahasyā bahudhā bhinnāḥ |
ekaśatam-adhvaryu-śākhāḥ, sahasravartmā sāmavedaḥ ||
ekaviṁśatidhā bāhvṛcyaṁ, navadhātharvaṇo vedaḥ |[35]

However, during these 5,000 years and more, many *śākhās* have been lost. Out of the 1,131 *śākhās*, only 13 *śākhās* (*ṚV* - 2, + *ŚYV* - 2, + *KYV* - 4, + *SV* - 3, + *AV* - 2) are preserved in form, content and purity (see list in this chapter). As per a survey made in 1980, it was estimated that in India and Nepal, there are only 1,750 Vedic *puṇḍit*s and about 650 *vidyārthī*s learning the Vedas through *adhyayana*.

The *Ṛgveda*, the oldest one, although has more number of *mantras*, it has less number of recensions developed, compared to *Yajus* and *Sāma*. The reason attributed to this is, *Ṛgveda* is a reservoir of laudatory *mantra*s dedicated to various Vedic deities. *Mantra*s meant for rituals in *Yajurveda* had more probability of branching out to different recensions (101) than the laudatory *mantra*s of *Ṛgveda*. Similarly, singing style being still more different, *Sāmaveda* branched out to as vast as a 1,000(-recorded) recensions.

Of the 21 *śākhās* of *Ṛgveda*, until recently only one *Śākhā* was extant — the Śākala-Śākhā, or the Aitareya-Śākhā, since the *Aitareya Upaniṣad* occurs in it. Āśvalāyana-Śākhā has since been revived and printed and is available. References of few

35. *Ma.Bh.-Paspaśāhnikam.*

other recensions are available, namely Bāṣkala (available in fragments), Sāṁkhāyana (or Sāṁkhyāyana), and Māṇḍūkāyana from their available Brāhmaṇa, Āraṇyaka and/or Śrauta-Sūtras. As per some reports Sāṁkhāyana-Śākhā is still available.

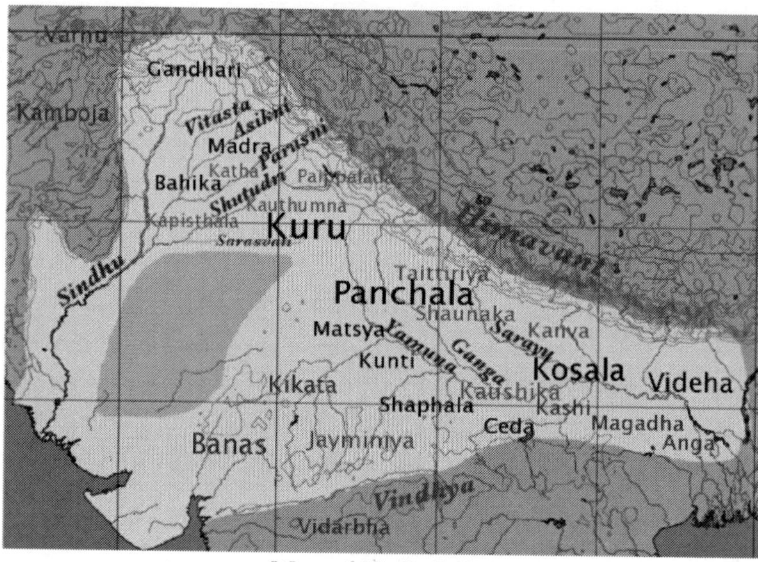

Map of Vedic India

Of the 15 *śākhās* of *Śukla-Yajurveda*, only two are extant — Kāṇva-Śākhā having a large following in Maharashtra and Odisha, and Mādhyandina-Śākhā popular in north India.

Of the 94 or 86 *śākhās* of *Kṛṣṇa-Yajurveda*, only four *śākhās* are available, Taittirīya, Kaṭha, Maitrāyaṇī and Kapiṣṭhala. Taittirīya has a large following in south India. Maitrāyaṇī has a small following in Maharashtra.

Of the 1,000 *śākhās* of *Sāmaveda*, we have lost 997 *śākhās*. Currently we have Kauthuma, Jaiminīya (or Talavakāra) and Rāṇāyanīya *śākhās*.

The Kauthuma-Śākhā is followed in Gujarat and Odisha. In Maharashtra, there is a small following of Rāṇāyanīya. Jaiminīya has a small following in Karnataka, Tamil Nadu and Kerala.

At one time, the apprehension was that none of the 50 *śākhās* of *Atharvaveda* was extant. However, on enquiry it was discovered that there was a brāhmaṇa in Sinor, Gujarat, who was conversant with Śaunaka-Śākhā of this Veda. Kāñcī Maṭha sent students from Tamil Nadu to learn the same from him. The manuscript of Paippalāda-Śākhā in Oḍiā script was discovered by Durgamohan Bhattacharya in Odisha, who edited *kaṇḍikā* 1-4 (into Devanāgarī script) during his lifetime, which has been published by Calcutta College, Calcutta in 1974 titled *Atharvavedīya Paippalāda Saṁhitā*.

Subsequently, his son Deepak Bhattacharya independently edited *kāṇḍa*s 1-15 (out of 20 *kāṇḍas*) titled *Paippalāda Saṁhitā of the Atharvaveda* which has been published by The Asiatic Society in 1997.

Recently, Kunja Bihari Upadhyaya, from Puri, Odisha, himself a Paippalāda *Ś*ākhādhyāyī has published (in 2009) the *Atharvaṇaveda-Paippalāda-Saṁhitā* in its entirety of 20 *kāṇḍa*s, after referring to at least four palm-leaf manuscripts. It is the result of commitment and dedication of 25 years. We have however lost the accent marks for the *Paippalāda Saṁhitā*.

According to Vyāsa's arrangement, though it is obligatory for a person to learn only one *śākhā*, it does not mean that there is a prohibition on learning more. The intention is that at least one *śākhā* must be studied. Even after Vyāsa's time, there have been examples of Vedic scholars (*puṇḍit*s) mastering more than one *śākhā* from the four Vedas. In northern India, there are many with titles 'Caturvedī', 'Trivedī', 'Dwivedī'. At least one of their ancestors would have been one. A person descended from a family well versed in the four Vedas is called a 'Caturvedī'. In Bengal, he is called a Chattopadhyaya or Chatterji. Those who have mastered three Vedas are called 'Trivedis'. 'Duve' 'Dube' and 'Dave' are derived from 'Dwivedi' who have mastered two Vedas. It is like having surnames 'Vājapayī'[36] and 'Somayājulu'[37] and 'Agnihotrī.'[38] Today it is very rare to see a single person who has learned even one Veda, but the fact that members of some families still like to call themselves 'Trivedīs' or 'Caturvedīs' shows that in the past there must have been someone in their family who knew three or four Vedas respectively.

Incidentally, it takes eight years to learn, i.e. memorise even one recension of a Veda (Saṁhitā).

List of Saṁhitās Extant Now

The *mantras* of the Saṁhitā are meant to be recited in different ritualistic performances, and often express the loftiest visions of the Vedic seers about the cosmic world and the aspects associated with it. Although mere recitation of the texts is supposed to have an unseen spiritual power, their application was mostly with reference to some rituals or sacrifices. Hence, they are included in the *karma-kāṇḍa*. A bird's eye-view is

1	*Ṛgveda*	i	*Śākala Saṁhitā*
2	*Ṛgveda*	ii	*Āśvalāyana Saṁhitā*
3	*Śukla-Yajurveda*	i	*Mādhyandina Saṁhitā*
4	*Śukla-Yajurveda*	ii	*Kāṇva Saṁhitā*
5	*Kṛṣṇa-Yajurveda*	i	*Taittirīya Saṁhitā*
6	*Kṛṣṇa-Yajurveda*	ii	*Kāṭhaka Saṁhitā*
7	*Kṛṣṇa-Yajurveda*	iii	*Maitrāyaṇī Saṁhitā*
8	*Kṛṣṇa-Yajurveda*	iv	*Kapiṣṭhala Saṁhitā*
9	*Sāmaveda*	i	*Kauthuma Saṁhitā*
10	*Sāmaveda*	ii	*Jaiminīya Saṁhitā*
11	*Sāmaveda*	iii	*Rāṇāyanīya Saṁhitā*
12	*Atharvaveda*	i	*Śaunaka Saṁhitā*
13	*Atharvaveda*	ii	*Paippalāda Saṁhitā*

36. One who has performed a *Vājapeya* sacrifice gets a title of 'Vājapāyī'.
37. One who has performed a *Somayāga* is a 'Somayājī'.
38. One who performs the *nitya-agnihotra* ritual is titled an 'Agnihotrī'.

presented here to have a comprehensive knowledge about the different Saṁhitās.

The Saṁhitās of all the four Vedas together have around 20,490 *mantras*. *Ṛgveda* (Śākala) — 10,552; *Śukla-Yajurveda* — 2,086; *Sāmaveda* (Rāṇāyanīya) — 1,875; and *Atharvaveda* (Śaunaka) — 5,977.

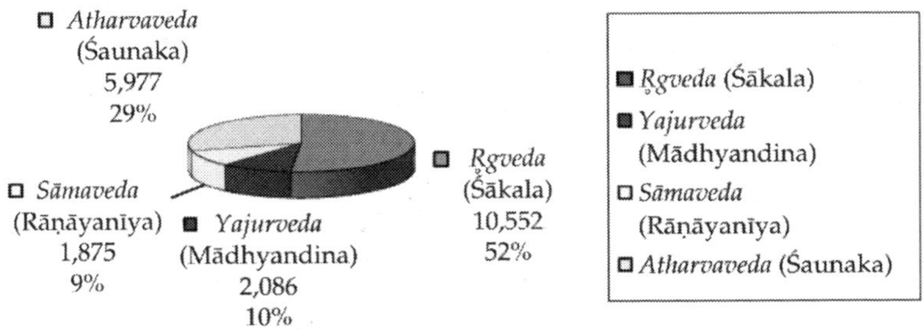

Chart of Vedic Corpus

Brāhmaṇas, Āraṇyakas and Upaniṣads

As stated earlier, in addition to the Saṁhitās, Vedic literature includes Brāhmaṇas, Āraṇyakas and Upaniṣads. The Brāhmaṇas offer explanations, whether exegetical, mythological or polemical, of the ritual prescriptions. The Āraṇyakas and the Upaniṣads are completely different in spirit. Āraṇyaka means forest-texts; products of these thinkers when they had retired into forest retreats for philosophical meditation. The term *upaniṣad*, likewise means the sitting down (of the disciple) near (the teacher, for a secret communication), and the progressive evolution of the meaning made the Upaniṣad a sacred session or sacred doctrine.

Some women also participated in these discussions, and we get vivid description in the *Bṛhadāraṇyaka Upaniṣad* where Gārgī Vācaknvī (daughter of Vacaknu), a *brahmavādinī* questions Yājñavalkya about the basic reality pervading the whole world to a point of exasperation. She dares to raise questions a second time even after being reprimanded, and finally she declares Yājñavalkya to be the unchallenged *brahmajñānī*.

Incidentally, the style of presentation of the subject matter in the Upaniṣads was subsequently seen in Greece by Socrates (470-399 BCE), who taught in a dialogue style, where probing and sustained query compel the response to refine itself in a finer and deeper perception.

THE BRĀHMAṆAS

The Brāhmaṇas are mostly in prose, comprising detailed descriptions of the sacrificial rites, the modes of their performance, as well as comment on their meanings and connected themes. Commentator Bhaṭṭa Bhāskara (eleventh century) in *Taittirīya Saṁhitā* has defined Brāhmaṇa as *brāhmaṇa-nāma karmaṇas-tan-mantrāṇāṁ ca vyākhyāna-granthaḥ.* The subject matter of Brāhmaṇas has been aptly stated by commentator Śabara in a verse as follows:

hetur-nirvacanaṁ nindā praśaṁsā saṁśayo vidhi ।
parakriyā purākalpo vyavadhāraṇa-kalpanā ॥
upamānaṁ daśaite tu vidhayo brāhmaṇasya tu ।
— *Śābarabhāṣyam* II.1.33

According to Sāyaṇācārya (fourteenth century), Brāhmaṇas contain eight types of topics as (i) *itihāsaḥ* (history), (ii) *purāṇam* (old stories), (iii) *vidyā* (esoteric knowledge about meditation), (iv) *upaniṣad* (secret knowledge), (v) *ślokaḥ* (verses), (vi) *sūtram* (aphorisms), (vii) *vyākhyānam* (explanations) and (viii) *anu-vyākhyānam* (elaborations). However, the *vidhiḥ* or rules and regulations about sacrificial ceremony are the primary concerns of the Brāhmaṇa-*grantha*s and all other factors contribute to this aspect.

Each *śākhā* of the Vedic Saṁhitās had its separate Brāhmaṇa. A total of 18 Brāhmaṇas are extant in their entirety: two belonging to *ṚV*, two to *ŚYV*, four to *KYV*, nine to *SV* and one to *AV*. They vary greatly in length. While the *Śatapatha Brāhmaṇa* constitutes five volumes in the 50-volume Sacred Books of the East, the *Vaṁśa Brāhmaṇa* can be printed on a single page. A short survey is presented here:

List of Brāhmaṇas Extant Now

Ṛgveda	Śākala-Śākhā	1	*Aitareya Brāhmaṇa*
	Sāṁkhyāyana-Śākhā	2	*Kauṣītaki or Sāṁkhyāyana Brāhmaṇa*
Śukla-Yajurveda	Mādhyandina-Śākhā	3	*Śatapatha-Mādhyandina Brāhmaṇa*
	Kāṇva-Śākhā		*Śatapatha-Kāṇva Brāhmaṇa* (has minor differences with *Mādhyandina Brāhmaṇa*)
Kṛṣṇa-Yajurveda (Taittirīya-Saṁhitā)	Taittirīya-Śākhā	4 5 6 7 8	*Taittirīya Brāhmaṇa* *Kaṭha Brāhmaṇa* *Maitrāyaṇī Brāhmaṇa* *Satyāyaṇī Brāhmaṇa* *Bhallaka Brāhmaṇa*
Sāmaveda (997 *śākhās* are lost)	Jaiminīya-Śākhā	9	*Jaiminīya /* or *Talavakāra Brāhmaṇa* (includes *Kenopaniṣad* as its integral part)
	Jaiminiya-Śākhā	10	*Ārṣeya Brāhmaṇa* (part of *Jaiminīya* or *Talavakāra Brāhmaṇa*)
	Kauthuma & Rāṇāyanīya	11	*Tāṇḍya* /or *Prauḍha*/ or *Pañcaviṁśa*/ or *Mahā Brāhmaṇa*
		12	*Ṣaḍviṁśa Brāhmaṇa* considered as an appendix to *Pañcaviṁśa*). 5th *prapāṭhaka* is *Adbhuta Brāhmaṇa*.
	Kauthuma-Śākhā	13	*Chāndogya* /or *Mantra*/ or *Upaniṣad Brāhmaṇa*
		14	*Sāmavidhāna Brāhmaṇa*
		15	*Devatādhyāya Brāhmaṇa*
		16	*Saṁhitopaniṣad Brāhmaṇa*
		17	*Vaṁśa Brāhmaṇa*
Atharvaveda	Paippalāda-Śākhā	18	*Gopatha Brāhmaṇa* (the only extant *Brāhmaṇa*)

As stated earlier, according to ancient scholars (Yāska and Āpastamba), the *mantras* or the Saṁhitās and their explanations in the Brāhmaṇas together constitute the Veda.[39] Thus, the Brāhmaṇas in general have been recognised as the Vedas, and the rituals are performed as per the instructions in the Brāhmaṇas.[40] The language, the style of expression of the Brāhmaṇas are quite different from those of the Saṁhitās, i.e. younger than the Mantra texts, but older than the Sūtra texts. Scholars date the Brāhmaṇas between 900-700 BCE, with some of the later Brāhmaṇas (such as *Śatapatha Brāhmaṇa*), dating around 600 BCE. Historically, it corresponds to the emergence of great kingdoms or *mahājanapada* (800-500 BCE) period.

The Brāhmaṇas are of great significance for studying the culture, language and religion of the Vedic period as they contain the basic interpretations of the Vedic *mantras*. They are glosses on the mythology, philosophy and rituals of the Vedas. As these are predominantly related to sacrificial explanations, they belong to the *karma-kāṇḍa* section.

The Brāhmaṇas are separate texts, being the first and the earliest commentaries on the Vedas/Saṁhitās. Only in case of *Kṛṣṇa-Yajurveda*, the Brāhmaṇa portion is integrated[I] into the Saṁhitā.

Batakrishna Ghosh has done a laudable work by collecting the fragments of 16 lost Brāhmaṇas, from quotations in *Veda-Bhāṣyas* and allied Vedic literature (*Collection of the Fragments of Lost Brāhmaṇas*, Calcutta, 1935). The names of these Brāhmaṇas are:

---

39. *mantra-brāhmaṇayor-veda-nāmadheyam*. — Āpastamba.
40. Swami Dayananda Saraswati, founder of the Ārya Samāj did not accept the Brāhmaṇas as Vedas. Cf. Introduction of *The Samaveda* by Devi Chand, p. xiv, published by Munshiram Manoharlal, New Delhi, 1961.

1. *Satyāyana*
2. *Bhallavi*
3. *Talavakāra* (*Sāmaveda*)
4. *Āhvaraka*
5. *Kaṅkati*
6. *Kalabavri*
7. *Caraka*
8. *Cagaleya*
9. *Jābāli*
10. *Paiṅgāyaṇi*
11. *Maṣasaravi*
12. *Maitrāyaṇīya* (*Sāmaveda*)
13. *Rauruki*
14. *Śaibali*
15. *Śvetāśvatara (Kṛṣṇa-Yajurveda)*
16. *Hāridrāvikā*

THE ĀRAṆYAKAS

The Āraṇyakas (Forest texts/Treaties) are so named since they had originated from sages by the contemplation in the serene atmosphere of secluded forests. Sāyaṇācārya in his commentary on *Taittirīya Āraṇyaka* has said that:

> *araṇyādhyayanād-etad āraṇyakam-itīryate* ।
> *araṇye tad-adhyet-ityevaṁ vākyaṁ pravakṣate* ॥

Āraṇyaka is to be recited by a *vratī* in the midst of a forest (*araṇya*). The importance of the Āraṇyakas has been glorified in the *Mahābhārata* as: *āraṇyakaṁ ca vedebhya auṣadhibhyo 'mṛtaṁ yathā.*[41]

Āraṇyaka section is designated as the *upāsanā-kāṇḍa*, since meditation and contemplation on the *prāṇa-vidyā* is predominant here. The metaphysical and esoteric significance

41. *Ma.Bhā.* I.265.

of the sacrifice is the chief concern of the Āraṇyakas. It is also known as Rahasya Brāhmaṇas or esoteric mystic Brāhmaṇas. Many Āraṇyakas belonging to different Vedas are now lost. The *Aitareya* and *Kauṣītaki Āraṇyaka*s belong to the *R̥gveda;* the *Taittirīya, Kaṭha* and *Maitrāyaṇī Āraṇyaka*s belong to *Kr̥ṣṇa-Yajurveda;* the *Śatapatha Āraṇyaka* and *Br̥hadāraṇyaka*s belong to *Śukla-Yajurveda; Jaiminīya* or *Talavakāra Āraṇyaka* belongs to Jaiminīya Śākha of *Sāmaveda. Atharvaveda* does not have any Āraṇyaka.

List of Āraṇyakas Extant Now

1	*R̥gveda*	*Aitareya Āraṇyaka*
2	*R̥gveda*	*Sāṁkhyāyana Āraṇyaka*
3	*Śukla-Yajurveda*	*Śatapatha Āraṇyaka*
4	*Śukla-Yajurveda*	*Br̥hadāraṇyaka*
5	*Kr̥ṣṇa-Yajurveda*	*Taittirīya Āraṇyaka*
6	*Kr̥ṣṇa-Yajurveda*	*Maitrāyaṇī Āraṇyaka*
7	*Sāmaveda* (*Jaiminīya-Śākha*)	*Jaiminīya or Talavakāra Āraṇyaka*
	Atharvaveda	*No Āraṇyaka*

THE UPANIṢADS

The Upaniṣads are otherwise called Vedānta (end of the Veda) as they form the last part of the Vedic literature. The Upaniṣads are regarded as the essence of the entire Vedic literature since the culmination of the Vedic philosophy and spiritual thoughts has been enshrined in them. The word *upaniṣad* actually means the secret teaching that is to be imparted closely and intimately leading to the ultimate truth. They are mostly in dialogue-form. They reveal the existence of the Absolute Truth (in all Upaniṣads), identity of the individual with the Absolute (in all Upaniṣads and explicitly in *Taittirīya, Chāndogya, Māṇḍūkya, Br̥hadāraṇyaka*), explain the cosmology (in *Taittirīya, Chāndogya*), fate of the individual *jīva* after death (as in *Kaṭha*). The Upaniṣads are the sum and substance of the Vedānta philosophy.

The Upaniṣads have dominated Indian philosophical thought, as also its religious and cultural life. Although currently there are around 250 Upaniṣads claiming to belong to one or the other of the Vedas, the celebrated commentator of the Upaniṣads, Śaṅkara Bhagavadpāda has recognised only 14 of them to be authoritative and authentic. He has written commentaries on ten[42] of them, and has quoted four[43] others in his commentaries.

List of Principal Upaniṣads Extant Now

1	*Ṛgveda (Aitareya Āraṇyaka)*	*Aitareya Upaniṣad*
2	*Ṛgveda (Sāṁkhyāyana Āraṇyaka)*	*Kauṣītaki Upaniṣad*
3	*Śukla-Yajurveda Saṁhitā*	*Īśāvāsya Upaniṣad*
4	*Śukla-Yajurveda (Bṛhadāraṇyaka)*	*Bṛhadāraṇyaka Upaniṣad*
5	*Kṛṣṇa-Yajurveda (Taittirīya Āraṇyaka)*	*Taittirīya Upaniṣad*
6	*Kṛṣṇa-Yajurveda (Taittirīya Āraṇyaka)*	*Mahānārāyaṇa Upaniṣad*
7	*Kṛṣṇa-Yajurveda (Maitrāyaṇī Āraṇyaka)*	*Maitrāyaṇī Upaniṣad*
8	*Kṛṣṇa-Yajurveda* (Kaṭha-Śākhā)	*Kaṭhopaniṣad*
9	*Kṛṣṇa-Yajurveda* (Śvetāśvatara-Śākhā)	*Śvetāśvatara Upaniṣad*
10	*Sāmaveda* (Kauthumīya-Śākhā)	*Chāndogya Upaniṣad*
11	*Sāmaveda* (Jaiminīya-Śākhā)	*Kenopaniṣad*
12	*Atharvaveda* (Paippalāda-Śākhā) *Gopatha Brāhmaṇa*	*Praśnopaniṣad*
13	*Atharvaveda* (Paippalāda-Śākhā) *Gopatha Brāhmaṇa*	*Muṇḍaka Upaniṣad*
14	*Atharvaveda* (Paippalāda-Śākhā) *Gopatha Brāhmaṇa*	*Māṇḍūkya Upaniṣad*

42. *īśa-kena-kaṭha-praśna-muṇḍaka-māṇḍūkya-tittiriḥ* ।
aitareyaṁ ca chāndogyaṁ bṛhadāraṇyakaṁ tathā ॥ — *Muk.Up.* I.1.20

43. *Śvetaśvatara, Kauṣītaki, Maitrāyaṇī.*

While the composition of the Brāhmaṇa and Āraṇyakas ceased with the end of Vedic period, large number of Upaniṣads were composed even after the Vedic period. Most of the major Upaniṣads are considered to be of the Vedic or *mahājanapada* period; rest of the Upaniṣads in the list of *Muktikā Upaniṣad* are considered to be of Common Era and attached to the four Vedas.

The Upaniṣads often interpret the polytheistic and ritualistic Saṁhitās in philosophical and metaphorical ways to explore the abstract concept of the Absolute (*Brahman*) and the individual self (*jīva*) introducing Vedānta philosophy, one of the major trends in later Hinduism.

Endnote

I. Which reportedly became the point of contention between the Guru Vaiśampāyana and his disciple Yājñavalkya, who went ahead and authored/compiled the *Śukla-Yajurveda* through the Grace of the Sun God.

2

Ṛgveda

Ṛgveda Saṁhitā

THE *Ṛgveda* is the basis of the entire Vedic literature. It represents the most ancient poetry not only of India, but also of the entire Indo-European family. The word *ṛk* means the laudatory hymn {*ṛcā* (plural form) for hymns}, and the collection of laudatory hymns is the *Ṛgveda*. The only *śākhā*-recension of the *Ṛgveda* that is extant now is Śākala-Śākhā. Currently, the *Ṛgveda* means *Ṛgveda-Śākala Saṁhitā.*

Ṛgveda Nomenclature

There are two types of nomenclature in the division of the *Ṛgveda*. One is *maṇḍala* division; the other is *aṣṭaka* division. The *maṇḍala* nomenclature is considered more systematic than the latter. There are 1,028 *sūkta*s (hymns) in 85 *anuvāka*s

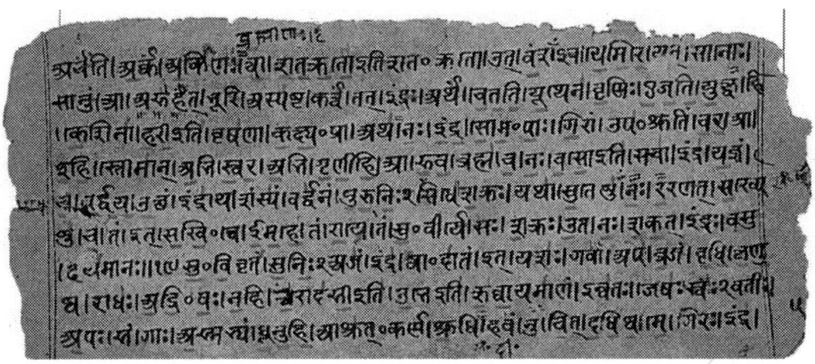

An 18th century manuscript of the *Ṛgveda*

(recitations/chapters) in the 10 *maṇḍalas*. *Sūkta* is a subdivision of an *anuvāka*, and every *sūkta* has some *mantras*.

Maṇḍala	Envisioned by	No. of Sūktas/ Hymns	No. of Ṛcā[1]/ Verses
I (various *ṛṣis*)	Various *ṛṣis*	191	2,006
II (*vaṁśa-maṇḍala*)	Gṛtsamada Śaunahotra Āṅgirasa/later Gṛtsamada Śaunaka Bhārgava	43	429
III (*vaṁśa-maṇḍala*)	Viśvāmitra Gāthina	62	617
IV (*vaṁśa-maṇḍala*)	Vāmadeva Gautama	58	589
V (*vaṁśa-maṇḍala*)	Atri Bhauma	87	727
VI (*vaṁśa-maṇḍala*)	Bharadvāja Bārhaspatya	75	765
VII (*vaṁśa-maṇḍala*)	Vasiṣṭha Maitrāvaruṇi	104	841
VIII (Kaṇva)	Mainly Ṛṣi Kaṇva & his descendants & other *ṛṣis*	92	1,636
IX *Pavamāna maṇḍala*	Various *ṛṣis*	114	1,108
X (various *ṛṣis*)	Various *ṛṣis*	191	1,754
Sub-Total		**1,017**	**10,472**
Bālakhilya		11	80
Total		**1,028**	**10,552**

In *aṣṭaka*, the nomenclature is purely mechanical. There are eight *aṣṭaka*s or 'eighths' of about equal length, each *aṣṭaka* is subdivided into eight *adhyāya*s (chapters), thus totalling 64 *adhyāya*s, and each *adhyāya* consists of *varga*s (groups) totalling to 2,006[2] *vargas*, of five to six *mantra*s each.

In *maṇḍala* nomenclature, the *mantra*s of the *Ṛgveda* are grouped into 10 books called *maṇḍala*, each *maṇḍala* being divided into *sūkta*s or hymns, and each *sūkta* comprising a number of *mantra*s. There are 1,028 *sūkta*s, hymns (1,017 hymns

1. The number of *ṛcā* in each of the ten *maṇḍala* and the total number of *ṛcā* 10,552 as per *Sarvānukramaṇī* of Kātyāyana.
2. *Anu.anu.* 38.

Aṣṭakas	Adhyāyas	No. of Sūktas/ Hymns	No. of Mantras/ Ṛcā/Verses
I	8	121	1,370
II	8	119	1,147
III	8	122	1,209
IV	8	140	1,289
V	8	129	1,263
VI	8	124	1,650
VII	8	116	1,263
VIII	8	146	1,281
Sub-Total	**64**	**1,017**	**10,472**
Bālakhilya		11	80
Total		**1,028**	**10,552**

+ 11 Bālakhilya hymns joined at the middle of the eighth *maṇḍala*). Each *sūkta* has roughly 10 *mantras*, the shortest has only one *mantra*, while the longest *sūkta* has 58. As per *Anuvākānukramaṇī* of Sage Śaunaka, there are in all 10,580[3] *mantras*, 153,826[4] words and 4,32,000[5] syllables in the *Ṛgveda*. On an average, a *mantra* has 15 words and every word has three syllables. Our sages had calculated these divisions so minutely that there was no scope left for any interpolation or misreading. The number of hymns varies in different *maṇḍalas*. While the first *maṇḍala* has 191 *sūktas* containing 2,006 *mantras*, roughly one-fifth of the entire text, the second *maṇḍala* has only 43 *sūktas*, containing 429 *mantras*. The tenth *maṇḍala* interestingly has 191 *sūktas*, like the first *maṇḍala*, possible explanation of which by scholars is provided later in this

3. *Anu.anu.* 43. Number of *mantras* as per Śaunaka 10,580, and as per Kātyāyana is 10,552 (which is of the Śākala-Śākhā). This number is reconciled in both *aṣṭaka* and *maṇḍala* nomenclature.
4. *Anu.anu.* 45.
5. Ibid.

chapter. The general characteristics of these 10 *maṇḍala*s are not identical. The first, eighth and tenth *maṇḍala* have been envisioned by many seers of different families, and contain various *mantra*s relating to various subjects and deities. The second to seventh *maṇḍala* are termed as family books (*vaṁśa-maṇḍala*s) by the Western scholars. They form one group, and each one of them is attributed in its entirety to one individual seer and his family. These seers respectively are, (i) Gṛtsamada, (ii) Viśvāmitra, (iii) Vāmadeva, (iv) Atri, (v) Bharadvāja, (vi) Vasiṣṭha and the subsequent seers of their families. Kaṇva and his family form the predominant group of seers of the eighth *maṇḍala*. The whole of ninth *maṇḍala* contains hymns addressed to Pavamāna Soma, hence is known as Pavamāna Maṇḍala; its seers belong to different families. This again appears to have been extracted out of each *maṇḍala*, and compiled into one *maṇḍala*, hence the seers in this case belong to different families.

Various Śākhās of the Ṛgveda

As stated in the introductory chapter, in each of the four Vedas, there are different *śākhā*s and in the various *śākhā*s there are *pāṭhabheda*s or *pāṭhāntara*s. There may be more *sūkta*s in some *pāṭha*s than in others. There may also be differences in the order of the *mantra*s. Each *śākhā* comprises its Saṁhitā, the Brāhmaṇa, and the Āraṇyaka.

Ṛgveda was allotted to Paila, by Veda Vyāsa, for preservation and propagation. There were reportedly 21 *śākhā*s of *Ṛgveda*. However, the *Caraṇavyūha* of Śaunaka mentions only five[6] of them, i.e. (i) Śākala, (ii) Bāṣkala, (iii) Sāṁkhyāyana, (iv) Āśvalāyana, and (v) Māṇḍūkāyana.

I. ŚĀKALA-ŚĀKHĀ

The *Ṛgveda* that we have today in print form belongs to Śākala-Śākhā. Currently, Kerala has the tradition of chanting of this *śākhā*.

6. . . . *eteṣām śākhāḥ pañcavidhā bhavanti. āśvalāyanī, sāṅkhāyanī, śākalā, bāṣkalā, māṇḍūkāyanāśceti* — *Ca.Vy.* I.8.

II. BĀṢKALA-ŚĀKHĀ

Bāṣkala Saṁhitā is available in fragments. There are reportedly 1,025 *sūktas* (1,028 in Śākala) in this *śākhā*. *Bāṣkala Saṁhitā* differs from the *Śākala Saṁhitā* in three respects — (i) arrangement of the hymns, (ii) the presence of seven Bālakhilya hymns as an integral part of the text, and (iii) the presence of additional Saṁjñāna-Sūkta comprising 15 *mantras* at the end of the text. Thus, *Bāṣkala Saṁhitā* incorporates the Saṁjñāna-Sūkta of *Śākala Saṁhitā*, and adds one more Saṁjñāna-Sūkta to it, so to speak.[7] While the concluding *mantra* of the Śākala-Śākhā is, *samāni va ākuti-* (Sañjāna-Sūktam), in the *Bāṣkala* it is *tachaṁyorāvr̥ṇīmahe.* A Kāśmīrī manuscript of this *śākhā* is available at Pune.

III. SĀṀKHYĀYANA-ŚĀKHĀ

Manuscripts of this *śākhā* are reportedly available as referred by N.S. Sonatakke (in 1940), S.D. Satavalekar and others.[8] Its Brāhmaṇa and Āraṇyaka versions have been published, and are available. In the published Śākala and Sāṁkhyāyana-Śākhā, there is some difference only in the sequence of *mantras*. For instance, in the Śākala, the *R̥k-pariśiṣṭa* and Bālakhilya are separate from the Saṁhitā portion, whereas they are included in the Saṁhitā in Sāṁkhyāyana. The Gr̥hya-Sūtra and Śrauta-Sūtra of this *śākhā* are available.

IV. ĀŚVALĀYANA-ŚĀKHĀ

A manuscript exists with accents and *padapāṭha*. It was available until the seventeenth century, since the Saṁhitā and Brāhmaṇa of this *śākhā* are referred in the list of Kavindrācārya of the seventeenth century.[9] The Gr̥hya-Sūtra and Śrauta-Sūtra of this *śākhā* are available.

7. http:// vishalagarwal.voiceof dharma.com/uttamapatala.html.
8. Ibid.
9. *R̥gveda Saṁhitā*, vol. I, Introduction, Sriram Sharma.

At the time of going to the press, it is very pleasing to know that eminent Vedic scholar, Braj Behari Chaubey has revived and edited the Āśvalāyana-Śākhā with *padapāṭha* and proper accent marks; and the same has been published by the Indira Gandhi National Centre for Arts and D.K. Printworld, New Delhi. The verses of the 10 *maṇḍala*s are given in their original form, and have been examined critically in a thorough study. The English and Hindi translations of the additional (212) *mantra*s of the *Āśvalāyana Saṁhitā* are also presented with the original Sanskrit verses.

With the publication of the *Āśvalāyana Saṁhitā*, a complete picture of a new *Ṛgveda-Śākhā-Saṁhitā* has come to the fore for the first time. In comparison to *Śākala Saṁhitā*, the *Āśvalāyana Saṁhitā* has 212 additional *mantras*, among which some occur in the common *sūkta*, and the remaining form 16 additional complete *sūkta*s. Among the additional *sūkta*s special mention may be made of Kapiñjala-Sūkta (II.44), Lakṣmī-Sūkta (V.88-89), Pavamāna-Sūkta (IX.68), Hiraṇya-Sūkta (X.130), Medhā-Sūkta (X.155), and Mānasa-Sūkta (X.171).

Currently, Āśvalāyana-Śākhā is recited by the Nambudiri brāhmaṇas in Kerala. In Gujarat, brāhmaṇa families belonging to Sāṁkhyāyana and Āśvalāyana *śākhā*s are still there.[10]

V. MĀṆḌŪKĀYANA-ŚĀKHĀ

As per Bhagavat Dutta and Gangasagar Ray, the Saṁhitā of this *śākhā* was available earlier; however, it is no more extant.

VI. AITAREYA-ŚĀKHĀ

Based on the existence of *Aitareya Brāhmaṇa*, *Aitareya Āraṇyaka* and *Aitareya Upaniṣad*, many scholars are of the opinion that there was an Aitareya-Śākhā existing at one point of time.

10. Sriram Adhikari, *Veda Kathāṅka*, p. 162, Gita Press.

Subject Matter of Ṛgveda Saṁhitā

In the *Ṛgveda*, a little over half of its contents consist of hymns to Agni (around 250 *sūkta*s) and Indra (around 200 *sūkta*s). Other important deities to whom hymns are dedicated are the Aśvins, Savitṛ, Sūrya, Varuṇa, Uṣas, Pūṣan, the Maruts, Rudra, Soma, Viṣṇu, and the Viśvedevā.

There are some philosophical hymns in the tenth *maṇḍala*, such as, Puruṣa-Sūktam (X.90), Hiraṇyagarbha-Sūktam (X.121), Nāsadīya-Sūktam — the hymn of creation (X.129); five funeral hymns (X.14-18), of which X.15 is to the departed spirits. In the first *maṇḍala*, the entire hymn (I.164) by Ṛṣi Dīrghatamas addressed to the Viśvedevā and other *devatā*s is highly philosophical, and portions of it are frequently quoted in the Upaniṣads.[11]

Occurrence of seeds of Upaniṣadic thoughts are found in the *Ṛgveda*. This has been noticed and identified by the scholars.

> . . . Upaniṣad is later than the Saṁhitās, and later than the Brāhmaṇas, but the first germs of Upaniṣad doctrines go back to at least as far as the *mantra*-period, which conservatively has been fixed between 1000 and 800 BCE. Concepts corresponding to the general teaching of the Upaniṣads occur in certain hymns of the *Ṛgveda Saṁhitā*,[12] they must have existed therefore before that collection was finally closed. One hymn in the Saṁhitā, of the *Ṛgveda* (I.191)[I] was designed by Kātyāyana, the author of *Sarvānukramaṇikā*, as an Upaniṣad.[13]

In *Ṛgveda*, around 20 *sūkta*s are there, based on which stories and dramas have been written in later times. These *sūkta*s are

11. *dvā suparṇā sayujā sakhāyā samānaṁ vṛkṣaṁ pari ṣasvajāte* |
    tayor-anyaḥ pippalaṁ svādvatti-anaśnan-anyo abhi cākaśīti ||
    — *ṚVS* I.164.20 = *Muṇ. Up.* III.1.1
12. *asataḥ sad-ajāyata* = *ṚVS* X.72.2, 3=*Ch. Up.* VI.2.1.
13. Cf. Sacred Books of the East, vol. I, Introduction, p. lxvi.

mainly in the form of dialogues, because of which they are popularly known as 'Saṁvāda-Sūktas.' Some of the famous Saṁvāda-Sūktas (dialogue-hymns) are Purūravā-Urvaśī-Saṁvāda (X.95), Yama-Yamī-Saṁvāda (X.10), Saramā-Paṇi-Saṁvāda (X.108), Viśvāmitra-Nadī-Saṁvāda (III.33), etc.[14] Kālidāsa's famous drama *Vikramorvaśīya* is based on Purūravā-Urvaśī-Saṁvāda (X.95).

The long wedding hymn (X.85), known as Sūryā-Sāvitrī-Sūktam containing 47 *mantra*s is quite noteworthy.

Many *sūktas/mantra*s are eulogy of gifting/charity, called *dānastuti*s (e.g. VI.27.8 and X.62.8-11). As per *Ṛk-Sarvānukramaṇī*, there are 22 *dānastuti*s. Modern researchers claim the existence of at least 68 *sūkta*s containing *dānastuti*. They further claim that these *stuti*s laud the charitable kings. However, as per Vedic tradition (*siddhānta*), these *stuti*s are meant to prompt and propel people to gift. Interestingly, as a corollary to the *dānastuti*, there is a Śraddhā-Sūktam (X.151) composed by Ṛṣikā Śraddhā Kāmāyanī lauding the value of *śraddhā*.

Apart from hymns dealing with the evils of gambling (X.34), and a few individual verses having secular character, the Ṛgvedic text is essentially sacrificial in character.

Ṛṣi, Devatā, Chandas

Each *sūktam* of *Ṛgveda* has several *mantra*s, and a header having three factors, namely,

i. *Ṛṣi* (or *ṛṣi*s) to whom the *sūktam* was revealed.

ii. The cosmic powers or the *devatā*s to whom it is addressed.

iii. The metres of the various *mantra*s. Although the metres

---

14. Few other dialogue-hymns are — Agastya-Lopāmudrā (*ṚV* I.179), Vaśukrapatnī-Indra-Vaśukra (*ṚV* X.28), Indrāṇī-Indra-Vṛṣākapi (*RV* X.86), Vāmadeva-Indra-Aditi (*ṚV* IV.18).

of the *Ṛgveda mantra*s are about 15, most of the *mantra*s are in one of the seven specific metres, namely, Gāyatrī, Triṣṭubh, Jagatī, Uṣṇik, Anuṣṭubh, Bṛhatī, Virāṭ (Virāj), which are listed in *ṚV* X.130.4-5. Gāyatrī, Triṣṭubh and Jagatī, together, furnish two-thirds of the total number of *mantra*s in *ṚVS*. The importance of the *Ṛgveda* has been extolled by the *Taittirīya Saṁhitā*, as the Ṛgvedic *mantra*s have authoritative dominance over any other Saṁhitā[15] in performance of any sacrifice.

The details of number of *sūkta*s in 10 *maṇḍala*s are furnished below:

Maṇḍala I (191 Sūktas)

Maṇḍala I has 191 *sūkta*s. The *sūkta*s 65-73 of Parāśara Śāktya (son of Śakti and grandson of Vasiṣṭha) are the most lyrical in the *Ṛgveda*. The first *aṣṭaka,* having 121 hymns serves as an excellent introduction to the entire *Ṛgveda*. This *aṣṭaka/maṇḍala* has several *mantra*s that are quoted in various Upaniṣads.[16]

Sūktas	Ṛṣi
1-10	Madhuchandā Vaiśvāmitra (son or descendant of Viśvāmitra)
11	Jetā Mādhucchandas (son of Madhuchandā)
12-23, I.13 - Āprīsūktam of the Kāṇvas	Medhātithi Kāṇva (descendant of Kaṇva)
24-30	Śunaḥśepa[II] Ājīgarti/later Devarāta Vaiśvāmitra[III]
31-35	Hiraṇyastūpa Āṅgirasa
36-43	Kaṇva Ghaura (Ghora's son, other son being Pragatha)
44-50	Praskaṇva Kāṇva (Kaṇva's son or descendant)
51-57	Savya Āṅgirasa (descendant of Aṅgiras)
58-64	Nodhā Gautama (of Gotama's lineage)

15. *yad vai yajñasya sāmnā yajuṣā kriyate śithilaṁ tat yadṛcā tad dṛḍham.* — *Tai.Sa.* VI.5.20.3

16. *ṚVS* I.164.20 = *Muṇ. Up.* III.1.1.

65-73 (most lyrical in content)	Parāśara Śāktya (son of Śakti, grandson of Vasiṣṭha)
74-93	Gotama Rāhūgaṇa
94-98, 101-04, 106-15	Kutsa Āṅgirasa (descendant of Aṅgiras)
99	Kāśyapa Mārica
100	Vārṣāgira, Ṛjrāśvāmbariṣa, Sahadeva, Bhayamāna, Surādhas (collective vision)
105	Kutsa Āṅgirasa or Trita Āptya
116-25	Kakṣīvān Dairghatamas Auśija (son of Ṛṣi Dīrghatamas and Uśija, a maid of king of Aṅga)
126	1-5 - Kakṣīvān Dairghatamas, 6 - Svanaya Bhāvayavya 7 - Romaśā (*ṛṣikā*)
127-39	Parucchepa Daivodāsī
140-64 I.142 - Āprīsūktam of the Āṅgirasas	Dīrghatamā[17] Aucathya (son of Ṛṣi Ucathya and Mamatā)
165	Indra, Marudgaṇa and Agastya Maitrāvaruṇi
166-69, 171-78, 180-91, I.188 - Āprīsūktam of the Agastyas I.191-Viṣoghnopaniṣad[18]	Agastya Maitrāvaruṇi
170	1-3, Indra, 4 - Indra or Agastya, 2, 5 - Agastya Maitrāvaruṇi
179	1-2 - Lopāmudrā (*ṛṣikā*), 3-4 - Agastya Maitrāvaruṇi, 5-6 - Agastya's *śiṣya* — a *brahmacārī*

Maṇḍala II (43 Sūktas)

As stated earlier, *Maṇḍala* II to VII have been designated as *vaṁśa-maṇḍala* (family-books) by the Western researchers. In the IInd *maṇḍala,* all the 43 *sūkta*s have been revealed to Ṛṣi Gṛtsamada Śaunahotra Āṅgiras (subsequently known as

---

17. Dīrghatamas, means 'long darkness', meaning blind.
18. Was titled by Kātyāyana, the author of *Sarvānukramaṇikā*, as an Upaniṣad.

Gṛtsamada Śaunaka Bhārgava), or to his descendants or disciples. These 43 *sūkta*s are dedicated to Agni, Indra, Āditya, Mitrāvaruṇa, Varuṇa, Viśvedevā and the Maruts. This *maṇḍala* is also known as Gṛtsamada *maṇḍala*. Interesting stories about him are available in the *Ṛgveda, Atharvaveda, Aitareya Brāhmaṇa, Śatapatha Brāhmaṇa, Bṛhaddevatā*[19] (of Śaunaka), *Ṛgveda-Sarvānukramaṇī* (of Kātyāyana), *Mahābhārata* and *Gaṇeśa Purāṇa*. From these texts we know, Maharṣi Gṛtsamada Śaunahotra Āṅgiras was the biological son of Ṛṣi Śunahotra of Āṅgiras *gotra*, and his parental title was Śaunahotra, and *gotra* title was Āṅgiras. Later, he was adopted by Ṛṣi Śunaka due to Indra's efforts, and came to be known as Gṛtsamada Śaunaka (adopted parent's title) Bhārgava (adopted parent's *gotra* title). Gṛtsamada's special relationship with Indra is available in the *Ṛgveda*. Around 16 *sūkta*s of this *maṇḍala* are dedicated to Indra. Once he effortlessly vanquished two *asura*s by praising Indra. This is narrated in *ṚV*. II.12, famously known as Sajanīya-Sūktam, since most of the *mantra*s (12 of them) end with the refrain *sa janāsa indraḥ*. The famous *mantra* — *gaṇānāṁ tvā gaṇapatiṁ havāmahe* — is in this *maṇḍala* (*ṚV*. II.23.1), where Gaṇeśa has been invoked as Bṛahmaṇaspati.

Sūktas	Ṛṣi
1-3, 8-26, 30-43 II.3 - Āprīsūktam of the Gṛtsamadas	Gṛtsamada Śaunahotra Āṅgiras /later Gṛtsamada Śaunaka Bhārgava
4-7	Somāhuti Bhārgava
27-29 (28.10 – Duḥsvapna-nāśana)	Kūrma Gārtsamada/or Gṛtsamada

Maṇḍala III (62 Sūktas)

All the 62 *sūkta*s of the IIIrd *maṇḍala* have been revealed to Ṛṣi Viśvāmitra Gāthina, his eight descendants 'the Vaiśvāmitras', and his father, Gāthin Kauśika. The deities in this *maṇḍala* are — Agni, Indra, Aditi, Uṣā, the Aśvins, Ṛbhu and Viśvedevā. This *maṇḍala* has the famous *Gāyatrī-mantra* (*ṚV* III.62.10)

19. Index of the 'many gods'.

envisioned by Viśvāmitra. More than 500 *mantras* were envisioned by him. His name is mentioned in other Vedic texts like *Aitareya Āraṇyaka, Taittirīya Saṁhitā,* etc. His *mantra* (*R̥V* III.53.12) is said to protect the clan of the Bhāratas or the people of Bhārata (*bhāratam̐ janam*). His father, Gāthin Kauśika is also a *r̥ṣi* of the *R̥gveda.* Viśvāmitra belonged to Kuśika *gotra*[20] and was a Kauśika. He was the chief priest in the sacrifice performed by King Sudās. An interesting story about his birth is in the Purāṇas. His sons (R̥ṣabha Vaiśvāmitra, Kata Vaiśvāmitra, Devaśravā, Devarāṭa Bhārata, Prajāpati Vaiśvāmitra) also being seers, brought great fame to the Kuśika lineage, and Viśvāmitra himself thus became a *gotrakāra r̥ṣi.*

There is no explicit mention of the supposed enmity between *r̥ṣi*s Viśvāmitra and Vasiṣṭha in the *R̥gveda Saṁhitā.* However, the enmity between Viśvāmitra with Śakti, son of Vasiṣṭha is detailed in some portions of *R̥VS.* Detail of this enmity however is mentioned in *Taittirīya Saṁhitā* VII.4.7.1 and *Pañcaviṁśa Brāhmaṇa* IV.7.3, VIII.2.3, where Vasiṣṭha's sons were killed by King Sudās, and subsequently Vasiṣṭha defeating Sudās.

R̥ṣi Viśvāmitra is an example of what a person can achieve in the same life, through *tapas.* In the same life, from a kṣatriya he became a brāhmaṇa, from a *rājarṣi* to a *brahmarṣi* and obtained the honour of being a *saptarṣi.* All this is attributed to his *Gāyatrī japa.*

Sūktas	R̥ṣis
1-12, 24-25, 27-30, 32, 34, 35, 37, 39-53, 57-61, III.4 – Āprīsūktam Of the Vaiśvāmitras	Viśvāmitra Gāthina (30, 34, 39 — seen/composed later)
13-14	R̥ṣabha Vaiśvāmitra (son of Viśvāmitra)
15-16	Utkīla Kātya
17-18	Kata Vaiśvāmitra

20. *R̥VS.* III.26.1, *R̥VS* III.30.20, *R̥VS* III.53.9.

19-22	Gāthī Kauśika (21 — seen/composed later)
23	Devaśravā and Devarāṭa Bhārata
26	Viśvāmitra Gāthina and Ātmā
31	Viśvāmitra Gāthina or Kuśika Eṣirathi
33 - Viśvāmitra-Nadī-Saṁvāda	1, 2, 3, 5, 9, 11, 12, 13 Viśvāmitra, 4, 6, 7, 8, 10 Nadyaḥ (*ṛṣikās*)
36	Viśvāmitra Gāthina & Ghora Āṅgiras (36 — seen/composed later)
38	Viśvāmitra Gāthina or Prajāpati Vaiśvāmitra/Vācya (seen/composed later)
54-56	Prajāpati Vaiśvāmitra or Prajāpati Vācya
62 62.10 *Gāyatrī-mantra*	1-15 Viśvāmitra Gāthina, 16-18 Viśvāmitra Gāthina or Jamadagni Bhārgava

Maṇḍala IV (58 Sūktas)

All the 58 *sūktas* of Maṇḍala IV have been revealed to Vāmadeva and his three descendants, the Vāmadevyaḥ. The *sūktas* invoke Agni, Indra, Varuṇa, Soma, the Ṛbhus, Dadhikāṇa, Viśvedevā and Uṣā. The hymns have a high degree of symbolism. In addition, they appear to be in the spirit of *loka-kalyāṇa*. Vāmadeva has revealed about himself in the *Ṛgveda*. The two *ṛcā* (*ṚVS* IV.27.1-2) were envisioned by him while he was still in his mother's womb.[21] The famous declaration — *ahaṁ manurabhavaṁ, sūryaścāhaṁ, kakṣivān ṛiṣiraśmi vipraḥ, ahaṁ kutsaṁ-ārjuneyaṁ nṛyuñje'haṁ kaviruśanā paśyatā mā*[22] — is in this *maṇḍala*. His choice of coming to this world is described by him.[23] He did not want to be born in the normal way, hurting his mother. He came out through her side taking

21. *ṚVS*, IV.27.1-2.
22. *ṚVS* IV.26.1.
23. *ṚVS* IV.18.

the form of an eagle. Indra was upset with him for this action; however, Vāmadeva pleased him with his laudatory hymns. Once, when Vāmadeva fell into dire poverty, Indra gave him solace. This is movingly described by Vāmadeva in *R̥VS* IV.18.13.

Another *r̥k* (*R̥VS* IV.16.10) describes the story, where Indra had made Kutsa his lookalike out of affection, and how Śaci was confused seeing two Indras sitting together on the throne.

The famous *Sauri-R̥k* addressed to Sūrya is in this *maṇḍala* — *haṁsaḥ śuciṣad, vasur-antarikṣasad, hotāvediṣad, atithir-duroṇasat. . ..*[24] This famous *mantra* is repeated in *Śukla-Yajurveda* X.24, XII.14, *ŚYV*-(Kāṇva-Śākhā) XIII.5.18, XV.6.25, *Taittirīya Saṁhitā* I.8.15.2, IV.2.1.5, *Aitareya Brāhmaṇa* IV.20, *Taittirīya Āraṇyaka* X.10.2 *in toto.* The *Pañcadevatā-mantra* — *catvāri śr̥ṅgā trayo asya pādā, dve śīrṣe sapta hastāso asya,*[25] — belongs to this *maṇḍala.*

Maharṣi Vāmadeva was the son of R̥ṣi Gotama. He is treated as a *gotrakāra-r̥ṣi.*

Sūktas	R̥ṣi
1-41, 45-58 40.5 — *Sauri r̥cā* 58.3 — *Pañcadevatā-mantra*	Vāmadeva Gautama
18	1 Indra, 2nd half of 4 and 7 Aditi (*r̥ṣikā*), 2, 3, 1st half of 4, 5, 6, 8-13 Vāmadeva Gautama
26	1-3 Vāmadeva Gautama or Indra 4-7 Vāmadeva Gautama
42 (*Ātmastuti*)	Trasadasyu Paurukutsya
43-44	Purumīḷha Sauhotra, Ajamīḷha Sauhotra

Maṇḍala V (87 Sūktas)

All the 87 *sūkta*s of this *maṇḍala* have been revealed to R̥ṣi Atri Bhauma and his 35 descendants, the Ātreyāḥ. This *maṇḍala* is

24. *R̥VS* IV.40.5.
25. *R̥VS* IV.58.3.

also known as Ātreya-*maṇḍala*. The *sūktas* are addressed to Agni, Indra, Marut, Viśvedevā and Savitā.

Atri is considered the *mānasa-putra* of Caturmukha Brahmā and was born from his eyes.[26] He is one of the *saptarṣis*. He is also considered as one of the Prajāpatis. His wife, Anasūyā was the daughter of Prajāpati Kardama and his wife Devahūti. The famous sage Durvāsā, is the son of Maharṣi Atri and Devī Anasūyā.

Atri had a special connection with the Aśvins. While doing *tapas* when he became old, the Aśvins made him young and strong.[27] Further, he was released from the *asuras* by the Aśvins.[28] These facts are mentioned in the *Ṛgveda*. His sons are also seers of many *sūktas* of this *maṇḍala*. The *sūkta* *ṚV*. V.51.11-15 of this *maṇḍala* is known as Kalyāṇa-Sūkta or Svasti-Sūkta seen by Svasti Ātreya. The famous *mantra: viśvāni deva savitar-duritāni parā suva, yad bhadraṁ tanna ā suva*[29] is in this *maṇḍala*.

Sūktas	**Ṛṣi**
1	Budha/Gaviṣṭhira Ātreya
2	Kumāra Ātreya and/or Vṛṣa Jāna/Jāra Ātreya
3-6 V.5 - Āprīsūktam of the Ātreyas	Vasuśruta Ātreya
7-8	Iṣa Ātreya
9-10	Gaya Ātreya
11-14	Sutaṁbhara Ātreya
15	Dharuṇa Āṅgirasa
16-17	Pūru Ātreya
18	Mṛktavāha Dvita Ātreya

26. *akṣaṇo'triḥ* — *Śrī.Bhā*. III.12.24.
27. *ṚVS* X.143.1.
28. *ṚVS* X.143.2.
29. *ṚVS* V.82.5.

19	Vavrī Ātreya
20	Prayasvān Ātrigaṇa
21	Sasa Ātreya
22	Viśvasāmā Ātreya
23	Dyumna Viśvacarṣaṇī Ātreya
24	Bandhu, Subandhu, Śrutabandhu, Viprabandhu (Gaupāyana or Laupāyana)
25-26	Vasūyu Ātreya
27	Tryaruṇa Traivṛṣṇa, Trasadasyu Paurukutsya, and Aśvamedha Bhārata/or Atri Bhauma
37-43, 76-77, 83-86	Atri Bhauma
28	Viśvavāra Ātreyī (*ṛṣikā*)
29	Gaurivīti Śāktya
30	Babhru Ātreya
31	Avasyu Ātreya
32	Gātu Ātreya
33-34	Saṁvaraṇa Prājāpatya
35-36	Prabhūvasu Āṅgirasa
37-43	Atri Bhauma
44	Avatsāra Kāśyapa, 10-13 -various Ātreyas
45	Sadāpṛṇa Ātreya
46	Pratikṣatra Ātreya
47	Pratiratha Ātreya
48	Pratibhānu Ātreya
49	Pratiprabha Ātreya
50-51	Svasti Ātreya
52-61, 81-82 (V.61 — *Dānastuti*)	Śyāvāśva Ātreya
62	Śrutivida/Śrutavid Ātreya
63-64	Arcanānā Ātreya

65-66	Rātahavya Ātreya
67-68	Yajata Ātreya
69-70	Urucakri Ātreya
71-72	Bāhuvṛkta Ātreya
73-74	Paura Ātreya
75	Avasyu Ātreya
78	Saptavadhri Ātreya
79-80	Satyaśravā Ātreya
87	Evayāmarut Ātreya

Maṇḍala VI (75 Sūktas)

Sixth *maṇḍala* is one of the *vaṁśa-maṇḍala*, and the 75 *sūkta*s were revealed to Ṛṣi Bharadvāja and his sons/descendants. Of these, 765 *mantra*s have been envisioned by Bharadvāja. Additionally, in *Atharvaveda*, 23 *mantra*s were visioned by Bharadvāja. Ten of his sons and daughter Rātrī Bhāradvājī are the other seers of this *maṇḍala*. Rātrī Bhāradvājī is the seer of the famous Rātrīsūktam[30] that is chanted in *Durgā-Saptaśatī* Caṇḍī ritual. His ten sons are — Ṛjiśvān, Garga, Nara, Pāyu, Vasu, Sasa, Shirambitha, Śunahotra, Sapratha and Suhotra. As per *Ṛk-Sarvānukramaṇī*, Ṛṣikā Kaśipā was also Ṛṣi Bharadvāja's daughter. Thus, 12 of his children were seers — *mantradraṣṭāraḥ*.

Bharadvāja's father was Bṛhaspati and mother was Mamatā. Bharadvāja studied grammar from Indra and taught the same with commentary to many *ṛṣi*s. This is mentioned in *Ṛktantra* and *Aitareya Brāhmaṇa*. Caraka has mentioned that Bharadvāja also studied Āyurveda. He has written *Āyurveda Saṁhitā*. He learnt Dharmaśāstra from Mahraṣi Bhṛgu and authored *Bhāradvāja Smṛti*. This text is mentioned in *Mahābhārata* Śāntiparva 182.5.

30. *ṚVS* X.127.

Sūktas	Ṛṣi
1-14,16-30, 37-43, 53-74 (VI.27.8 — *Dānastuti*) (VI.63 — *Dānastuti*)	Bharadvāja Bārhaspatya
15	Bharadvāja Bārhaspatya or Vitahavya Āṅgirasa
31-32	Suhotra Bhāradvāja
33-34	Śunahotra Bhāradvāja
35-36	Nara Bhāradvāja
44-46, 48	Śaṁyu Bārhaspatya
VI.47 — *Dānastuti*	Garga Bhāradvāja
49-52	Ṛjiśvā Bhāradvāja
75	Pāyu Bhāradvāja

Maṇḍala VII (104 Sūktas)

This *maṇḍala* has 104 *sūkta*s revealed to Vasiṣṭha and his 12 descendants, the Vāsiṣṭhas. This *maṇḍala* is also known as 'Vāsiṣṭha-Maṇḍala.' The *sūkta*s are addressed to Agni, Indra, Varuṇa, the Aśvins, Mitrā-Varuṇa, Dyāvā-Pṛthīvi, Āditya, Viśvedevā, Vāstoṣpati, Savitā, Bhaga and Uṣā. Vasiṣṭha manifested from the power of both Mitrā-Varuṇa through Urvaśī.[31] Vasiṣṭha's wife Arundhatī is given great respect in our tradition. She shares a place in the *saptarṣi-maṇḍala*[32] near Vasiṣṭha.[33]

Many of the *sūkta*s seen by Vasiṣṭha, end with *yūyaṁ pāta svastibhiḥ sadānaḥ*.[34] This portion has been repeated more than 100 times, and shows the compassion of Ṛṣi Vasiṣṭha who has prayed for the welfare and auspiciousness of the whole humankind.

---

31. *ṚVS* VII.33.11.
32. The Great Bear containing the seven stars – Kratu, Pulaḥ, Pulastya, Atri, Aṅgirā, Vasiṣṭha (and Arundhatī), and Bharadvāja.
33. The sixth star.
34. *ṚVS* VII.1.20, 25.

Similarly, the *ṚVS* VII.35.1-13 is known as Śānti-Sūktam, where Vasiṣṭha has prayed to all the *devatās*, individually for auspiciousness. This *sūktam* also ends with *yūyaṁ pāta svastibhiḥ sadā naḥ*.

Then there is Bhāgya-Sūktam *ṚV*. VII.41, containing seven *ṛcā*, where Vasiṣṭha has invoked all the *devatās* and Bhaga for prosperity and well-being. This is repeated in *Taittirīya Brāhmaṇa* II.8.9.

The 101st and 102nd *sūktas* of this *maṇḍala* are addressed to Parjanya, and are known as 'Parjanya-Sūktas', chanting of which continuously for five nights brings rains.

The famous *mṛtyuñjaya-mantra*: *tryaṁbakaṁ yajāmahe sugandhiṁ puṣṭivardhanam* (VII.59.12), was also seen by Vasiṣṭha. The *mantra*: *paśyema śaradaḥ śataṁ, jivema śaradaḥ śatam*[35] prayer is also by Vasiṣṭha.

Sūktas	**Ṛṣi**
1-31, 34-100, 103-104 VII.2 — Āprīsūktam of the Vāsiṣṭhas VII.18.22-25 — *Dānastuti* 55 — *Prasvāpinī Upaniṣat*	Vasiṣṭha Maitravaruṇi 55[IV] — addressed to celestial canine, Saramā's son
32	Vasiṣṭha Maitrāvaruṇi and/or Śakti Vāsiṣṭha 32.26 — first half Śakti Vāsiṣṭha,[V] Second half Vasiṣṭha Maitrāvāruṇi
33	1-9 Vasiṣṭha Maitrāvaruṇi, 10-14 sons of Vasiṣṭha (addressed to Vasiṣṭha)
101-02 Parjanya-Sūktas	Vasiṣṭha Maitrāvaruṇi or Kumāra Āgneya

Maṇḍala VIII (103 Sūktas)

The 103 (92+11 *khila*)) *sūktas* of this *maṇḍala* have been revealed to various *ṛṣis*. As per *prādhānyena vyapadeśā bhavanti* analogy, this *maṇḍala* is attributed to Ṛṣi Kaṇva and his descendants. Eighth *maṇḍala* contains eleven supplementary *sūktas* that are commonly known as 'Bālakhilya-Sūktas', on which Sāyaṇa's commentary is not available.

35. *ṚVS* VII.66.16.

Sūktas	Ṛṣi
1 VIII.1.32-33 — *Dānastuti*	1-2 Pragātha (Ghaura) Kāṇva, 3-29 Medhātithi Kāṇva, Medhyātithi Kāṇva, 30-33 Āsaṅga Plāyogī, 34 Śaśvati Āṅgirasī (*ṛṣikā*)
2 VIII.2.41 — *Dānastuti*	Medhātithi Kāṇva and Priyamedha Āṅgiras
3	Medhyātithi Kāṇva
4	Devātithi Kāṇva
5	Brahmātithi Kāṇva
6,11	Vatsa Kāṇva
7	Punarvatsa Kāṇva
8	Sadhvaṁsa Kāṇva
9	Śaśakarṇa Kāṇva
10, 48, 62-65	Pragātha Kāṇva
12	Parvata Kāṇva
13	Nārada Kāṇva
14-15	Goṣūkti Kāṇvāyana, Aśvasūkti Kāṇvāyana
16-18	Irimbiṭhi Kāṇva
19-22, 103 VIII.19.36-37 — *Dānastuti* VIII.21.17-18 — *Dānastuti*	Sobhari Kāṇva
23-25 VIII.24.28-30 — *Dānastuti*	Viśvamanā Vaiyaśva
26	Viśvamanā Vaiyaśva or Vyaśva Āṅgirasa
27-28, 30-31	Manu Vaivasvata
29	Manu Vaivasvata or Kaśyapa Mārīca
32	Medhātithi Kāṇva
33	Medhyātithi Kāṇva
34	Nīpātithi Kāṇva 16-18-Sahasra Vasurociṣ Āṅgirasa
35-38	Śyāvāśva Ātreya
39-41	Nābhāka Kāṇva

42	Nābhāka Kāṇva or Arcanānā Ātreya
43-44	Virūpa Āṅgirasa
45	Triśoka Kāṇva
46 VIII.46.21-24 — *Dānastuti*	Vaśa Aśvya
47	Trita Āptya
49 — Bālakhilya-Sūkta	Praskaṇva Kāṇva
50 — Bālakhilya-Sūkta	Puṣṭigu Kāṇva
51 — Bālakhilya-Sūkta	Śruṣṭigu Kāṇva
52 —Bālakhilya-Sūkta	Āyu Kāṇva
53, 57-58 — Bālakhilya-Sūktas	Medhya Kāṇva
54 — Bālakhilya-Sūkta	Mātariśvā Kāṇva
55 — Bālakhilya-Sūkta VIII.55-3 — *Dānastuti*	Kṛśa Kāṇva
56 — Bālakhilya-Sūkta VIII.56.2-3 — *Dānastuti*	Pṛṣadhra Kāṇva
59 — Bālakhilya-Sūkta	Suparṇa Kāṇva
60-61	Bharga Prāgātha
66	Kali Prāgātha
67	Matsya Sāmmada /or Mānya Maitrāvaruṇī/or many Matsya Jālanaddha
68-69 VIII.68.14-19-*Dānastuti*	Priyamedha Āṅgirasa
70	Puruhanmā Āṅgirasa
71	Sudīti and/or Purumīḷha Āṅgirasa
72	Haryata Prāgātha
73	Gopavana Ātreya or Saptavadhri
74 VIII.74.15 — *Dānastuti*	Gopavana Ātreya
75	Virūpa Āṅgirasa
76-78	Kurusuti Kāṇva
79	Kṛtnu Bhārgava
80	Ekadyū Naudhasa
81-83	Kusīdī Kāṇva
84	Uśanā Kāṇva

85	Kṛṣṇa Āṅgirasa
86	Kṛṣṇa Āṅgirasa or Viśvaka Kārṣṇī
87	Kṛṣṇa Āṅgirasa /or Dyumnīka Vāsiṣṭha or Priyamedha Āṅgirasa
88	Nodhā Gautama
89-90	Nṛmedha Āṅgirasa and Purumedha Āṅgirasa
91	Apālā Ātreyī (*ṛṣikā*)
92	Śrutakakṣa or Sukakṣa Āṅgirasa
93	Sukakṣa Āṅgirasa
94	Bindu Āṅgirasa or Pūtadakṣa Āṅgirasa
95	Tiraścī Āṅgirasa
96	Tiraścī Āṅgirasa or Dyutāna Māruta
97	Rebha Kāśyapa
98-99	Nṛmedha Āṅgirasa
100	Nema Bhārgava, and 4, 5 Indra
101	Jamadagni Bhārgava
102	Prayoga Bhārgava or Agni Bārhaspatya or Agni Pāvaka or Gṛhapati (son of Sahasa) and Yavistha; or any one of them

Maṇḍala IX (114 Sūktas)

The 114 *sūktas* of this *maṇḍala* have been revealed to various *ṛṣis*. All *sūktas* are addressed to the same deity Pavamāna Soma.[VI] Hence, this *maṇḍala* is known as Pavamāna-*maṇḍala*.

Maṇḍala IX is a late *maṇḍala*, which was compiled by combing out the hymns dedicated to Pavamāna Soma from earlier *maṇḍalas*.

Sūktas	**Ṛṣi**
1	Madhucchandā Vaiśvāmitra
2	Medhātithi Kāṇva
3	Śunaḥśepa Ājīgarti
4, 69	Hiraṇyastūpa Āṅgirasa

5-24 IX.5 — Āprī sūktam of the Kāśyapas	Asita Kāśyapa or Devala Kāśyapa
25	Dr̥ḷhacyuta Āgastya
26	Idhmavāha Dār̥ḍhacyuta
27, 29	Nr̥medha Āṅgirasa
28	Priyamedha Āṅgirasa
30	Bindu Āṅgirasa
31	Gotama Rāhūgaṇa
32	Śyāvāśva Ātreya
33-34, 102	Trita Āptya
35-36	Prabhūvasu Āṅgirasa
37-38	Rahūgaṇa Āṅgirasa
39-40	Br̥hanmati Āṅgirasa
41-43	Medhyātithi Kāṇva
44-46	Ayāsya Āṅgirasa
47-49, 75-79	Kavi Bhārgava
50-52	Ucathya Āṅgirasa
53-60	Avatsāra Kāśyapa
61	Amahīyu Āṅgirasa
62	Jamadagni Bhārgava
63	Nidhruvi Kāśyapa
64, 91-92	Kaśyapa Mārīca
65	Bhr̥gu Vāruṇi or Jamadagni Bhārgava
66	Śata Vaikhānasa
67	*Sapta R̥ṣayaḥ* — (i) Bharadvāja Bārhaspatya, (ii) Kaśyapa Mārica, (iii) Gotama Rāhūgaṇa, (iv) Atri Bhauma, (v) Viśvāmitra Gāthina, (vi) Jamadagni Bhārgava, (vii) Vasiṣṭha Maitrāvaruṇi, Pavitra Āṅgirasa or Vasiṣṭha Maitrāvaruṇi or both
68	Vatsaprī Bhālandana
70	Reṇu Vaiśvāmitra

71	Ṛṣabha Vaiśvāmitra
72	Harimanta Āṅgirasa
73, 83	Pavitra Āṅgirasa
74	Kakṣīvān Dairghatamas Auśija (son of Dīrghatamā and Uśija)
80-82	Vasu Bhāradvāja
84	Prajāpati Vācya
85	Vena Bhārgava
86	1-10 Akṛṣṭāmāsā *ṛṣis*, 11-20 Sikatā and Nivāvarī, 21-30 Pṛṣni-Aja *ṛṣis*, 31-40 Three Akṛṣṭāmāsā *ṛṣis*, 41-45 Atri Bhauma, 46-48 Gṛtsamada Bhārgava Śaunaka
87-89	Uśanā Kāvya
90	Vasiṣṭha Maitrāvaruṇi
93	Nodhā Gautama
94	Kaṇva Ghaura /or Kaṇva Āṅgirasa
95	Praskaṇva Kāṇva
96	Pratardana Daivodāsī
97	1-3 Vasiṣṭha Maitrāvaruṇi, 4-6 Indrapramati Vāsiṣṭha, 7-9 Vṛṣagaṇa Vāsiṣṭha, 10-12 Manyu Vāsiṣṭha, 13-15 Upamanyu Vāsiṣṭha, 16-18 Vyāghrapāda Vāsiṣṭha, 19-21 Śakti Vāsiṣṭha, 22-24 Karṇaśruta Vāsiṣṭha, 25-27 Mṛḷīka Vāsiṣṭha, 28-30 Vasukra Vāsiṣṭha, 31-44 Parāśara Śāktya, 45-58 Kutsa Āṅgirasa
98	Ambarīṣa Vārṣāgira, Ṛjiśvā Bhāradvāja/or Āṅgirasa
99-100	Rebhasūnū Kāśyapa
101	1-3 Andhīgu Śyavāśvi, 4-6 Yayāti Nāhuṣa, 7-9 Nahuṣa Mānava, 10-12 Manu Sāṁvaraṇa, 13-16 Prajāpati Vaiśvāmitra/or Prajāpati Vācya
102	Trita Āptya
103	Dvita Āptya

104	Parvata Kāṇva and Nārada Kāṇva/ or Śikhaṇḍinī (two celestial nymphs daughters of Kaśyapa, both *ṛṣikās*
105	Parvata Kāṇva and Nārada Kāṇva
106	1-3 Agni Cākṣuṣa, 4-6 Cakṣu Mānava, 7-9 Manu Āpsava
107[36]	*Sapta Ṛṣayaḥ*[VII] — (i) Bharadvāja Bārhaspatya, (ii) Kaśyapa Mārica, (iii) Gotama Rāhūgaṇa, (iv) Atri Bhauma, (v) Viśvāmitra Gāthina, (vi) Jamadagni Bhārgava, (vii) Vasiṣṭha Maitrāvaruṇi
108	1-2 Gaurīvīti Śāktya, 3, 14-16 Śakti Vāsiṣṭha, 4-5 Ūru Āṅgirasa, 6-7 Ṛjiśvā Bhāradvāja, 8-9 Ūrdhvasadmā Āṅgirasa, 10-11 Kṛtayaśā Āṅgirasa, 12-13 Ṛṇañcaya
109	Agni Dhiṣṇya Aiśvara
110	Tryaruṇa Traivṛṣṇa and Trasadasyu Paurukutsya
111	Anānata Pārucchepi
112	Śiśu Āṅgirasa
113-14	Kaśyapa Mārica

Maṇḍala X (191 Sūktas)

Chronologically, the hymns in Maṇḍala X were composed in the final period of the *Ṛgveda*, long after the period of the other nine *maṇḍalas*; so long after them that, its language alone, in spite of attempts at standardisation, is sufficient proof to establish its late position.

This *maṇḍala* has 191 *sūktas*. Many famous *sūktas* of *Ṛgveda* are found in this *maṇḍala*. The listing below has all the names:

36. The seven *ṛṣis* have individually seen one *ṛk* each in this Sūkta IX.107, and collectively rest of the *ṛcā*.

Sūktas	Ṛṣi
1-7	Tritā Āptya
8	Triśirā Tvāṣṭra
9	Triśirā Tvāṣṭra or Sindhudvīpa Āmbarīṣa
10 Yama-Yamī-Saṁvāda[VIII]	1, 3, 5, 7, 11, 13 Yamī Vaivasvatī (*ṛṣikā*) 2, 4, 8-10, 12, 14 Yama Vaivasvata
11,12	Havirdhāna Āṅgi
13	Vivasvān Āditya
14	Yama Vaivasvata
15	Śaṅkha Yāmāyana
16	Damana Yāmāyana
17	DevaśravāYāmāyana
18	Saṅkusuka Yāmāyana
19	Mathita Yāmāyana /or Bhṛgu Vāruṇi / or Cyavana Bhārgava
20-26	Vimada Aindra/ or Vimada Prājāpatya/or Vasukṛt Vasukra
27, 29	Vasukra Aindra (son of Indra)
28	1 Indrasnuṣā Vasukra Patnī (*ṛṣikā*), 2, 6 , 8, 10, 12 Indra, 3, 4, 5, 7, 9, 11 Vasukra Aindra (son of Indra)
30-33	Kavaṣa Ailūṣa
34 — *Sūktam* on a Gambler	Kavaṣa Ailūṣa or Akṣa Maujavān
35-36	Luśa Dhānāka
37	Abhitapā Saurya
38	Indra Muṣkavān
39-40	Ghoṣā Kakṣīvatī (*ṛṣikā*)
41	Suhastya Ghauṣeya (son of Ṛṣikā Ghoṣā Kakṣīvatī)
42-44	Kṛṣṇa Āṅgirasa

45-46	Vatsapri Bhālandana
47	Saptagu Āṅgirasa
48-50	Indra Vaikuṇṭha
51,53	Devagaṇa and Agni Saucīka
52	Agni Saucīka
54-56	Bṛhaduktha Vāmadevya
57-59	Bandhu, Subandhu, Śrutabandhu, Viprabandhu (Gaupāyana or Laupāyana)
60	1-5, 7-12 Bandhu, Subandhu, Śrutabandhu, Viprabandhu (Gaupāyana or Laupāyana), 6 Agastya-svasā (*ṛṣikā*)
61-62 X.62.8-11 — *Dānastuti*	Nābhānediṣṭha Mānava
63-64	Gaya Plāta
65-66	Vasukarṇa Vāsukra
67- 68	Ayāsya Āṅgirasa
69-70 X.70 — *Āprīsūktam* of the Bhāratas	Sumitra Vadhryaśva
71	Bṛhaspati Āṅgirasa
72	Bṛhaspati Laukya/or Bṛhaspati Āṅgirasa/or Aditi Dākṣāyanī (*ṛṣikā*)
73, 74	Gaurivīti Śāktya
75	Sindhukṣit Praiyamedha
76	Jaratkarṇa Airāvata (a Snake)
77-78	Syumaraśmi Bhārgava
79-80	Agni Saucīka /or Agni Vaiśvānara /or Saptivājaṁbhara
81-82	Viśvakarmā Bhauvana
83, 84	Manyu Tāpas
85 — Sūryā-Sāvitrī-Sūktam (used at the time of wedding)	Sūryā Sāvitrī (*ṛṣikā*)

Vedic wedding being performed chanting Sūryā-Sāvitrī-Sūktam

86	8, 11, 12, 13, 14, 19, 20, 21, 23 Indra, 1, 7 Vṛṣākapi Aindra, 2, 3, 4, 5, 6, 9, 10, 15-18, 22 Indrāṇī (*ṛṣikā*)
87	Pāyu Bhāradvāja
88	Mūrdhanvān Āṅgirasa /or Mūrdhanvān Vāmadevya
89	Reṇu Vaiśvāmitra
90 — Puruṣa-Sūktam	Nārāyaṇa
91	Aruṇa Vaitahavya
92	Śāryāta Mānava
93	Tānva Pārtha
94	Arbuda Kādradeya (a Snake)
95 — Purūravā-Urvaśī Saṁvāda	1, 3, 4, 6, 7, 8, 9, 10, 12, 14, 17 Purūravā, 2, 5, 7, 11, 13, 15, 16, 18 Urvaśī (*ṛṣikā*)
96	Baru Āṅgirasa/or Sarvahari Aindra
97	Bhiṣak Ātharvaṇa
98	Devāpi Ārṣṭiṣeṇa
99	Vamra Vaikhānasa
100	Duvasyu Vāndana
101	Budha Saumya

102	Mudgala Bhārmyaśva
103 — Apratiratha-Sūktam	Apratiratha Aindra (son of Indra)
104	Aṣṭaka Vaiśvāmitra
105	Durmitra /or Sumitra Kautsa
106	Bhūtāṁśa Kāśyapa
107 — *Dānastuti*	Divya Āṅgirasa/or Dakṣiṇā Prājāpatyā (*ṛṣikā*)
108 — Saramā-Paṇi-Saṁvāda	2, 4, 6, 8, 10-11 Saramā Devaśunī (*ṛṣikā*) 1, 3, 5, 7, 9 Paṇi (group of Asuras)
109	Juhū-Brahmajāyā (*ṛṣikā*)/ or Urdhvanābhā Brāhma
110, 167 110 — Āprīsūktam of the Bhṛgus	Jamadagni Bhārgava/ or Rāma Jāmadagnya
111	Aṣṭrādaṁṣṭra Vairūpa
112	Nabha Prabhedana Vairūpa
113	Śata Prabhedana Vairūpa
 Indus Valley Seal probably depicting *Ṛgveda* X.114.9 114[37]	Sadhri Vairūpa /or Gharma Tāpas
115	Upastuta Varṣṭihavya
116	Agniyuta Sthaura /or Agniyūpa Sthaura
X.117 — *Dānastuti* *Dhana-Annadāna-Praśaṁsā*	Bhikṣu Āṅgirasa
118	Urukṣaya Āmahīyava

37. *ṚVS* X.114.9 is depicted in an Indus Valley. See *In Search of the Cradle of Civilization* by David Frawley, p. 34.

119 — *Ātmastuti*	Lava Aindra
120	Bṛhaddiva Ātharvaṇa
121 — Hiraṇyagarbha-Sūktam	Hiraṇyagarbha Prājāpatya
122	Citramahā Vāsiṣṭha
123	Vena Bhārgava
124	2, 3, 4 Agni; 1, 5, 9 Agni, Varuṇa, and Soma
125 — Devīsūktam/*Ātmastuti* (also chanted in *Dugāsaptaśatī Caṇḍī*)  Durgā Saptaśatī Caṇḍī Karma	Vāgambhṛṇī (*ṛṣikā*)
126	Kulmalabarhiṣa Śailūṣi/or Āhomuk Vāmadevya
127 — Rātri Sūktam (also chanted in *Durgāsaptaśatī Caṇḍī*)	Kuśika Saubhara/ or Rātri Bhāradvājī (*ṛṣikā*)
128	Vihavya Āṅgirasa
129 — Nāsadīya-Sūktam-(Hymn of Creation)	Prajāpati Parameṣṭhi
130	Yajña Prājāpatya
131	Sukīrti Kākṣivata
132	Śakapūta Nārmedha
133	Sudās Paijavan

134	1, 5, 1st part of 6 Māndhātā Yauvanāśva, 2nd part of 6, 7 Godhā (*ṛṣikā*) (6th *mantra* was envisioned by Māndhātā Yauvanāśva and Godhā)
135	Kumāra Yāmāyana
136	Vātaraśana Munis, i.e. 1 Jūti, 2 Vātajūti, 3 Viprajūti, 4 Vṛṣāṇaka, 5 Karikrata, 6 Etaśa, 7 Ṛṣyaśṛṅga
137	*Sapta Ṛṣayaḥ*[38] — (i) Bharadvāja Bārhaspatya, (ii) Kaśyapa Mārīca, (iii) Gotama Rāhugaṇa, (iv) Atri Bhauma, (v) Viśvāmitra Gāthina, (vi) Jamadagni Bhārgava, (vii) Vasiṣṭha Maitrāvaruṇi
138	Aṅga Aukha
139 — *Ātmastuti*	Viśvāvasu Devagandharva
140	Agni Pāvaka
141	Agni Tāpasa
142	Śārṅgagaṇa (1-2 Jaritā, 3-4 Droṇa, 5-6 Sārisṛkva, 7-8 Stambamitra)
143	Atri Sāṁkhya
144	Suparṇa Tārkṣyaputra/or Ūrdhvakṛṣṇa Yāmāyana
145 — *Sapatnī-Vādhana Upaniṣad*	Indrāṇī (*ṛṣikā*)
146	Devamuni Airaṁmada
147	Suvedasa Śairīṣa
148	Pṛthuvainya
149	Arcan Hairaṇyastūpa
150	Mṛḷīka Vāsiṣṭha
151 — Śraddhā-Sūktam	Śraddhā Kāmāyanī (*ṛṣikā*)
152	Śāsa Bhāradvāja
153	Indramātaraḥ (*ṛṣikās*) — Deva-bhaginis

38. The seven *ṛṣis* have individually seen one *ṛk* each in this *sūkta* X.137.

154 — Bhāvavṛtta-Sūktam	Yamī Vaivasvatī (*ṛṣikā*)
155 — Alakṣmīghna-Sūktam	Śirimbiṭha Bhāradvāja
156	Ketu Āgneya
157	Bhuvana Āptya /or Sādhana Bhauvana
158	Cakṣu Saurya
159-*Ātmatuṣṭi*	Śaci Paulomī (*ṛṣikā*)
160	Pūraṇa Vaiśvāmitra
161	Yakṣmanāśana Prājāpatya
162	Rakṣohā Brāhma
163	Vivṛha Kāśyapa
164 — Duḥsvapna-nāśana-Sūktam	Pracetā Āṅgirasa
165	Kapota Nairṛta
166	Ṛṣabha Vairāja /or Ṛṣabha Śakvara
167	Viśvāmitra and Jamadagni
168	Anila Vātāyana
169	Śabara Kākṣīvata
170	Vibhrāṭ Saurya
171	Iṭa Bhārgava
172	Saṁvarta Āṅgirasa
173	Dhruva Āṅgirasa
174	Abhīvarta Āṅgirasa
175	Ūrdhvagrāvā Ārvudi (a Snake)
176	Sūnu Ārbhava
177	Pataṅga Prājāpatya
178	Ariṣṭanemi Tārkṣya
179	1 Śibi Auśīnara, 2 Pratardana Kāśirāja, 3 Vasumanā Rohidaśva
180	Jaya Aindra
181	1 Pratha Vāsiṣṭha, 2 Sapratha Bhāradvāja, 3 Gharma Saurya
182	Tapumūrdhā Bārhaspatya

183	Prajāvān Prājāpatya
184	Tvaṣṭā Garbhakartā/ or Viṣṇu Prājāpatya
185	Satyadhṛti Vāruṇi
186	Ula Vātāyana
187	Vatsa Āgneya
188	Śyena Āgneya
189	Sārparājñī (*ṛṣikā*)
190 — Bhāvavṛtta-Sūktam	Aghamarṣaṇa Mādhucchandas
191	Saṁvanana

Ṛgveda-Khila[39]-Sūktas

Different texts have different *khila-sūktas*, with many common hymns. Vaidika Samshodhana Mandala (VSM), Pune, and C.G. Kashikar have published a critical edition of the *khila-sūktas*. All these *khila-sūktas* belong to the four other nearly extinct Ṛgvedic *śākhās*, namely Bāṣkala, Āśvalāyana, Sāṁkhāyana (or Sāṁkhyāyana), and Māṇḍūkāyana, as evidenced by the fact that many ancient texts like the Brāhmaṇas and *Bṛhaddevatā* refer to the *mantras* in these *khila* hymns. Thus, these *khila* hymns are part of the *Ṛgveda* in a strict sense, and are not merely popular hymns that were later on appended to the *Ṛgveda* by their admirers as is commonly believed.

In *Śākala Saṁhitā*, there are 36 *sūktas* named as *Ṛk-pariśiṣṭa*. Some of the well-known *khila-sūktas*, commonly chanted are: Śri-Sūktam, Medhā-Sūktam, Rātrī-Sūktam, Sauparṇās, Śiva-Saṁkalpa-Sūktam, Hṛdaya-Sūktam and Sañjāna-Sūktam. The *khila* hymns in *adhyāyas* 5 to 7, namely the *nivids*, *purorucas* and *praiṣas* belong to the oldest *Ṛgveda* period as per some scholars. Some like Mahānāmni, Bālakhilya and Kuntāpa belong to the end of the Ṛgvedic period.

39. *khila-lakṣaṇam — paraśākhīyaṁ svaśākhāyām-apekṣāvaśāt-paṭhyate tat khilam-ucyate.*
— *Ma.Bhā.Śā.* 323.10, Nīlakaṇṭha *ṭīkā*.

The eight Bālakhilya-Sūktas in the eighth *maṇḍala* (VIII.49 to VIII.56), are also part of *adhyāya* 3 of the *khila;* except that the accent marks of these verses in the standard *Ṛgveda* text differ from those in the *khila*. The accent marks for the same *khila-sūkta*s found in different books, are substantially different.

Bālakhilya-Sūktas

ṚV. VIII.49 to VIII.59 are the eleven Bālakhilya-Sūktas. R.T.H. Griffith has placed the 11 Bālakhilya/Vālakhilya Sūktas at the end of the VIIIth *maṇḍala* and has explained thus:

> I place at the end of this book, the eleven hymns, called the *vālakhilya,* which are usually inserted after hymn 48. These hymns are not reckoned in the division into *maṇḍala* (books) and *anuvāka*s (chapters), and Sāyaṇa does not notice them in his commentary.[40]

The Bālakhilya-Sūktas are traditionally chanted during *svādhyāya* by the Ṛgvedic scholars.

Āprī-Sūktas[41]

The composers of *Ṛgveda* are divided into 10 families. The basis, on which these 10 families are identified, is the fact that each family has its own *āprīsūktam*.

An *āprīsūktam* is a particular type of ritual hymns 'consisting of invocations to a series of deified objects, (i) *idhma* or *samiddha agni,* (ii) *tanūnapāt,* (iii) *narāśaṁsā,* (iv) *iḷā,* (v) *barhi,* (vi) *divyadvāra,* (vii) *uṣāsānaktā,* (viii) *divyahotā pracetas,* (ix) the three *devīs* — *sarasvatī, iḷā, bhāratī,* (x) *tvaṣṭā,* (xi) *vanaspati,* (xii) *svāhākṛti,* and are said to be introductory to the animal sacrifice'.[42]

---

40. *The Hymns of the Ṛgveda,* R.T.H. Griffith, vol. II, p. 199.
41. *The Ṛgveda: A Historical Analysis,* Ch 2, Composers of the Ṛgveda, Shrikant G. Talageri.
42. *Hymns of Ṛgveda,* R.T.H. Griffith, vol. I, fn I.13.

The 10 *āprīsūktas*, and the 10 families of composers to whom they belong are shown in the table below.

	Sūktam	Ṛṣi	Family
1	I.13	Medhātithi Kāṇva	The Kāṇvas (Kevala-Āṅgirasas)
2	I.142	Dīrghatamā Aucathya	The Āṅgirasas
3	I.188	Agastya Maitrāvaruṇi	The Āgastyas
4	II.3	Gṛtsamada Āṅgirasa Saunahotra/later Gṛtsamada Śaunaka Bhārgava	(Kevala-Bhṛgus)
5	III.4	Viśvāmitra Gāthina	The Viśvāmitras
6	V.5	Vasuśruta Ātreya	The Atris
7	VII.2	Vasiṣṭha Maitrāvaruṇi	The Vāsiṣṭhas
8	IX.5	Asita Kāśyapa or Devala Kāśyapa	The Kāśyapas
9	X.70	Sumitra Vadhryaśva	The Bharatas
10	X.110	Jamadagni Bhārgava	The Bhṛgus

Incidentally, repetition of three consecutive verses of the *āprisūktas* III.4.8-11 seen by Viśvāmitra Gāthina, in VII.2.8-11 seen by Vasiṣṭha Maitrāvaruṇi, is considered to be the longest repetition in *Ṛgveda*.

The composers of the *Ṛgveda* were members of 10 priestly families, and each family had its own *āprīsūktam* composed by a member of that family. In later times, during the performance of any sacrifice, at the point where an *āprīsūktam* was to be recited, the sacrifice conducting *ṛṣi* was required to recite the *āprīsūktam* of his own family.

Women Ṛṣis (Ṛṣikās) in Ṛgveda Saṁhitā[43]

	Ṛṣikās (alphabetically)	Sūktas
1	Aditī or Aditi-Dākṣyāyanī	IV.18. 2nd half of 4 & 7 (2 ½ *mantras*) X.72 (9 *mantras*)
2	Agastya-svasā (sister of Agastya)	X.60.6 (1 *mantra*)
3	Apālā Ātreyī (daughter of Atri)	VIII.91 (7 *mantras*)
4	Dakṣiṇā Prājāpatyā	X.107 (11 *mantras*)
5	Godhā	X.134.7 (1 *mantra*)
6	Ghoṣā Kakṣīvatī, a princess, daughter of Kakṣivān	X.39 (14 *mantras*) X.40 (14 *mantras*)
7	Indrāṇī (consort of Indra)	X.86 (12 *mantras*) X.145 (6 *mantras*) (*sapatnī-vādhana*)
8	Indramātaraḥ (mothers of Indra)	X.153 (5 *mantras*)
9	Juhū-Brahmajāyā (wife of Bṛhaspati)	X.109 (7 *mantras*)
10	Kaśyapī/Śikhaṇḍinī (two daughters of Kāśyapa, celestial nymphs)	IX.104 (6 *mantras*)
11	Lopāmudrā (wife of Agastya)	I.179.1 & 2 (2 *mantras*)
12	Nadyaḥ (the Rivers)	III.189 (3 *mantras*)
13	Rātri-Bhāradvājī (daughter of *ṛṣi* Bharadvāja)	X.127 (8 *mantras*) (Rātri-Sūktam — also chanted in *Durgāsapataśatī*)
14	Romaśā (daughter of Bṛhaspati and wife of King Svanaya Bhāvayava)	I.126.7 (1 *mantra*)
15	Sūryā Sāvitrī (daughter of Sūrya)	X.85 (47 *mantras*) (used in Wedding)
16	Saramā Devaśunī	X.108 (6 *mantras*) (Saramā-Paṇi-Saṁvāda)
17	Sārparājñī	X.189 (3 *mantras*)

43. Cf. R.L. Kashyap's *Ṛgveda Mantra Saṁhitā*, p. 25.

18	Śaśvatī Āṅgirasī (daughter of Āṅgiras, wife of Āsaṅga)	VIII.1.34 (1 *mantra*)
19	Śaci Paulomī	X.159 (6 *mantras*) (Ātmatuṣṭi-addressed to Self)
20	Śraddhā Kāmāyanī	X.151 (5 *mantras*) (Śraddhā-Sūktam)
21	Urvaśī (a celestial nymph)	X.95 (8 *mantras*) (Purūravā-Urvaśī-Saṁvāda)
22	Vāgambhṛṇī	X.125 (8 *mantras*) (Devī-Sūktam)
23	Vaśukrapatnī /Indrasnuṣā (wife of Vaśukra, daughter-in-law of Indra)	X.28.1 (1 *mantra*)
24	Viśvavāra Ātreyī	V.28 (6 *mantras*)
25	Yamī Vaivasvatī (sister of Yama)	X.10 (8 *mantras* - Yama-Yamī-Saṁvāda), X.154 (5 *mantras*)

Some Popular Sūktas and Mantras in the Ṛgveda

The *ṚVS* has 1,028 *sūkta*s containing 10,552 *mantras*. Very few people have the opportunity, time or inclination to read all the *mantras*. Some of the well-known *sūkta*s and *mantra*s are presented here, divided into six categories. During their recitation, persons regularly attending temple-chantings may recognise some *mantra*s or *sūkta*s, but may not be able to identify them or even know that they are in the *ṚVS*. The titles of the six sections are self-explanatory.

1. *Mantra*s for Peace and well-being
2. *Mantra*s for Specific Benefits
3. General Information
4. *Mantra*s in *Navagraha Pūjā*
5. *Mantra*s in *Tantra* (*Daśa-Mahā-Vidyā*s)
6. *Mantra*s in *Sandhyā* Worship

ṚK-MANTRAS FOR PEACE AND WELL-BEING

Puruṣa-Sūktam	X.90
Gāyatrī-mantra	III.62.10
All *sūktas* of Maṇḍala IX (addressed to Pavamāna Soma)	IX.1-IX.114
Śānti-mantras	I.90.9 (*śaṁ no mitra śaṁ varunaḥ*), VII.35.1 to 13 (*saṁ na . . . .*), VIII.18.8 & 9, VIII.38.7, VIII.48.4 (*śaṁ no bhava hṛda*), X.9.4 (*śaṁ no devirabhiṣṭaya*), X.37.10 (*śaṁ no bhava cakṣasā*)
Svasti-mantras	I.1.9 (*sa naḥ piteva*), I.89.6 (*svasti na indro vṛddhaśravāḥ*), V.51.11 to 15 (*svasti-mantras*), X.35.3 to 12, X.63.3 to 14, X.178.1 & 2
(*Bhadramantrāḥ*) *Mantras* for happiness and well-being	I.1.6, I.89.8, I.115.3, IV.6.6, IV.11.1, IV.21.9, V.30.12, VI.64.2, VII.93.28, VII.96.3, VIII.19.20, VIII.29.19, IX.97.2, X.3.3, X.20.1, X.25.1, X.69.7, X.164.2, *khila* 2.2
Śri-Sūktam	*Khila* II.6
Aghamarṣaṇa-mantrāḥ (Purification *mantrāḥ*)	X.9.1 to 3
Brahmaṇaspatiḥ or *Gaṇapatiḥ*	I.40.1, II.23.1 (*gaṇānāṁ tvā gaṇapatim*), II.24.11 to 16, II.25, II.26, X.72, X.112.9
Durgā	I.99.1, I.189.2
Atreḥ Gāyatrī (*Gāyatrī* of Atri)	V.82.1
Haṁsa-mantraḥ /or *Sauri Ṛk* (He is everywhere)	IV.40.5
Viśvam-āryam	IX.63.5
Rudraḥ-Śivaḥ	I.43.1, 2, 4 to 6, I.114, II..33, V.42.11, VII.46, VII.59.12 (*tryambakaṁ yajāmahe*)
Sarasvatī (Goddess of inspiration)	I.3.10 to 12, I.164.49, II.30.8, II.41.16 to 18, VI.61, VII.95, VII.96, X.17.8 & 9

Savitṛ (Creator)	I.35.2 to 11, II.38, III.62.10 to 12, IV.53 & 54, V.81 82, VI.71, VII.45, X.149
Śiva-saṁkalpa	*Khila* IV.11
Sūrya (Sun, the basis of all life)	I.50, I.115, I.164.46, VII.63, VII.66, X.37, X.158, X.170
Viṣṇu	I.22.16 to 21, I.154, I.155.5 to 6, I.156, VII.99.1 to 3 & 7, VII.100

ṚK-MANTRAS FOR SPECIFIC BENEFITS

These *mantra*s are meant for specific benefits like developing one's will-power, healing, ease of childbirth, etc. They are taken from Kātyāyana's *Sarvānukramaṇī*, Śaunaka's *Ṛgvidhāna* and Śrī Aurobindo's *The Secret of the Veda*. Their efficacy under appropriate conditions is a fact of experience.

Agniḥ (will-power)	I.1, I.65, I.73, I.96, I.189.1, IV.4.1, V.24, IV.9.8, V.2.9, VI.3.1 to 8, VI.48.1, VII.1.1, VII.13.1, VII.41, VIII.18.9, VIII.44.1, VIII.71.1, X.1.1, X.20.1, X.25.1, X.45, X.141, X.142
Annam (Food)	I.187
Dhana-Annadānam (Gift of Food)	X.117
Duḥsvapna-nāśanam (Averting Bad Dreams)	II.28.10, X.164
Āpaḥ (Water for Dynamical Energies)	I.164.42, I.23.16 to 23, VII.47 & 49, X.9, X.17
Āyudham (Battle & Weapons)	VI.75, X.103, X.152
Ānandaḥ (Happiness)	I.89, I.90
Śiśujanma, Garbhasrāva-nivāraṇam (Childbirth)	I.101, V.78, X.106, X.162
Śiśavaḥ (Children)	II.32.4
Garbhadhānam (Child's Conception)	X.184.1 to 3

Dānam (Reaching Out)	I.125, VI.27.8, VI.47.22 to 25, VII.98.22 to 25, VIII.1.30 to 33, VIII.2.41 to 42, VIII.3.21 to 24, VIII.4.19 to 21, VIII.5.37 to 39, VIII.6.46 to 48, VIII.21.17 to 18, VIII.24.28 to 30, VIII.46.1 to 4 and 21 to 24, VIII.55, VIII.68.14 to 19, VIII.74.13 to 15, X.33.4 & 5, X.62.8 to 11, X.117
Vasatiḥ (Dwelling)	X.32.7
Prajākāmaḥ (Desire for Children)	V.46.7 & 8
Roganāśaḥ (Destruction of Disease)	X.85.31, X.97, X.161, X.163
Ajñāna-nāśaḥ (Destruction of Ignorance)	X.177
Tejovardhanam (Developing Splendour)	VIII.101, X.128
Śaraṇāgatiḥ (Developing Surrender)	I.50.13, VI.51.8
Pācana-kriyā (Digestion of food)	III.26.7
Duḥkhanāsaḥ (Dispel misery)	I.97
Abhaya-pradānam (Dispel fear)	VII.55, VIII.30.1, VIII.61.13 to 18
Devirdvārāḥ (Divine Inner doors)	I.13.6, I.142.6, I.188.5, II.3.5, III.4.5, V.5.5, VII.2.5, IX.5.5, X.70.5, X.110.5
Ratiḥ (Enjoyment)	I.179.5 & 6
Śraddhā (Faith)	X.151
Agni-Śamanam (Fire extinguishing)	I.70.1
Araṇyāni (Forests & Woods)	X.146
Pāśatraya-vimocanam (release from triple cords of Bondage)	I.24.15, I.25.21, VII.88.7
Deva-sāmarasyam (Harmony of gods)	I.89, I.90, I.139, I.164, III.54, IV.55, VI.51
Asthi-cikitsā (Healing of bones)	VIII.1.12

Roga-Śamanam (Healing *mantras*)	I.50.11 to 13, II.33.1, VIII.48.5
Ārogyam (Health)	I.23.16, VII.51
Oṣadhiḥ (Herbs)	X.97
Protection from enemies	X.187
Sneha-vardhanam (Increase of affection)	I.74.2
Antar-devaśakti-vardhanam (Increase of Divine Power within Self)	I.135, VI.16.10 (*agna āyāhi vītaye gṛṇāno havyadātaye*)
Indraḥ-Divya-manomayasya adhirājaḥ (Lord of Divine Mind)	I.30.1 to 16, I.84.16 to 20, I.101, I.106.1 to 7, I.165.1, II.12.1, II.21.6, III.45, III.53.17 & 19 & 21, IV.25, 32, V.38, VI.46.1, VI.47.18 & 29 to 31, VII.32.22, VIII.32.1, VIII.35.1, VIII.46.1, VIII.81.1, VIII.93.4, X.89.1
Jñānam (Knowledge)	I.164, X.71
Jñānānanda (Joy of knowledge)	I.89
Vidyā-yaśaḥ (Literary/ Scholarly fame)	III.53.15
Dīrghāyuḥ (Long life)	I.10.11, I.24.11, I.51.15, III.53, X.18
Manyuḥ (Wrath)	X.83 & 84
Vivāhaḥ (Marriage)	X.85.6 to 47 (*Sūryā-Sāvitrī-Sūktam*)
Patnyā saha Patiḥ (Husband to wife)	X.85.36 (*Sūryā-Sāvitrī-Sūktam*)
Daṁpatī (Spoken by couple)	X.85.42 & 47 (*Sūryā-Sāvitrī-Sūktam*)
Patī Sāmrājñī (Wife as queen of all)	X.85.46 (*Sūryā-Sāvitrī-Sūktam*)
Viṣa-nāśana (Poison antidote)	I.191 (*Viṣoghnopaniṣad*)
Saṁjñānam (Prayer for unanimity)	X.191.3 to 4
Dhanakāmāḥ (Prayer for wealth)	I.96, X.31.2, X.73.1, X.155, *Khila* II.6

Ariṣad-vargaiḥ Rakṣaṇam (Protection from enemies)	IV.4, VII.104, VIII.16.1, X.87, X.118, X.169
Sapatnarakṣaṇam (Protection from rivals)	X.145
Aghamarṣaṇam (Purification)	I.97, X.9.1 to 3
Pūṣan (Recovery of lost persons)	I.23.13 to 15, I.42, I.138, VI.53, VI.54.10
Varṣā (Rain)	I.164.51, V.83, VII.101.1 & 6, VII.102 & 103, X.98
Sukhasya Nāvaḥ (Ship to felicity)	I.97.8, I.99.1, I.131.2, I.140.12
Somaḥ (*Karmānandaḥ*) (Joy of work)	I.43.8 to 9, I.91, III.62.13 to 15, VI.47.1 to 5, VIII.48.3 to 5, X.85.1 to 5
Guruḥ (Teacher)	III.26.9
Sukha-Prayāṇam (Safe travel)	IV.32, X.185
Uṣā (The dawn of Knowledge)	VII.75
Vāstu	VII.54, VII.55.1
Jayaḥ (Victory)	VIII.16.1
Vighnanāśaḥ (Ward off obstacles)	I.99.1, I.189.2, V.4.9
Udakāvāptiḥ (Water divining)	VIII.21.18, X.30.1
Yamaḥ	I.73.10, X.10, X.14, X.16, X.18.2, X.58, X.135
Daṁpatyāśiṣaḥ (Yearnings of a couple)	VIII.31.4 to 18

DETAILS OF FAMILIAR ṚK-MANTRAS

This section deals with answers to questions such as, 'Are *mantras* composed?', 'Who are the seven *ṛṣis*?' The listing given in this section is typical, not exhaustive.

Topic	Reference
Tvamgna Indro Varuṇaḥ (Agni as Indra, Varuṇa)	II.1.1 to 2, I.11, V.3.1
Aditiḥ	I.89.10, VIII.18.6, X.72.5 & 8 & 9, X.100, X.185
Aditiḥ and Ditiḥ	IV.2.11
Ādityaḥ	VIII.67.1
Agni's Guidance	I.189.1 (*agne naya supathā rāye asmān*) (repeated in *Īśāvāsyopaniṣad*)
Aśvinau (Devabhiṣajau) (Gods of Joy and Celestial Physicians)	I.46, I.112, I.116
Madhuvidyā (Joy)	I.90.6 to 8 (*madhu vātā ṛtāyate . . .*)
Bṛhaspatiḥ	III.62.4 to 18, VI.73
Gāvaḥ Jñānaṁ vā (Cows or Knowledge)	VI.28, VIII.101, X.169
Bhavavṛttam, Sṛṣṭiḥ (Creation) (Counter-form to all Forms)	X.129, X.130, X.154, X.190 VI.47.18 (*rūpaṁ-rūpaṁ-pratirūpo-*)
Bhūmiḥ (Earth)	I.22.15, VI.47.20
Deva-Mānava-maitrī (Friendship of gods)	I.26.3, I.89.2
Pitṛ-Putra-Rūpaḥ Devaḥ (Gods as fathers and sons)	I.1.9, I.31.10
Haṁsa-Mantraḥ / Sauri-Ṛcā	IV.40.5
Samanasā Ṛṣayaḥ (Harmony of all *ṛṣis*)	I.164.16, X.130.7
Hṛt Sūktam (Heart-inner)	*Khila* III.15
(Heart, mind and understanding)	I.61.2 (*hṛdā-manasā-maniṣā . . .*)
Svargaḥ (Ideal of heaven)	IX.113.11
Ekatā (Unity of all)	IV.26.1 & 2, X.125.1
Sphūrti (Inspiration)	See Sarasvatī
Sahajāvavodhaḥ (Intuition in heart)	I.24.12
Ila-Prajñāmayī Dṛṣṭi (Goddess of Revelation)	I.13.9, I.142.9, II.1.11
Ketuḥ (Intuition)	I.6.3
Medhā (Intelligence)	*Khila* IV.8

Jñānam (Knowledge)	I.89.1, IV.2.11, X.72.1 to 9
Cittim-acittim (Knowledge & ignorance)	IV.2.11
Jyotirhṛdayam (Light within heart)	VI.9.6
Mūrdhna Puṣkara (Lotus in the head)	VI.16.13
Mantrakṛt (*Mantras* are formed)	I.67.4, I.78.5, I.94.1, I.171.2, IX.114.2
Ṛṣikṛt (Men and women become *ṛṣis*)	I.31.16, IX.96.18
Nirṛtiḥ	X.49.1 to 3, X.59.4
Ānanda-sāgaraḥ (Ocean of joy)	IV.58.1
(One Truth, many forms)	X.114.5, I.164.46 (*indraṁ mitraṁ varunaṁ . . . ekaṁ sad viprā bahudhā vadanti. . .*)
Origin of *Ṛk mantra*	I.164.39 (*ṛce akṣare parame vyoman . . .*)
(Progress from peak to peak)	I.10.2 (*yat sānoḥ sānum aruhad . . .*)
Guhyanāma (Secret name)	IV.58.4
Niṇya Vacāṁsi (Secret word)	IV.3.16
Ṣaḍripavaḥ (Six enemies in symbols)	VII.104.22
Ātmā	I.34.7, 1.113.6, 1.115.6, 1.162.20, 1.163.6, 1.164.4, VII.87.2, VII.101.6, VIII.3.24, IX.2.10, IX.6.8, X.16.3, X.82.13, X.97.11, X.107.7, X.168.4
Śyenātmā (Soul as bird)	IV.26.4 to 7, IV.27.1 to 4
Vāk (Speech)	I.164.42 & 45, III.53.15 & 16, VIII.100.10 & 11, X.125
Sūryaḥ Vaiśvānaraḥ	X.88
The two birds	I.164.20 (*dvā suparṇā sayujā sakhāyā. . .*)
Vāyuḥ	II.42 & 43
Vibhūtiyogaḥ	IX.96.6
(Viśvāmitra protects the Bhāratīyas)	III.53.12 (*viśvāmitrasya rakṣati brahmedaṁ bhārataṁ janam*)

SOURCE OF MANTRAS OF NAVAGRAHA-SŪKTAM

Navagraha-Sūktam available in popular texts[44] and regularly chanted in temples is not available in the *Ṛgveda*, since the *graha*s (celestial bodies) were not yet treated as *devatā*s. They appear to have been compiled later in the post-Vedic period, being adaptations of various *ṛcā*. Their source can be identified and is furnished below:

1	Ādityaḥ	*ṚV* I.35.2 (*āsatyena rajasā*) *ṚV* I.12.1 (*agniṁ dūtaṁ vṛṇīmahe*)	Savitā, Agni
2	Aṅgārakaḥ	*ṚV* VIII.44.16 (*agnirmūrdhā divaḥ*) *ṚV* I.22.15 (*śyona pṛthivī bhavanṛkṣarā. . .*) IV.57.1 (*kṣetrasya patinā*)	Agni, Pṛthivī Kṣetrapati
3	Śukraḥ	*ṚV* VII.4.1 (*pra vaśśukrāya*) *ṚV* X.86.11 (*indrāṇīmāsu nāriṣu. . .*) *ṚV* I.7.10 (*indraṁ vo viśvataspari. . .*)	Agni Indra Indra
4	Somaḥ	*ṚV* I.91.16 (*ā pyāyasva sametu te viśvatassoma*) *ṚV* I.23.20 (*apsu mesomo abravid. . .*) *ṚV* I.164.4 (*gaurīmīmāya salilāni-*)	Soma Āpaḥ Viśvedeva
5	Budhaḥ	*ŚYV* XV.54 (*udbudhyasvāgne*) *ŚYV* XV.53 (*punaḥ kṛṇvanaḥ*) *ṚV* I.22.17 (*idaṁ viṣṇurvicakrame tredhā*)	Agni Agni Viṣṇu
6	Bṛhaspatiḥ	*ṚV* II.23.15 (*bṛhaspate ati yadaryo arhād. . .*) *ṚV* III.51.7 (*indra marutva iha pāhi soma*) *ŚYV* XIII.3 (*brahma jajñānaṁ prathamam-*)	Bṛhaspati Indra Āditya
7	Śanaiścaraḥ[45]	*ṚV* X.9.4 (*śan no devīrabhiṣṭaya*) *ṚV* X.121.10 (*prajāpate na tvadetānyanyo-*) *ṚV* X.14.4 (*imaṁ yama prastaramā hi. . .*)	Āpodevatā Prajāpati Yama
8	Rāhuḥ	*ṚV* IV.31.1 (*kayā naścitra ābhuvadūti-*) *ṚV* X.189.1 (*āyaṁ gauḥ pṛśnirakramī-dasanan. . .*) *ŚYV* XII.65 (*yaṁ te devī nirṛtirābabandha*)	Indra Sūrya Yajamāna
9	Ketuḥ	*ṚV* I.6.3 (*ketuṁ kṛṇvannaketave peśo. . .*) *ṚV* IX.96.6 (*brahmā devānāṁ padavīḥ. . .*) *ṚV* VI.6.7 (*sa citra citraṁ citayantamasme-*)	Indra Soma Agni

44. *Mantrapuṣpam* published by Ramakrishna Mission, Mumbai.
45. *Śanaiścaraḥ* means, that which moves slowly. Saturn takes 19 years to complete the circumambulation of the Sun.

ṚK-MANTRAS USED IN TANTRA (DAŚA-MAHĀVIDYĀ)[46]

The presence of *Ṛgveda mantras* in the tāntric rituals such as *navagraha-homam* or *daśa-mahā-vidyās* — the 10 great goddesses / powers causes surprise to many.

1	Kālī (*Kriyāśaktiḥ*)	X.127.2 (*orvapra amatya nivato*) *ṚV Khila* II.5 (*varṣantu te vibhāvari*)
2	Tārā (*Paśyantī Vāk*)	I.164.41 (*gaurīmimāya*) VIII.94.1 (*gaurdhayati marutām*)
3	Tripurasundarī (*Jnānaśaktiḥ*)	I.164.29 (*ayaṁ sa śiṅkte*)
4	Bhuvaneśvarī (*Icchāśaktiḥ*)	I.89.10 (*aditir-dyaur-ditir*)
5	Tripurabhairavī (*Parā Vāk*)	I.99.1 (*jātavedase*)
6	Chinnamastā (*Vajravairocanī*)	X.86.10 (*saṁhotraṁ sma purā*)
7	Dhūmāvatī (*Yoganidrā*)	I.38.6 (*mo ṣu ṇaḥ pārāvarā*) I.35.1 (*rātrī jagato niveśanīm*)
8	Bagalāmukhī (*Stambhana-Śaktiḥ*)	X.120.1 (*tadidāsa bhuvaneṣu*)
9	Mātaṅgī (*Vaikhari Vāk*)	I.3.12 (*aṛnaḥ sarasvati*) II.23.1 (*gaṇānāṁ tvā*)
10	Kamalātmikā (*Sundaryāstavam*)	*ṚV Khila* II.6 (Śrī-Sūktam) III.62.10 (*tat savitur vareṇyam*)

Ṛgveda-Saṁhitā-Bhāṣya and English Translations

ṚGVEDA-BHĀṢYAS

The commentaries on the *Ṛgveda* are those of Devaswāmi, Skandaswāmi (CE 630), his contemporaries Nārāyaṇa (CE 630) and Udgītha (CE 630), Veṇkaṭa Mādhava (CE 1050), Swāmi Ānanda Tīrtha, i.e. Madhvācārya (CE 1198-1278), Ātmānanda (CE 1250), Sāyaṇācārya (CE 1315-87). All these old Bhāṣyas are fortunately available today.

46. The information in this section is from Mahāvidyāsūtram, and other works of Śrī Vasiṣṭha Gaṇapati Muni.

Swāmi Ānanda Tīrtha, i.e. Madhvācārya gave a Bhāṣyam on the first 40 *sūktas* only of the first *maṇḍala* in verse. Ātmānanda wrote his commentary on 'Asyavamīya Sūkta' only.

ṚVS with commentaries of Skandaswāmi, Udgītha, Veṅkaṭa Mādhava and Mudgalācārya is published by VVR Institute, Hoshiarpur.

ṚVS with Sāyaṇa-Bhāṣya is published by Vaidika Samshodhana Mandala, Pune and is available.

The Bhāṣya of Dayananda Saraswati and Kapali Sastri belong to later period, and are useful additions. Swāmi Dayananda Saraswati's *Ṛgveda-Bhāṣya-Bhūmikā* (CE 1878) and *ṚVS-Bhāṣya* up to *Maṇḍala* VII.2.2 are also available. *Ṛgveda-Bhāṣya-Bhūmikā* is a prescribed text in many Indian universities. Kapali Sastry's *Siddhāñjana* is a favourite with scholars.

TRANSLATION IN INDIAN LANGUAGES

The *Ṛgveda* translation is available in Hindi done by Ramgovind Trivedi, Jayadev Sharma and S.D. Satavalekar. It has also been translated in Bengali by Romesh Chandra Dutta. There is a very fine Marathi translation with exhaustive notes by Siddheswar Shastri Chitrav.

WESTERN TRANSLATIONS

H.H. Wilson (CE 1786-1860) translated the complete *Ṛgveda* in 1850 in six parts along with *Sāyaṇa-Bhāṣya* titled *Ṛgveda, English Translation*. This is the oldest and the first English translation of the *Ṛgveda*. Currently, the translation along with original text of the *Ṛgveda*, is available in four volumes, edited by Ravi Prakash Arya and K.L. Joshi, and published by Saujanya Books, Delhi.

F. Max Müller (CE 1823-1900) translated the *Ṛgveda* along with Sāyaṇa-Bhāṣya between 1849-73 in six volumes. This set is currently available in Svādhyāya Maṇḍala. He also edited *Ṛgveda* with *pada-pāṭha.*

Ṛgveda has been translated into German by K.F. Geldner in four volumes.

R.T.H. Griffith (1826-1906) translated the *Ṛgveda* with popular commentary in two volumes titled *Hymns of the Ṛgveda.*

Ṛgveda Brāhmaṇas

In the *Ṛgveda,* three Brāhmaṇas, two Āraṇyakas and three Upaniṣads are extant. The Brāhmaṇas are, (i) *Aitareya Brāhmaṇa* (ii) *Kauṣītaki Brāhmaṇa* and (iii) *Sāṁkhyāyana Brāhmaṇa.*

i. *Aitareya Brāhmaṇa* consists of 40 *adhyāyas*, and each bunch of five *adhyāyas* is called a *pañcikā*. These are sub-divided into 285 *kaṇḍikās*. The work is mostly written in verse, and only partly in prose. The first 16 chapters deal with Agniṣṭoma sacrifice that lasts for one day. The next two chapters (17 and 18) describe Gavamāyana sacrifice that lasts for a whole year. Chapters 19-24, describe Dvādaśa. Chapters 25-32, are connected with *Agnihotra,* and the last few chapters describe Abhiṣeka (coronation ceremony). The 38th chapter describes consecration of Indra, and the 40th chapter refers to the benefits of entertaining a *purohita* (a Vedic priest). The longest and the most interesting description/story found in *Aitareya Brāhmaṇa,* is the story of Śunaḥśepa.

ii. *Sāṁkhyāyana Brāhmaṇa* has 30 *adhyāyas,* and each *adhyāya* is divided into many *khaṇḍas* (parts). Overall, there are 226 *khaṇḍas*. It treats in its 30 chapters, the entire sacrificial ritual in a systematic manner. The greatness and the many forms of Rudra are described herein.

iii. The entire *Kauṣītaki Brāhmaṇa* contains 30 *adhyāyas,* 272 *khaṇḍas* and 6,962 passages. There are three *daśakas,* with each *daśaka* comprising ten *adhyāyas* (like *pañcikās* in *Aitareya Brāhmaṇa*). *Kauṣītaki Brāhmaṇa* is of a later period than *Aitareya Brāhmaṇa*, and is considered its offshoot. Some scholars even consider *Kauṣītaki Brāhmaṇa* same as *Sāṁkhyāyana Brāhmaṇa*.

The text of *Kauṣītaki Brāhmaṇa* was edited by E.R. Srikrishna Sarma, and published in 1968, by Franz Steiner Venlog Gmbft, Wiesbaden (printed in West Germany). Srikant Sarma writes thus in the introduction:

> This text is based on twelve manuscripts. Sri Raman Nambudiri of Erkkara Mana, aged 76, a traditional scholar in Kerala consented to chant the entire text of *Kauṣītaki Brāhmaṇa* for recording. There are two schools of Ṛgvedins in Kerala, one designated as *Trissur Yogam* and the other as *Tirunāvāya Yogam*. These two schools have some small differences in the recitations of the *Ṛgveda*, as well as in ritual procedure. E. Raman Nambudiri belongs to *Kauṣītaki* School.

Ṛgveda Brāhmaṇa-Bhāṣyam

Sāyaṇa-Bhāṣya is available completely on *Aitareya Brāhmaṇa*. Ṣaḍguruśiṣya's *bhāṣyam* on *Aitareya Brāhmaṇa* is also available.

Ṛgveda Āraṇyakas

The two Āraṇyakas in the *Ṛgveda* are, (i) *Aitareya Āraṇyaka* and (ii) *Sāṁkhyāyana Āraṇyaka*. *Aitareya Āraṇyaka* contains five subsidiary Āraṇyakas.

Ṛgveda Āraṇyaka-Bhāṣyam

Sāyaṇa-Bhāṣya is available completely for *Aitareya Āraṇyaka*.

Aitareya Āraṇyaka — text with English translation with *ṭīkā* by A.B. Keith, published by Oxford is also available.

Ṛgveda Upaniṣads

We have *Aitareya Upaniṣad* from *Aitareya Āraṇyaka*, *Kauṣītaki*

Upaniṣad from *Sāṁkhyāyana Āraṇyaka,* and *Bāṣkala Mantropaniṣad* from Bāṣkala-Śākhā. *Aitareya Upaniṣad* is one of the 10 Upaniṣads on which Śaṅkara has written *bhāṣyam. Kauṣītaki Upaniṣad* has been referred by him. Some Bhāṣyam is also available on *Kauṣītaki Upaniṣad.*

Bāṣkala Mantropaniṣad, for a long time, was known only in Perso-Latin-German translations. Fortunately, one or two of its manuscripts have been found in southern India. They are full of inaccuracies, but the text is reconstructed and amended. The Āḍyār manuscripts make some interesting readings. This Upaniṣad, as already mentioned, is a part of the *Bāṣkala Saṁhitā,* which is available only in fragments.

Arrangement and Sequence of the Maṇḍalas

As per some of the Western scholars, the 1st and 10th *maṇḍala*s of the *Ṛgveda* are relatively modern, when compared to 2nd to 9th *maṇḍalas*. Their opinion is based on the facts that,

i. The language, and the use of metres in 1st and 10th *maṇḍala*s is different.

ii. There is visible novelty with respect to the *devatā*s, some novelty in the subject matter also.

iii. In 2nd to 9th *maṇḍalas,* there is use of *refa,* whereas in 1st and 10th *maṇḍalas, la-kāra* has been used in the place of *refa.*

iv. Similarly, 1st and 10th *maṇḍala*s especially contain *sūkta*s dedicated to abstract thoughts such as Śraddhā, Manyu in place of popular Vedic deities like Indra, Agni, Mitra, and Varuṇa.

A theory of the current arrangement of the Ṛgvedic *maṇḍala,* which I found extremely interesting, has been incorporated later in this chapter.

The general arrangement of the *Ṛgveda,* as it has come down to us, has the family hymns in the middle, the 'Pavamāna Soma' *maṇḍala* coming immediately afterwards. Generally, this arrangement is based on an ascending order in the number of hymns. If there is any deviation, there is an explanation. Thus, according to Madhvācārya, although the third *maṇḍala* by Viśvāmitra (62 hymns) is longer than the fourth *maṇḍala* by Vāmadeva (58 hymns), it is placed before the latter, as it contains the famous *Gāyatrī-mantra*. However, Viśvāmitra does not supersede Gr̥tsamada, the author of the second *maṇḍala*, since Gr̥tsamada was originally a kṣatriya, and through the grace of Indra became a brāhmaṇa, endowed with poetic vision.

The internal arrangement within a *maṇḍala* places the father's hymns first; the son's hymns follow. However, in the fifth *maṇḍala*, *sūkta*s 52-61 (10 *sūkta*s) and the following, composed by Śyāvāśva Ātreya,[IX] precede the *sūkta*s 63 and 64, composed by his father Arcanānā Ātreya. Here the order is reversed, probably because the son had composed far more hymns than the father had. Except in the eighth *maṇḍala*, and in the ninth, which is wholly devoted to 'Pavamāna Soma', everywhere hymns to Agni come first, then to Indra, followed by those addressed to other deities.

The Structure and Formation of the R̥gveda

The structure and formation of the *R̥gveda* can be summarised from various angles:

1. The order of the *maṇḍala*s
2. The formation of the *R̥gveda*
3. The chronology of the *maṇḍala*s

The Order of the Maṇḍalas

The chronological order of the *maṇḍala*s is VI (Bharadvāja), III (Viśvāmitra), VII (Vasiṣṭha), IV (Vāmadeva), II (Gr̥tsamada), V (Atri), VIII (Kaṇva), IX (combed out hymns of Soma), and X, with the chronological period of *maṇḍala* I spread out over the periods of at least four other *maṇḍala*s IV (Vāmadeva), II (Gr̥tsamada), V (Atri), VIII (Kaṇva).

It is obvious that the chronological order of the 10 *maṇḍala*s has not been followed in the arrangement of the *maṇḍala*s that have come down to us.

There is a consensus among the scholars that the six family-*maṇḍalas*, II to VII formed the original core of the *Ṛgveda,* and the four non-family-*maṇḍala*s, i.e. I, VIII, IX, X, were added to the corpus later.

The serial order of the non-family-*maṇḍala*s tallies with their chronological order. The only two problems are:

1. Why is *maṇḍala* I placed before, rather than after, the corpus of the family *maṇḍala*s?
2. The family-*maṇḍala*s are not arranged in chronological order; so what is the criterion adopted in their arrangement?

These questions can be answered as under:

1. *Maṇḍala* I, unlike the other non-family *maṇḍala*s, is not unambiguously later than the family-*maṇḍala*s in terms of composition and compilation. Many *upa-maṇḍala*s in this *maṇḍala* are contemporaneous with the later family-*maṇḍalas*, and some even precede them. It is in recognition of this fact that the compilers of the *Ṛgveda* placed it before the family-*maṇḍala*s.
2. The family-*maṇḍala*s were formulated into a text before the addition of non-family-*maṇḍala*s, and the criterion of their arrangement was not chronology, but size; Maṇḍala II is the smallest of the family-*maṇḍala*s with 429 *mantra*s, while Maṇḍala VII is the biggest with 841 *mantra*s.

The number of *mantra*s in the six family-*maṇḍala*s is II (429), III (617), IV (589), V (727), VI (765) and VII (841) respectively. Clearly, there is a lacuna here; Maṇḍala III (617 *mantra*s) has more *mantra*s than Maṇḍala IV (589 *mantra*s). The only logical explanation for this is that Maṇḍala-III originally, at the time of fixing of the arrangement of the family-*maṇḍalas*, had fewer *mantras* than Maṇḍala IV; but many more *mantras* were added to it at a later point of time, which upset the sequence.

Surprisingly, this is not just a matter of logic, the fact is directly confirmed in the *Aitareya Brāhmaṇa*, that is connected to *Ṛgveda*. According to *Aitareya Brāhmaṇa* VI.18, six *sūktas* (III — 21, 30, 34, 36, 38-39) were seen by Viśvāmitra at a later point of time, to compensate for certain other *sūktas*, which were seen by the Viśvāmitras, but were misappropriated by the Vāmadevas.

That is, after the text of the family-*maṇḍalas* was fixed, a dispute arose with the Vāmadevas, claiming that some of the *sūktas* included in the Vāmadeva *maṇḍala* were actually composed by the Viśvāmitras. The dispute was resolved by including some new *sūktas* into Maṇḍala III, by way of compensation, in lieu of the disputed *sūktas*.

If these six *sūktas* (III — 21, 30, 34, 36, 38-39), which have a total of 68 *mantras*, are excluded from the *mantra*-count of Maṇḍala III, we get more or less the original *mantra*-count of the six family-*maṇḍala* — 429, 549, 589, 727, 765, 841 in an ascending form.

The Formation of the Ṛgveda

The process of formation of the *Ṛgveda* took place in four stages:

1. The six-*maṇḍala Ṛgveda-maṇḍalas* II, III, IV, V, VI, VII — The family-*maṇḍalas*.
2. The eight-*maṇḍala Ṛgveda-maṇḍalas* I-VIII
   (a) Major interpolations — III.21, 30, 34, 36, 38-39 (originally seen by the Viśvāmitras, but appropriated by the Vāmadevas).

(b) Minor interpolations — References to Tṛksi kings in older *maṇḍalas*.

(c) Introductions — Old Bhṛgu hymns included in the *Ṛgveda* in Maṇḍala III.

3. The nine-*maṇḍala Ṛgveda* — Maṇḍalas I-IX.

   Major interpolations — The Bālakhilya-Sūktas VIII — 49-59.

4. The ten-*maṇḍala Ṛgveda* — Maṇḍalas I-X.

   Minor adjustments — Splitting and combining of hymns to symmetrical numbers (191 hymns each in Maṇḍala I and X) or astronomically or ritually significant numbers and sequences.

The completion of the fourth stage saw the full canonisation of the *Ṛgveda*, and the text was frozen into a form, which it has maintained to this day.

The Chronology of the Maṇḍalas

Now that the 10,552 *mantras* in ten *maṇḍalas* have been listed and the *ṛṣis* named, we have more or less some familiarity with the *maṇḍalas*, *sūktas*, the *ṛṣis*, the families and the subject matter of the *Ṛgveda*.

It is now clear[47] that the *Ṛgveda* was not composed in just one sitting, or in a series of sittings, by a conference of *ṛṣis;* the text, on the other hand, is clearly the result of many centuries of visualisation, comtemplation and composition. The question is how many centuries?

The Western scholars measure the periods of various *maṇḍalas*, in terms of decades, while some Indian scholars go to the other extremes, and measure them in terms of millennia and deca-millennia.

---

47. This part is totally based on the research of Shrikant G. Talageri from his book *The Ṛgveda: A Historical Analysis*, Chapter V.

A more rational, but still conservative estimate would be as follows:

1. There should be, at a very conservative estimate, a minimum time gap of at least six centuries, between the completion of the first nine *maṇḍala*s of the *Ṛgveda* and the completion of the last one, the tenth.
2. The period of the later *maṇḍala*s and *upa-maṇḍala*s (V, VIII, IX, and the corresponding parts of Maṇḍala I) should together comprise a minimum of three to four centuries.
3. The period of the middle *maṇḍala*s and *upa-maṇḍala*s (IV, II, and the corresponding parts of Maṇḍala I) and the time gap which must have separated them from the period of the later *maṇḍala*s, should likewise, comprise a minimum of another three or four centuries.
4. The period of Maṇḍalas III and VII, and the early *upa-maṇḍala*s of *maṇḍala* I, beginning around the period of King Sudās, should comprise at least two more centuries.
5. The period of Maṇḍala VI, from its beginnings in the remote past and covering its period of composition right up to the times of Sudās, must again cover a minimum of at least six centuries.

Thus, by a conservative estimate, the total period of composition of the *Ṛgveda* must have covered a period of at least two millennia.[48]

48. I am aware of the Witzel-Talageri controversy. Nevertheless, I have an open mind about Talageri's theory as on date.

Endnotes

I. 'This so-called hymn is a spell or charm said to have been recited by Agastya, when he suspected that he had been poisoned. Its silent repetition is said to have an effectual antidote against all venom in reptiles, insects, scorpions, roots, and artificial poisons.'

— cf. *The Hymns of the Ṛgveda*, vol. I, p. 255, R.T.H. Griffith.

II. The legend of Śunaḥśepa is told in full detail in the *Aitareya Brāhmaṇa* VII.17. A king named Hariścandra, worships Varuṇa in order to obtain a son, promising to sacrifice to him his first-born. A son is born, named Rohita; but the king delays the sacrifice until Rohita grows up, when his father communicates to him his intended fate. Rohita refuses submission, and spends several years in the forest away from home. There at last, he meets with Ājīgarta, a *ṛṣi* in great distress, and persuades him to part with his second son Śunaḥśepa to be offered as a substitute to Varuṇa. Śunaḥśepa is about to be sacrificed, when by the advice of Viśvāmitra, one of the officiating priests, he appeals to the gods, and is liberated. Cf. *The Hymns of the Ṛgveda*, vol. I, p. 30, R.T.H. Griffith.

III. Biological son of Ājīgarta, abandoned by him, and subsequently adapted by Ṛṣi Viśvāmitra.

IV. Birth of Vasiṣṭha — Vasiṣṭha and Agastya are the offsprings of Mitra and Varuṇa, whose seed fell from them at the sight of lovely nymph Urvaśī. Part of the seed fell into a jar, and part in water; from the former arose Agastya, who is therefore called *Kumbhayoni*, and from the water arose Vasiṣṭha. Cf. *The Student's Sanskrit-English Dictionary*, Vaman Shivram Apte, Nag Publisher, Delhi, 1987, p. 646.

V. The first half of *ṚVS* VII.32.26 was seen by Śakti, son of Vasiṣṭha while he was being thrown into the fire by the sons of King Sudās. He was burnt before he could see the second half, which was seen by his father Vasiṣṭha. *ṚV.Sā.Bh.* VII.32. This *mantra* *ṚVS* VII.32.26 is repeated in *Sāmaveda* 259, 1456 where it is attributed to Vasiṣṭha. Similarly, *ṚVS* VIII.32.26 and 27 is found in *Atharvaveda* XX.79.1-2, where they are attributed to either of Śakti or Vasiṣṭha.

VI. Deified *soma* juice, or to Soma, or Indu — the Moon, who as containing the celestial nectar, the drink of the gods, is identified with *soma* plant and its exhilarating juice. As the Moon-God pours down his ambrosial rain through the sieve of heaven, he is addressed and worshipped as Pavamāna (self-purifying), represented by *soma* juice as it undergoes purification by flowing through the wool, which is used as a filter or strainer — *Hymns of the Ṛgveda,* vol. II, p. 268, R.T.H. Griffith.

VII. The list of *saptarṣis* differs in the Vedic texts. The earliest list is in *Ja.Br.* II.218-221 listing — Vasiṣṭha, Bharadvāja, Jamadagni, Gotama, Atri, Viśvāmitra and Agastya. The next list is in *BṚ.Up* II.2.6 listing — Gautama, Bharadvāja, Viśvāmitra, Jamadagni, Vasiṣṭha, Kaśyapa and Atri. The *Go.Br.* I.2.8 lists — Vasiṣṭha, Viśvāmitra, Jamadagni, Gautama, Bharadvāja, Guṅgu, Agastya and Kaśyapa.

The list of *saptarṣis* also differs for each *manvantara*. The list of *saptarṣis* for the current seventh *manvantara,* i.e. *Śveta-Varāha-Kalpa* is — Gautama, Bharadvāja, Viśvāmitra, Jamadagni, Vasiṣṭha, Kaśyapa and Atri.

VIII. Commentators have glossed over the content of the Yama-Yamī-dialogue. After searching for years, I got the story, which goes as under — 'Yamī, the twin sister of Yama is regarded as the first of women, while her brother as the first of men born to Vivasvat (the Sun) and Saraṇyu, before Saraṇyu became afraid of her glorious husband. Yamī entreated her brother Yama to become her husband, as there were no others to perpetuate the human race. But Yama refused and died. Her sorrow at his loss was so great that to assuage her, the gods created night.' Cf. *The Yajurveda* by Devi Chand, Glossary and Index, p. 451.

I found the explanation in another book — 'The idea of primal incest is unavoidable in any creation story. Bards often cringe with embarrassment as they narrate the tale of the one who appeared first in the cycle of life, and the one who came second. The second is offspring, if born of the first. The second is sibling, if born with the first. Either way, it is incest.' Cf. *The Goddess in India,* Devdutt Pattanaik, Inner Traditions, Rochester, Vermont, p. 12.

IX. Story about Śyāvāśva becoming a seer described in *Bṛhaddevatā* V.50-V.80 is described here — There was a royal seer by the name Rathavīti Dārbhya. That king being about to sacrifice, went to Atri and propitiated him (50). And making known his identity and the object he had in view, as he stood with folded hands, he chose the seer Arcanānas, the son of Atri, to officiate as (his) priest (51). He, accompanied by his son, went to the king for the performance of the sacrifice. Now the son of Arcanānas, Atri's son was Śyāvāśva, (52) who had been gladly taught by his father all the Vedas with their members (*aṅga*) and subordinate members (*upāṅga*). Then Arcanānas having gone with his son, performed the sacrifice for the king (53). And as the sacrifice was in progress, he saw the illustrious daughter of the king. The thought occurred to him that the princess might become his daughter-in-law (54). Then the heart of Śyāvāśva too became fixed on her; and so he said to the institutor of the sacrifice: 'Ally yourself with me, O king' (55). The king wishing to give his daughter to Śyāvāśva, said to his royal consort: 'What is your opinion? I (desire to) give the girl to Śyāvāśva (56). For a son of Atri would be no contemptible (*adurbala*) son-in-law for us.' She on her part said to the king: 'I have been born in a family of royal seers; (57) one who is not a seer should not be our son-in-law; this (youth) has not seen formulas. Let the girl be given to a seer: she would thus become a mother (*ambā*) of the Veda; for a (certain) seer regards one who sees formulas as a father of the Veda (58). The king, after conferring with his wife, refused him (saying), 'No one is worthy to be (our) son-in-law who is not a seer' (59). The seer, being rejected by him, returned, when the sacrifice was over; but the heart of Śyāvāśva returned not from the girl (60). So these two returned; they both met Śaśīyasī and Taranta (Vaidadaśvi) and king Purumīḷha (Vaidadaśvi) (61). Now the two kings Taranta and Purumīḷha were seers, sons of Vidadaśva. These two kings themselves paid homage to the two seers (62). And the King (Taranta) showed the seer's son to his royal consort; and with Taranta's approval she gave manifold wealth, (63) goats and sheep, cows and horses, to Śyāvāśva, did Śaśīyasī. Father and son, (thus) honoured by the institutors of the sacrifice, went to their hermitage to Atri (64). And they saluted Atri, the great seer, of brilliant splendour. (But) Śyāvāśva thought: "Because I have not seen (any) formula, (65) I have, alas! not obtained the maiden beautiful in all her limbs. Could I but become a seer of formulas, my joy would be great" (66) to him as he thus reflected in the forest, the host of the Maruts appeared. He saw standing at his (*ātmanaḥ*) side, quite (*iva*) similar in form (67) and equal in age, the Maruts, with gold on their breasts. Seeing the gods similar in age, with the figures of men, (68) Śyāvāśva astonished, then asked the Maruts, 'Who are ye?' Then, however, he became aware that they were the divine Maruts, the sons of Rudra. (69) Having observed (this), he also praised them with the (stanzas) 'They that ride' (*ya īṁ vahante: Ṛ V* V.61.11). For the seer it is considered a great transgression on his part, (70) that, as soon as he had seen them, he did not praise them, and that he asked them, 'Who are ye?' Being praised and being delighted with their praise, the sons of Pṛṣni (the Maruts) as they went along (71) taking off the gold from their breasts, gave it to him. Now when the Maruts had gone thence, the illustrious Śyāvāśva (72) went in thought to the daughter of Rathavīti. He only just (*sadyaḥ*) a seer, wishing to declare himself to Rathavīti, (73) commissioned Night on a message with the two (stanzas) 'This is my song of praise' (*etaṁme stomam* — *Ṛ V* V.61.17-18). And to her (Night) who did not see Rathavīti, he discerning (him) with the eye of a seer, (74) said, 'Here he dwells, on a delightful ridge of the Himavat.' Urged by the goddess night, after learning his instructions, (75) the son of Darbha, taking the girl with him, approached Arcanānas, and after clasping his feet, standing bend forward with folded hands, (76) he announced his name (saying), 'I am Rathavīti, son of Darbha. Inasmuch as I refused you formerly when you desired an alliance with me, (77) forgive me for that. I pay homage to you; and do not, adorable one, be wroth with me. You are the son of a seer, a seer yourself, you are adorable one, the father of a seer (78). Come, accept this (girl) as a daughter-in-law.' So said the king, and himself honouring him with water to wash his feet (*pādya*), with the water of hospitality (*arghya*) and with a mixture of honey (*madhuparka*), (79) and giving him 100 white steeds, he dismissed him to his home. And the seer, on his part, having praised Śaśīyasī and Taranta and King Purumīḷha with the six (stanzas) 'May she gain' (*sanat*, *Ṛ V* V.62-72) departed to his abode (80).

ṚGVEDA – Original *Śākhās*

Ṛṣi Paila

(21 as per *Caraṇavyūha)*

Ṛgveda Śākala-Saṁhitā 1,028 *sūktas*, 10,580 *ṛcā*, 153,826 words, 432,000 syllables (as per Śaunaka) 10 *maṇḍalas*/ or 8 *aṣṭakas*	***Brāhmaṇa***	***Āraṇyaka***	***Upaniṣad***	***Mahāvākya***	***Śāntimantraḥ***	**Priest**
Available *Śākhās*						*Ṛtvik*
Śākala Saṁhitā (extant)	*Aitareya* (extant)	*Aitareya*	*Aitareya*	*prajñānāṁ brahma* (*Ai.Up*. V.3)	*vaṅg me manasi pratiṣṭhitā*	
Bāṣkala-Saṁhitā (in fragments)			*Bāṣkala*			
Āśvalāyana-Saṁhitā (extant after revival)						
Sāṁkhyāyana Saṁhitā (extinct)	*Kauṣītaki* (extant)/or *Sāṁkhyāyana*	*Kauṣītaki*/or *Sāṁkhyāyana*	*Kauṣītaki* (extant)			
Māṇḍūkāyana Saṁhitā (extinct)	*Paiṅgi*					

3

Śukla-Yajurveda

Yajurveda Saṁhitā

THE *Yajurveda* is the collection of *yajus* or sacrificial formulae and mainly deals with Vedic rituals, sacrifices and the role of rituals in life. The *yajus* are defined as *aniyatākṣarāvasāno yajuḥ*, or *gadyātmako yajuḥ* or *śeṣe yajuḥ śabdāḥ*,[1] all of which refer to the unique character of *Yajurveda* as consisting of prosaic portions.

According to *Śatapatha Brāhmaṇa*,[2] the *Yajurveda* has two prominent schools (i) Brahma *sampradāya* and (ii) Āditya *sampradāya*. The *Śukla-Yajurveda* is the representative of *Āditya sampradāya*, and the *Kṛṣṇa-Yajurveda* is the representative of Brahma *sampradāya*.

The division of *Yajurveda* into two as *Śukla* and *Kṛṣṇa* is due to the compilation. While in *Kṛṣṇa-Yajurveda* the *mantras* are along with the Brāhmaṇa portion, *Śukla-Yajurveda* contains only the *mantras*; hence the title *Kṛṣṇa*, meaning mixture (of *mantra* and Brāhmaṇa).

There is however, a Purāṇic story regarding the division of *Yajurveda*. This story is available in the introduction to *Mahīdhara-Bhāṣya* on *Śukla-Yajurveda*'s *Mādhyandina Saṁhitā*: 'In the beginning, Satyavatī's son Pārāśara Vyāsa compiled the Vedic corpus and divided it into four sections — *Ṛk*, *Yajus*,

1. *Ja.Sū*. II.1.37.
2. *ādityānīmāni śuklāni yajūṁṣi vājasaneyena yājñavalkyenā-khyāyante.* — *Śa.Br*. XIV.9.5.33

Maharṣi Yājñavalkya

Sāma and *Atharva*, and taught them to Paila, Vaiśampāyana, Jaimini and Sumantu. Vaiśampāyana taught *Yajurveda* to Yājñavalkya and others. Once for some reason, Vaiśampāyana was displeased with Yājñavalkya and ordered him to return the Veda taught by him. As per the order of his *guru*, Yājñavalkya by his yogic power gave a form to his knowledge and threw up. The other disciples of Vaiśampāyana took the form of *Tittīri* birds and swallowed it. Since then, those *yajus mantra*s are known as *Kr̥ṣṇa-Yajurveda*. On the other hand, Yājñavalkya performed deep penance and pleased Lord Sun. Satisfied with his penance; Lord Sun took the form of *vāji* (horse) and taught him *yajus* during noon (*madhyāhna*). Thus, the *yajus* received from Āditya was known as *Śukla-Yajus*. Having received it during noon, it was known as *Mādhyandina*, and since taught by Āditya in the form of *vāji*, *Vājasaneyī*. Sāyaṇācārya has also accepted this contention. This is validated in *Śatapatha Brāhmaṇa*.[3]

Out of 101 *śākhā*s of *Yajurveda* as declared by Patañjali, only six *śākhā*s are available now. The *Śukla-Yajurveda* has two extant *śākhā*s, (a) Kāṇva-Śākhā and (b) Mādhyandina-Śākhā out of fifteen (i) Kāṇva, (ii) Mādhyandina, (iii) Sabīya, (iv) Sthapayanīya, (v) Kasara, (vi) Pauṇḍaravasta, (vii) Avantika, (viii) Paramavatika, (ix) Pārāśarya, (x) Vaidheya, (xi) Vaineya, (xii) Aakheya, (xiii) Vaijeya, (xiv) Gālava, (xv) Baijava *śākhā*s. The *Kr̥ṣṇa-Yajurveda* has four extant *śākhā*s as Taittirīya, Kāṭhaka,

3. *Śa.Br.* XIV.9.5.33.

Kapiṣṭhala, and Maitrāyaṇī out of 86 *śākhās*. The *Taittirīya Saṁhitā* is the most popular among *Kṛṣṇa-Yajurveda* recensions.

Śukla-Yajurveda

As stated above, there were 101 *śākhā*s of *Yajurveda*, out of which *Kṛṣṇa-Yajurveda* had 86, and *Śukla-Yajurveda* had 15 *śākhā*s as per *mahābhāṣyakāra* Patañjali. However, currently only four *śākhā*s of *Kṛṣṇa*, and two *śākhā*s of *Śukla* are available.

Śukla-Yajurveda Saṁhitā Śākhās

As stated earlier, *Śukla-Yajurveda* is also known as *Vājasaneyī Saṁhitā*. In Śaunaka's *Caraṇavyūha*, Sāyaṇācārya has given the names of the 15 *śākhā*s — (i) Kāṇva, (ii) Mādhyandina, (iii) Sabīya, (iv) Sthapayanīya, (v) Kapala, (vi) Pauṇḍravatsa, (vii) Avatika, (viii) Paramavatika, (ix) Pārāśarya, (x) Vaidheya, (xi) Vaineya, (xii) Audheya, (xiii) Gālava, (xiv) Vaijava, and (xv) Kātyāyanīya. The names do not exactly match with the earlier list. Currently, only two *śākhā*s of *Śukla-Yajurveda* are extant — (i) Kāṇva-Śākhā and (ii) Mādhyandina-Śākhā. These two Saṁhitās have 40 *adhyāya*s each. Kaṇva and Madhyandina were the two principal disciples.

KĀṆVA SAṀHITĀ

Kāṇva Saṁhitā is popular in Maharashtra and Tamil Nadu. *Kāṇva Saṁhitā* contains 40 *adhyāyas*, 328 *anuvākas*, 2,086 *mantras*, with many repetitions of texts. *Kāṇva Saṁhitā* is specially adopted and revered by the Pāñcarātra Āgama system of worship in the temples. *Kāṇva Saṁhitā* has been published by 'Anandavana' of Chennai, and Audh in Maharashtra.

MĀDHYANDINA SAṀHITĀ

Mādhyandina is popular mainly in the northern India. Its pronunciation is audibly different, i.e. *sahasra-śīrṣā puruṣaḥ* is chanted as *sahasra-śīrkhā purukhaḥ* (*ṣa-kha-yor abhedaḥ*). *Mādhyandina Saṁhitā* contains 1,975 *mantra*s (111 *mantras* less than *Kāṇva Saṁhitā*).

Subject Matter of Śukla-Yajurveda

An enumeration of the various topics that form the contents of *Śukla-Yajurveda Saṁhitā*, or the *Vājasaneyī Saṁhitā* containing 40 *adhyāyas* (chapters) in both the recensions, will be useful as presenting an outline of the entire *śrauta* ritual.

Chapters	Topics
I.1-II.28	*Darśa-Pūrṇamāsa* (new and full-moon sacrifices)
II.29-34	*Piṇḍa-Pitṛyajña* (sacrifice to the manes)
III.1-8	*Agnihotra and Punarādheya* (establishment and re-establishment of the fires)
III.9-10	*Agnihotra* (fire-sacrifice) offered in the morning and evening. III.35 *Gāyatrī-mantra*[4]
III.11-43	*Agnyupasthāna* (homage to the fires, usually performed at the evening fire-service only)
III.44-63	*Cāturmāsyāni* (four-month or seasonal sacrifices to be offered once every four months, at the beginning of each of the three seasons: spring, rains, and autumn). III.60 is the *Mahā-mṛtyuñjaya-mantra.*
IV.1-VIII.23	*Somayāga* sacrifices in general, which, including the animal sacrifice as a part of it, has many varieties, the *Agniṣṭoma* being the most typical of them. Different varieties of *Agniṣṭoma*s are described in this section.
IX.1-34	*Vājapeya* (draught of strength)
IX.35-X.30	*Rājasūya*
X.31-34	*Caraka-Sautrāmaṇi*
XI-XVIII	*Agnicayana*
XVI	*Śrī Rudra-Praśna*
XVIII	*Camaka Praśna*
XIX-XXI	*Sautrāmaṇi-Yajñavidhāna*
XXII-XXV, and XXIX	*Aśvamedha* XXII.9 — *Gāyatrī-mantra*
XXVI-XXIX	*Khila-mantras*

4. The *Gāyatrī-mantra* occurs four times in *ŚYV*. III.35, XXII.9, XXX.2, and XXXVI.3.

XXX	*Puruṣamedha* XXX.2 — *Gāyatrī-mantra*
XXXI.1-22	*Puruṣasūktam*[5]
XXXII	*Sarvamedha-yajña*
XXXIII.55- XXXIV.58	*Anārabhyādhīta*
XXXIV.1-6	*Śiva-Saṁkalpa-Sūktam/Upaniṣad*
XXXIV.34-40	*Bhāgyasūktam*[6]
XXXV	*Pitṛmedha*
XXXVI- XXXVIII	*Pravargya-bhāga/Pravargya-agnikāṇḍa* XXXVI.3 — *is Gāyatrī-mantra*
XXXIX	All the 13 *mantras* relate to cremation.
XL	*Īśāvāsyopaniṣad*

Śukla-Yajurveda Saṁhitā-Bhāṣya and English Translation

On *Śukla-Yajurveda Mādhyandina Saṁhitā*, we have an old *bhāṣya* by Uvvaṭa (eleventh century) and by Mahīdhara (CE 1588). Mahīdhara's *Bhāṣya* is named *Vedadīpa*. This *bhāṣya* is very lucid and simple and has the influence of Uvvaṭa. *ŚYVS* with Uvvaṭa and Mahīdhara's *Bhāṣya* is published by MLBD and is available.

Sāyaṇa's *Bhāṣya* is on *Kāṇva Saṁhitā*.

ENGLISH TRANSLATION OF YAJURVEDA

Vājasaneyī Saṁhitā in Mādhyandina and Kāṇva-Śākhā with Mahīdhara's *Bhāṣya*, edited by A. Weber, was reprinted in 1972, by the Chowkhamba Sanskrit Series Office, Varanasi.

R.T.H. Griffith has translated *Yajurveda* titled *Hymns of the White Yajurveda of Vājasaneyī-Saṁhitā* into English with a popular commentary.

---

5. *ŚYV* XXX.1-16 is repetition of *ṚV* Puruṣasūktam (*ṚV* X.90). *ŚYV* XXX.17 to 22 are the 6 extra *ṛcā* that have now become regular part of the Puruṣasūktam that is being chanted now.
6. Repetition of Bhāgyasūktam (*ṚV* VII.41), both seen by Vasiṣṭha.

MODERN COMMENTARY AND TRANSLATIONS

Swami Dayananda Saraswati (CE 1824-83) has written *bhāṣyam* on *ŚYV-Mādhyandina Saṁhitā*. *ŚYV* is available with Hindi commentary by S.D. Satavalekar.

Devi Chand has translated the *Śukla-Yajurveda* into English with original Sanskrit texts.

Śukla-Yajurveda Brāhmaṇa

Śatapatha Brāhmaṇa (of a 'hundred paths' or chapters) is the only Brāhmaṇa connected to *Śukla-Yajurveda*. It is an extensive Brāhmaṇa available in both the *śākhās*, i.e. Mādhyandina (has 14 *kāṇḍas*) and Kāṇva (has 17 *kāṇḍas*). In size, this is as big as the *Ṛgveda*. There are only minor differences between these two *śākhās*. This Brāhmaṇa is considered very important in exposition of the texts of the Vedas in general. Besides its theological significance, it has enormous social, cultural and geographical importance. Practically it is an encyclopedia of Vedic sacrifices.

> From the historical point of view, the *Śatapatha Brāhmaṇa* of 100 chapters is the most important Vedic text, next to *Ṛgveda Saṁhitā*. The most interesting legend of the deluge in which Manu came into possession of a little fish, which asked him to rear it, and promised to save him from the coming flood is told there in detail. The stories of Urvaśī and Purūravā and of Bharata, the son of Śakuntalā and Duṣyanta are also found there. It also mentions Janamejaya, the celebrated king of the Kurus, and gives geographical data pertaining to the spread of Brāhmanical system to various parts of India.[7]

In the Mādhyandina-Śākhā (of 14 *kāṇḍas*, 68 *prapāṭhakas*, 100 *adhyāyas*, 438 *brāhmaṇas* and 7,624 *kaṇḍikās*), the first nine *kāṇḍas* — books constitute a close and continuous commentary,

---

7. Cf. *A Short History of Sanskrit Literature*, by T.K. Ramachandra Aiyar, published by R.S. Vadhyar & Sons, 1977.

quoting, explaining, and liturgically employing the *mantras* of the first 18 chapters of the *Śukla-Yajurveda* (*Vājasaneyī*) *Saṁhitā*. The next four *kāṇḍas* deal with the *agni-rahasya* (mystery of the fire-altar), *upanayana* (initiation, *svādhyāya* (Vedic study), *prāyaścittas* (expiations), Saṁhitā-formulae of the *Sautrāmaṇi* rite, *Aśvamedha*, *Puruṣamedha*, *Sarvamedha*, and *Pitṛmedha* (sacrifice to the manes) and the death-ceremonies, including the raising of a burial-mound to the dead. In the last (14th) *kāṇḍa*, the first three chapters comment on the *Pravargya* ceremony in the Saṁhitā, while the last six chapters (4th to 9th) constitute the *Bṛhadāraṇyaka Upaniṣad*.

Śatapatha Brāhmaṇa[8] Kāṇva-Śākhā		**Śatapatha Brāhmaṇa Mādhyandina-Śākhā**	
S/No.	Names of the 17 *kāṇḍas*	S/No.	Names of the 14 *kāṇḍas*
1.	*Ekapadika*	1.	*Haviryajña*
2.	*Haviryajña*	2.	*Ekapadika*
3.	*Uddhari*	3.	*Adhvara*
4.	*Adhvara*	4.	*Graha*
5.	*Graha*	5.	*Sava*
6.	*Vājapeya*	6.	*Ukhasambharaṇa*
7.	*Rājasūya*	7.	*Hastighaṭa*
8.	*Ukhasambharaṇa*	8.	*Chiti*
9.	*Hastighaṭa*	9.	*Sañciti*
10.	*Chiti*	10.	*Agnirahasya*
11.	*Sañciti*	11.	*Aṣṭādhyāyī*
12.	*Agnirahasya*	12.	*Madhyamā*
13.	*Aṣṭādhyāyī*	13.	*Aśvamedha*
14.	*Madhyamā*	14.	*Bṛhadāraṇyaka* (also an Upaniṣad)
15.	*Aśvamedha*		
16.	*Pravargya*		
17.	*Bṛhadāraṇyaka* (also an Upaniṣad)		

8. *Yogeeswara Yajnavalkya*, p. 397, by E.R. Krishnamurti.

In Kāṇva-Śākhā (of 17 *kāṇḍas*, 104[9] *adhyāyas*, 446 *brāhmaṇas* and 5,865 *kaṇḍikās*), the 3rd-6th chapters of the 17th *kāṇḍa* constitute the *Bṛhadāraṇyaka Upaniṣad*.

Śatapatha Brāhmaṇa Kāṇva-Śākhā[10]

S/ No.	Names of the *kāṇḍas*	No. of *adhyāyas*	No. of *brāhmaṇas*	No. of *kaṇḍikās*
1.	*Ekapadika*	6	22	376
2.	*Haviryajña*	8	32	572
3.	*Uddhari*	2	22	124
4.	*Adhvara*	9	36	628
5.	*Graha*	8	38	475
6.	*Vājapeya*	2	7	100
7.	*Rājasūya*	5	19	288
8.	*Ukhasambharaṇa*	8	27	509
9.	*Hastighaṭa*	5	16	257
10.	*Chiti*	5	20	241
11.	*Sañciti*	7	20	441
12.	*Agnirahasya*	6	28	286
13.	*Aṣṭādhyāyī*	8	31	252
14.	*Madhyamā*	9	29	382
15.	*Aśvamedha*	8	44	308
16.	*Pravargya*	2	8	180
17.	*Bṛhadāraṇyaka* (also an Upaniṣad)	6	47	446
		104	**446**	**5,865**

Śukla-Yajurveda Brāhmaṇa-Bhāṣyam and English Translation

The Mādhyandina-Śākhā of this *Śatapatha Brāhmaṇa*, with

9. Still named *Śatapatha*, as per *chatri-nyāya*.

10. *Yogeeswara Yajnavalkya*, p. 398, by E.R. Krishnamurti.

extracts from *bhāṣyas* of Sāyaṇa, Harisvāmīn and Drāviḍagaṅga was published by A. Weber in 1855.

Satyabrata Sāmasrami's edition of this with *Sāyaṇa-Bhāṣya* was published in 1912.

There is also a gloss by Kavindracarya Saraswati on this Brāhmaṇa.

Julius Eggeling has translated *Śatapatha Brāhmaṇa* into English titled *The Śatapatha Brāhmaṇa According to the Text of the Mādhyandina School* in five volumes. It was published by MLBD in 1966 and is available.

Out of the 50 volumes of the famous Sacred Books of the East, 5 volumes, i.e. vols. 12, 26, 41, 43 and 44 are translations of *Śatapatha Brāhmaṇa.*

Śukla-Yajurveda Āraṇyaka

The fourteenth *kāṇḍa* of *Śatapatha Brāhmaṇa* of *Śukla-Yajurveda* is an Āraṇyaka titled *Bṛhadāraṇyaka*. As its very name implies, it is *Bṛhat* — voluminous in extent. It is both, an Āraṇyaka and an Upaniṣad.

Śukla-Yajurveda Upaniṣads

There are two important Upaniṣads in *Śukla-Yajurveda* — *Īśāvāsya* and *Bṛhadāraṇyaka*. The last (40th) chapter of *Śukla-Yajurveda Kāṇva Saṁhitā* is the famous *Īśāvāsya*[1] *Upaniṣad*, very short but deep in content. This is the only Upaniṣad that comes at the end of a Saṁhitā, to the delight of all Vedāntins. (This is so because the Ārya Samājīs do not accept the Upaniṣads as part of the Vedas). All other Upaniṣads come at the end of an Āraṇyaka or are part of the Brāhmaṇa[11] portion. The other Upaniṣad, as stated above, is *Bṛhadāraṇyaka Upaniṣad*. It is both, an Āraṇyaka as well as an Upaniṣad.

---

11. *Muṇḍaka, Māṇḍūkya* and *Praśna Upaniṣad* belong to *Gopatha Brāhmaṇa* of *Atharvaveda* (Paippalāda-Śākhā).

In Kāṇva-Śākhā (of 17 *kāṇḍas*), the 3rd-6th chapters of the 17th *kāṇḍa* constitute the *Bṛhadāraṇyaka Upaniṣad.* Śaṅkara Bhagavadpāda has adopted the Kāṇva text while writing his *Bhāṣyam* on the *Bṛhadāraṇyaka Upaniṣad.*

Endnote

I. Dara Shikoh, the elder brother of Aurangzeb, was a Sanskrit scholar. He translated the *Īśāvāsyopaniṣad* into the Persian. He was a seeker of Truth, and in his search for the Truth, studied the Quran, the *Old Testament*, the *New Testament*, and the Vedas with the help of some *puṇḍits*. As a result of his search, he made the following remarks, 'After gradual research, I have come to the conclusion that long before all heavenly books like the Quran, the *Old Testament* and the *New Testament*, etc. God had revealed to the Hindus, through the *ṛṣis* of yore, of whom Brahmā was the Chief, his four Books of Knowledge, the *Ṛgveda*, the *Yajurveda*, the *Sāmaveda* and the *Atharvaveda*.'

'A fortunate person, who relinquishing the selfishness of his polluted mind, for the sake of God, being free from bias, will study my translation of the *Īśopaniṣad*, the Word of God, will attain salvation and be free from death, fear and misery.'

For such sayings, the Muslim *mullahs* declared him a heretic and had him killed.

ŚUKLA-YAJURVEDA – Original *Śākhās*
Ṛṣi Yājñavalkya
(15 as per *Caraṇavyūha)*

Saṁhitā	**Brāhmaṇa**	**Āraṇyaka**	**Upaniṣad**	**Mahāvākya**	**Śāntimantraḥ**	**Priest**
Available ***śākhās***						
Kāṇva (2,086 *mantras*)	*Śatapatha-Kāṇva* (100 chapters) as big as *Ṛgveda*		*Īśāvāsya* (40th chapter)			*Adhvaryu*
Mādhyandina (1,975 *mantras,* 100 less than Kāṇva)	*Śatapatha-Mādhyandina* (100 chapters)	*Bṛhadāraṇyaka*	*Bṛhadāraṇyaka*	*ahaṁ brahmāsmi* (*Bṛ.Up.* I.4.10)	*pūrṇamadaḥ* *pūrṇamidam*	
			Jābāla			
			Paiṅgala			

4

Kṛṣṇa-Yajurveda

Kṛṣṇa-Yajurveda Saṁhitā Śākhās

As per *Caraṇavyūha*, there were 86 *śākhās* of *Kṛṣṇa-Yajurveda*. Veda Vyāsa had allotted these 86 *śākhās* to Vaiśampāyana for preservation and propagation. We have the names of 27 of them[1]— (i) Jābāla, (ii) Baudheya, (iii) Aukhya, (iv) Āpastambīya, (v) Baudhāyanīya, (vi) Satyaṣadīya, (vii) Hiraṇyakeśīya, (viii) Ankheyi, (ix) Kaṇḍikā, (x) Caraka, (xi) Ahvaraka, (xii) Kaṭa, (xiii) Prācyakaṭa, (xiv) Guruvistara Kaṭa, (xv) Carayaṇīya, (xvi) Varayaṇīya, (xvii) Varatanterveya, (xviii) Śveta, (xix) Śvetāśvatara (extinct, only the Upaniṣad is available), (xx) Maitrāyaṇīya, (xxi) Mānasa, (xxii) Dundubha, (xxiii) Cekeya, (xxiv) Varṣa, (xxv) Hārdyaveya, (xxvi) Śyāma, (xxvii) Śyāmāyanīya. There were 59 (86 minus 27) more *śākhās* of *Kṛṣṇa-Yajurveda* names of which are not available.

Currently we have only four Saṁhitās — (i) *Taittirīya Saṁhitā* (extant), (ii) *Maitrāyaṇīya Saṁhitā* (extant), (iii) *Kaṭha Saṁhitā* (extant), and (iv) *Kapiṣṭhala-Kaṭha Saṁhitā* (in fragments). The form and description of the rituals therein remain the same, with some minor differences in readings here and there.

TAITTIRĪYA SAṀHITĀ

Taittirīya Saṁhitā is meticulously preserved in Andhra Pradesh,

1. *Yogeeswara Yajnavalkya*, p. 131, bye E.R. Krishnamurti.

Tamil Nadu, and Maharashtra. It contains seven *kāṇḍas* (books), 44 *prapāṭhakas* (lessons), 631 *anuvākas*, 2,198 *praśnas*, 1,29,290 *padas* (words) and 253,868 *akṣaras* (letters).[2] The seven *kāṇḍas* are — (i) *Saumya*, (ii) *Prājāpatya*, (iii) *Vyāsadeva*, (iv) *Āgneya*, (v) *Āgneya Brāhmaṇa*, (vi) *Saumya Brāhmaṇa*, and (vii) *Kāmyaka*.

The Brāhmaṇa, Āraṇyaka, Upaniṣads, Śrauta-Sūtras and Gṛhya-Sūtras are intact. Incidentally, *Taittirīya Saṁhitā* is not exclusively a Saṁhitā, but also includes Brāhmaṇa portions.

MAITRĀYAṆĪ SAṀHITĀ (EXTANT)

Maitrāyaṇī Saṁhitā is popular in Gujarat and southern India. It is also known as Kalāpa-Śākhā. It is in hymns as well as in prose. It has four *kāṇḍas*. The concluding *kāṇḍa* is known as *khila-kāṇḍa*. There are 54 *prapāṭhakas*. Of the 2,144 *mantras*, 1,701 are extracted from the *Ṛgveda*.

KAṬHA SAṀHITĀ (EXTANT)

Patañjali has said that there were Kaṭha-vācakas (story-tellers) in each village — *grāme grāme kāṭhakaṁ kalāpakaṁ ca procyate*.[3] Currently it is not so popular. This Saṁhitā is divided into five *kāṇḍas* — Iṭhimikā, Mādhyamikā, Orāmikā, Yājyānuvākyā and Aśvamedhādi-anuvacana. This Saṁhitā has 40 *sthānakas*, 13 *anuvacana*, 843 *anuvākas*, 3,091 *mantras*. The total of its *mantras* and *brāhmaṇas* are 18,000.

KAPIṢṬHALA-KAṬHA SAṀHITĀ (IN FRAGMENTS)

Reference to Ṛṣi Kapiṣṭhala is available in *Pāṇini-Sūtra* — *kapiṣṭhalo gotre* (*As.* VIII.3.91). The present village Kaithala, situated on the west of the dry river Sarasvatī, once flowing near Kurukṣetra, is presumed to be the old Kapiṣṭhala. This Saṁhitā is divided into six *aṣṭakas*, 48 *adhyāyas*. The eight

2. *Yogeeswara Yajnavalkya*, p. 128, by E.R. Krishnamurti.
3. *Ma.Bh.* IV.3.101.

*adhyāya*s of the 1st *aṣṭaka* are available completely, whereas other *adhyāya*s of other seven *aṣṭaka*s are in fragments.

At present, there are no followers of *Kapiṣṭhala-Kaṭha*. A single original manuscript of the Saṁhitā, in fragments now is preserved in the Banaras Sanskrit College. Since the authorities have never allowed its removal from the library, copies have been made at different times for the use of various scholars. Of the copies that have gone to Europe, Weber's seems to be the first, copied before CE 1800. L Von Schroeder used the copy of P.V. Bradke, after whose death it passed into the possession of F. Knauer.

F. Keilhorn also had a copy made for him in 1881 and later presented it to the Gottingen University Library. The last is W. Caland's copy, made in 1908. This shows how these scholars toiled to get a copy of the rare Saṁhitā from India. Raghuvira has given us a beautiful critical edition of this Saṁhitā text. Except for Kapiṣṭhala-Kaṭha, the other three Saṁhitās of *Kṛṣṇa-Yajurveda* are commonly studied in southern India and southern Maharashtra.

Subject Matter of Kṛṣṇa-Yajurveda

The first two *adhyāya*s contain *mantra*s relating to Daraśa and Paurṇamāsa. The third *adhyāya* contains *mantra*s relating to Agnihotra and Cāturmāsya. The details of preparing the *yajñavedī* are available in this. *Adhyāya*s 22 to 25 contain *mantra*s for *Aśvamedha-Yāga*. *Adhyāya*s 32 and 33 have *mantra*s for *Sarvamedha-Yāga* and the 34th *adhyāya* has Śiva-Saṁkalpa *mantra*. *Adhyāya* 35 has

A Vedic *yajña* in process by a group of *Kṛṣṇa-Yajurveda* priests

Pitṛmedha *mantras*. *Adhyāyas* 36 to 38 have *mantras* for *Pravargya-Yāga*. It also has *mantras* on *Somayāga, Vājapeya, Rājasūya, Sautrāmaṇi*, etc.

Additionally, it has a number of *sūktas* of high order, not found in the *Ṛgveda*. For example, the popular Śrī Rudram *mantras* are from the *Yajurveda*. The *Ṛgveda* contains five *sūktas* known as *Pañcarudra*, but when *Śrī Rudram* is mentioned, we recollect the *mantras* to this deity in the *Yajurveda*. This is why a great Śaivite like Appaya Dīkṣita laments why he was not born a *Yajurvedīn* — he was a *Sāmavedīn*. The Puruṣa-Sūkta of *Ṛgveda* (containing 16 *mantras*) occurs with additional six *mantras* in the *Yajurveda*. Today, it is generally understood to be a Yajurvedic *sūkta*-hymn.

As it is related to Adhvaryu priest, it is also otherwise known as *Adhvayarva-Veda*.

Śvetāśvatara Saṁhitā is now extinct. The Upaniṣad of this *śākhā* is available, which is the source of many ideas of the *Bhagavad-Gītā*.

Kṛṣṇa-Yajurveda Saṁhitā-Bhāṣya and English Translation

The earliest commentaries on *KYS* are by Bhavasvāmi, Guhadeva and Kṣara, but their *bhāṣyas* are lost to us. Bhaṭṭa Bhāskara (eleventh century), an erudite scholar of the Vedic lore, named his *bhāṣya* on *Taittirīya Saṁhitā* as *Jñāna-Yajña*. This *bhāṣya*, along with Sāyaṇa's, is now being critically edited and published by Vaidika Samshodhana Mandala, Pune.

When it comes to *Kṛṣṇa-Yajurveda*, Sāyaṇa reigns supreme. This was his Veda and Taittirīya was his *śākhā*. Sāyaṇa has given us *bhāṣyas* on *Taittirīya Saṁhitā, Taittirīya Brāhmaṇa* and *Taittirīya Āraṇyaka*.

Prativādi Bhayankaram Annaṅgarācārya of Kāñcī, who lived up to his 93rd year, and passed away in 1983, a prolific writer, was an authority on Taittirīya-Śākhā of *Kr̥ṣṇa-Yajurveda*. He had done a unique research on this text, and proved that the splitting of words and accents were based on a logical principle and evolved his own formulae. He has authored many books in Sanskrit on this subject.

Another scholar who is widely respected is Agnihotram Rāmānuja Tātāchāriar, of Kumbakonam, Tamil Nadu, who has mastered all the branches of the *Yajurveda* and other religious texts. He keeps himself abreast with modern thoughts and is a student of comparative religion. This virtue has given him a breadth of outlook in his philosophical expositions in Sanskrit, Tamil, and English.

Taittirīya Saṁhitā was rendered in English by A.B. Keith in 1914. An authorised Indian reprint of this book is available.[4]

Kr̥ṣṇa-Yajurveda Brāhmaṇa

Taittirīya Brāhmaṇa of *Kr̥ṣṇa-Yajurveda* is a continuation of *Taittirīya Saṁhitā*, and is aptly named as *anu-brāhmaṇa* by tradition. It contains only the later additions to the Saṁhitā, including the sacrifice to the *nakṣatra*s, the horse-sacrifice, the *Sautrāmaṇi*, and the symbolic *Puruṣamedha*. The *Taittirīya Brāhmaṇa* is divided into three *kāṇḍa*s, which are further divided into 28 *prapāṭhaka*s and 338 *anuvāka*s. *Taittirīya Brāhmaṇa* is also separately available. This text was published in 1890 in Calcutta and in 1899 in Poona.

Maitrāyaṇī Brāhmaṇa is also available.

Some fragments of *Kāṭhaka Brāhmaṇa* are compiled under the title of *Kāṭhaka-Brāhmaṇa Saṅkalanam* by Suryakant.

---

4. *The Veda of the Black Yajus School Titled Taittirīya Saṁhitā*, English translation/ed.1914 by A.B. Keith, Harvard Oriental Series, dedicated to Charles Lanman.

KṚṢṆA-YAJURVEDA BRĀHMAṆA-BHĀṢYAM

Sāyaṇa-Bhāṣya is available on *Taittirīya Brāhmaṇa.*

Kṛṣṇa-Yajurveda Āraṇyakas

Kṛṣṇa-Yajurveda has (i) *Taittirīya Āraṇyaka,* (ii) *Maitrāyaṇī Āraṇyaka.* No Āraṇyaka of Kaṭha-Śākhā is available. *Taittirīya Āraṇyaka* is divided into eight *prapāṭhakas*. Rajendra Mitra brought out *Taittirīya Āraṇyaka* with *Sāyaṇa-Bhāṣya* in 1872. We have also Bhaṭṭa Bhāskara's *bhāṣya* on this.

KṚṢṆA-YAJURVEDA ĀRAṆYAKA-BHĀṢYAM

Sāyaṇa-Bhāṣya is available on *Taittirīya Āraṇyaka.*

Kṛṣṇa-Yajurveda Upaniṣads

Kṛṣṇa-Yajurveda has (i) *Taittirīya* and (ii) *Mahānārāyaṇa Upaniṣad* belonging to *Taittirīya Āraṇyaka,* (iii) *Maitrāyaṇī Upaniṣad* belonging to *Maitrāyaṇī Āraṇyaka* and (iv) *Kaṭhopaniṣad* of Kaṭha-Śākhā. The famous *Śvetāśvatara Upaniṣad* also belongs to *Kṛṣṇa-Yajurveda.*

Among all the Vedic texts, the Taittirīya-Śākhā of *Kṛṣṇa-Yajurveda* has preserved all its texts, from Saṁhitā to Sūtras in perhaps the most intact condition. It is heartening to find the oral tradition in respect of the entire Taittirīya corpus is still very much alive.

KṚṢṆA-YAJURVEDA – Original *Śākhās*
Ṛṣi - Vaisaṁpāyana
(94 as per *Caraṇavyūha)*

Saṁhitā	**Brāhmaṇa**	**Āraṇyaka**	**Upaniṣad**	**Mahāvākya**	**Śāntimantraḥ**	**Priest**
Available śākhās						
Taittirīya	*Taittirīya*	*Taittirīya*	*Taittirīya, Mahānārāyaṇa*	*satayaṁ-jñānam-anantaṁ-brahma. Ta.Up.* II.1	*śanno mitra śaṁ varuṇaḥ—*	*Adhvaryu*
Kaṭha	*Kaṭha*		*Kaṭha*		*sa ha nāvavatu—*	
Maitrāyaṇī	*Maitrāyaṇī*	*Maitrāyaṇī*	*Maitrāyaṇī*			
Kapiṣṭhala	*Satyāyanī*					
	Bhallaka		*Śvetāśvatara*			

5

Sāmaveda

Introduction

SĀMA denotes that which brings equipoise or tranquillity to the mind. *Sāmaveda* enables us to befriend the divine forces. Many of the *mantra*s of the *Ṛgveda* are intoned with a cadence in the *Sāmaveda*; thus, we have *sāmagāna*. While the *ṛcā* are chanted with the tonal difference of *udātta*, *anudātta* and *svaritta*s, the *sāman*s are intoned musically according to certain rules. Indian music, based on the seven notes (*saptasvara*), has its origin in *Sāmaveda*. All deities are pleased with *sāmagāna*. We become recipients of grace not only through the offerings made in the sacrificial fire, but also through the intoning of the *sāman*s by the Udgātā. *Sāmagāna* is particularly important to Soma sacrifices, in which the essence of the *soma* plant is offered as oblation.

Sāmaveda Saṁhitā

The *Sāmaveda* is musical in character. It is the collection of *sāman*s meant for the chanting of Udgātā priest in the sacrifice. As per the definition *gītiṣu sāmākhyā*,[1] *mantra*s set to music are known as *sāma*s. The *Sāmaveda* is called the *Vedapuṣpa*, the flower of the Vedas. The word *sāman* literally means calming, tranquillising, kind, or gentle words winning an adversary, conciliation, negotiation, etc. The *Sāmaveda*, as already mentioned, is a collection of Ṛgvedic hymns set to music. The

1. *Ja.Sū.* II.1.36.

order of the Ṛks in *Sāmaveda* is different from that in the *Ṛgveda*, and there are some variations. The chanting of this Veda indeed gives peace of mind, and exhilarates the listener. 'Of the Vedas, I am the *Sāma*'[2] says Lord Kṛṣṇa in the *Bhagavad-Gītā*. It is said that the music of the Hebrews has close resemblances to *Sāmaveda* chants. There is a close parallel in the styles of Hebrew chants with the Indian Vedic chants, particularly that of *Kauthuma Sāma* in southern India.

Division of Sāmaveda

The division of *Sāmaveda Saṁhitā* is of two types — *ārcika* and *gāna*. *Sāmaveda Saṁhitā* is divided into two *ārcika*s — (i) *Pūrvārcika* and (ii) *Uttarārcika*. *Ārcika* is a collection of *Ṛk* hymns.

Pūrvārcika contains *grāma-gāna* and *āraṇya-gāna*. *Uttarārcika* contains *ūhagāna* and *ūhyagāna*.

Gāna means song. There are four kinds of *gāna*s in the *Sāmaveda* — (i) *grāmagāna* (also called *veyagāna*) songs to be sung in the villages which are congregational, (ii) *araṇyagāna* — songs sung by the recluse in the forests (never sung in the villages), (iii) *ūhagāna* — songs based on the musical notes of *grāmagāna* and (iv) *ūhyagāna* — songs based on the musical notes of *araṇyagāna*.

Nomenclature of Sāmaveda (Rāṇāyanīya-Śākhā)

1	Pūrva-Ārcika (625 *mantras*)			Khaṇḍa
	Āgneyakāṇḍa / Parva	*Grāma-gāna*	I *Adhyāya*	12
	Aindrakāṇḍa / Parva	*Grāma-gāna*	II *Adhyāya*	12
		Grāma-gāna	III *Adhyāya*	12
		Grāma-gāna	IV *Adhyāya*	12
	Pavamāna-Kāṇḍa / Parva	*Grāma-gāna*	V *Adhyāya*	11
	Āraṇyaka-kāṇḍa / Parva	*Araṇya-gāna*	VI *Adhyāya*	5
	Mahānāmni Ārcika (*pariśiṣṭa*)			

2. *vedānāṁ sāmavedo'smi. Bh.Gī.* X.22.

2	Uttara-Ārcika (21 Adhyāyas, 1,225 mantras)	Ūhagāna & Ūhyagāna or Rahasyagāna		
	Prapāṭhaka I		I Adhyāya	6
			II Adhyāya	6
	Prapāṭhaka II		III Adhyāya	6
			IV Adhyāya	6
	Prapāṭhaka III		V Adhyāya	7
			VI Adhyāya	7
	Prapāṭhaka IV		VII Adhyāya	7
			VIII Adhyāya	6
	Prapāṭhaka V		IX Adhyāya	9
			X Adhyāya	12
	Prapāṭhaka VI		XI Adhyāya	3
			XII Adhyāya	6
			XIII Adhyāya	6
	Prapāṭhaka VII		XIV Adhyāya	4
			XV Adhyāya	4
	Prapāṭhaka VIII		XVI Adhyāya	4
			XVII Adhyāya	4
			XVIII Adhyāya	4
	Prapāṭhaka IX		XIX Adhyāya	5
			XX Adhyāya	7
			XXI Adhyāya	1

Āgneya-kāṇḍa contains *Ṛk-mantras* relating to Agni. *Aindra-kāṇḍa*, comprising three *adhyāyas*, contains hymns dedicated to Indra, hence the title *Aindra-kāṇḍa*. *Pavamāna-kāṇḍa* has only one *adhyāya* containing *ṛcā* dedicated to Soma. *Āraṇyaka-kāṇḍa*, is the sixth *adhyāya*, containing *mantras* in various metres dedicated to various deities, while retaining some homogeneity. The *ṛcā* of the first five *adhyāyas* are called *grāma-gāna*. The *ṛcā* of the sixth *adhyāya* are called *araṇya-gāna*, since these are sung only in the forests by the recluse.

Mahānāmni ārcika is a *pariśiṣṭa*, and is neither part of the *pūrvārdha* nor *uttarārdha*. It is an independent *ārcika*, placed in between the first and second part of the *Sāmaveda*, containing only 10 *mantras*.

Sāmaveda Saṁhitā Śākhās

Out of the 1,000 *śākhās* of *Sāmaveda* as stated by Patañjali,[3] as well as *Caraṇavyūha*,[4] only three *śākhās* are extant, namely, (i) Kauthuma, (ii) Rāṇāyanīya, and (iii) Jaiminīya.

KAUTHUMA-ŚĀKHĀ

The main Saṁhitā of *Sāmaveda* belongs to Kauthuma-Śākhā and is current in Gujarat. The Nāgara brāhmaṇas in Gujarat study this *śākhā*. With this come *Tāṇḍya Brāhmaṇa* and *Chāndogya Upaniṣad*.

RĀṆĀYANĪYA-ŚĀKHĀ

The Rāṇāyanīya-Śākhā prevalent in Maharashtra is the next popular *śākhā*. This is not very different from Kauthuma. However, in pronunciation it is different. While Kauthuma-school chant has it as *hāu* and *rāi*, Rāṇāyanīyas pronounce it as *hāvu* and *rāyi*. The number of *mantras* in Rāṇāyanīya-Śākhā is 1,875.

JAIMINĪYA/OR TALAVAKĀRA-ŚĀKHĀ

The third school Jaiminīya is popular in Karnataka and Tirunelveli and Tanjavur districts of Tamil Nadu. The total number of *mantras* are 1,687, and the number of *sāmagāna* are 3,861. Jaiminīya-Śākhā was almost on the verge of extinction. My spiritual *guru*, Swami Dayananda Saraswati (b. 1930), founder of 'Ārsha Vidyā' tradition revived it with much effort. This *śākhā* is now being taught in Ārsha Vidyā Gurukulam, Anaikatti, Coimbatore to a group of resident *brahmacārīs*.

There is not much of difference between the texts of the Kauthuma and Rāṇāyanīya *śākhās*. However, there is marked difference between Kauthuma and Jaiminīya *śākhās*. There

3. *sahasra-vartmā sāmaveda* says *Ma.Bh.Pa.Ah.*

4. *sāmavedasya kila sahasrabhedā āsit. Ca.Vy. Sāmaveda-khaṇḍa.*

Sāmaveda Jaiminīya-Śākhā being taught in Ārsha Vidyā Gurukulam, Coimbatore

are 2,722 songs in the Kauthuma, but 3,681 songs on Jaiminīya. Number of *mantra*s existing in these two *śākhā*s also varies a little.

		Kauthuma	**Jaiminīya**
		No. of songs	**No. of songs**
Pūrva-Ārcika	*Grāma-gāna*	1,197	1,232
Pūrva-Ārcika	*Āraṇya-gāna*	294	291
Pūrva-Ārcika	*Ūha-gāna*	1,026	1,802
Pūrva-Ārcika	*Ūhya-gāna*	205	356
	Total	**2,722**	**3,681**

The *Viṣṇu Purāṇa* gives an interesting compilation and expansion of the *Sāmaveda* and the *ṛṣis* associated with it from Veda Vyāsa onwards, and their division into (i) Northern *sāma*-singers (Udicya-Sāmaga) and (ii) Eastern *sāma*-singers (Prācya-Sāmaga).

> 'You shall now hear, Maitreya, how Jaimini, the pupil of Vyāsa, divided the branches of *Sāmaveda*. The son of Jaimini was Sumantu, and his son was Sukarman, who both studied the same Saṁhitā under Jaimini.'
>
> The latter composed *Sahasra Saṁhitā* (or compilation of a thousand hymns), which he taught to two disciples, Hiraṇyanābha, also named Kauśalya (of Kośala), and Pauṣyiñji. Fifteen disciples of the latter were the authors of

as many Saṁhitās. They were called the 'northern chanters of the *sāmans*.' As many more, also the disciples of Hiraṇyanābha, were termed the 'eastern chanters of the *sāmans*', founding an equal number of schools. Lokākṣi, Kuthumi, Kuṣidi, Kakṣivan and Lāṅgali were among the pupils of Pauṣyiñji, and by them, and their disciples many other branches were formed. Whilst another scholar of Hiraṇyanābha named Kṛti taught 24 Saṁhitās to as many pupils, and by them again was *Sāmaveda* divided into numerous branches.[5]

Subject Matter of Sāmaveda

There are 1,875 (1,504+272+99) *sāmans* in the *Sāmaveda* (Rāṇāyanīya-Śākhā), out of which 1,504 are from *Ṛgveda*, 272 are repetitions, and only 99 of them are independent of *Ṛgveda*. The *Ṛk mantras* are modified into the songs of *sāmans* by appropriate addition of *stobha* letters as *ha, u, i, o, au,* etc. This Saṁhitā is compiled exclusively for ritual purposes. According to *Bṛhadāraṇyaka Upaniṣad*, the word *sāma* comprises *sa* which means *Ṛk*, and *am* which means *gāndhārādi-svaraḥ*. Thus, *Sāmaveda* is the musical intonation of the *ṛcā*, which are sung during the sacrifice. According to *Chāndogya Upaniṣad*, there are seven types of *sāmas* — *hṛṅkāraḥ, prastāvaḥ, ādi, udgītha, pratihāraḥ, upadravaḥ,* and *nidhāna*.

The *mantras, ṛṣis*, and *devatās* in *Sāmaveda* are in many cases different from those of *Ṛgveda*.

Sāmaveda-Bhāṣya and English Translations

On the *Sāmaveda*, the well-known commentaries are those of Mādhava (seventh century), Guṇaviṣṇu (thirteenth century), Bharata Swāmi (CE 1303), Sāyaṇa (CE 1315-1387), Mahāswāmi (around fourteenth century), and Śobhākar Bhaṭṭa (before CE 1408).

---

5. After H.H. Wilson, *The Viṣṇu Purāṇa*, English translation, 3rd edn., Calcutta, 1961, p. 277.

Sāyaṇa has written *Bhāṣyam* on the extant *Rāṇāyanīya Saṁhitā*.

The *Sāmaveda* (Rāṇāyanīya-Śākhā) was first translated by Stevenson in English as early as in 1842, which was followed by the translation of Theodore Benfey in 1848, and R.T.H. Griffith in 1893. Griffith's English translation of the *Sāmaveda*, with a popular commentary, is titled *Hymns of the Sāmaveda*.

MODERN COMMENTARY AND TRANSLATIONS

Hindi translation of *Sāmaveda* by Bhagadevācārya as also *Sāmaveda* with Hindi commentary by S.D. Satavalekar are both available.

Satyabrata Sāmaśrami had brought out an edition with Sāyaṇa's commentary as early as in 1873. His texts titled *Sāmaveda Saṁhitā* with the commentary of Sāyaṇa is available in five volumes. His translations of the Brāhmaṇas however were in Bengali, hence could not be of a wider appeal.

Devi Chand has translated the *Sāmaveda* into English with original Sanskrit Texts.

Sāmaveda Brāhmaṇa and Bhāṣyas on Them

Sāma-Saṁhitā is not of much significance since it is a collection from the *Ṛgveda*. However, we have an abundance of Brāhmaṇa in the *Sāmaveda*, preserved intact with *Sāyaṇa-Bhāṣya*. These are as per table below:

	Śākhā	**Brāhmaṇas**		**Bhāṣya**
1	Jaiminīya	*Jaiminīya* or *Talavakāra Brāhmaṇa* (includes *Kenopaniṣad* as its integral part)	As important as *Śatapatha Brāhmaṇa*	*Sāyaṇa-Bhāṣya* titled *Vedārtha-Prakāśa*
2	Jaiminīya	*Ārṣeya Brāhmaṇa* (part of *Jaiminīya* or *Talavakāra Brāhmaṇa*)	3 *prapāṭhakas* (is an index to the hymns of *Sāmaveda*)	*Sāyaṇa-Bhāṣya* titled *Vedārtha-Prakāśa*

3	Kauthuma/ and Rāṇāyanīya	*Tāṇḍya* or *Prauḍha* or *Pañcaviṁśa* or *Mahā-Brāhmaṇa*	25 *prapāṭhakas*	*Sāyaṇa-Bhāṣya* titled *Vedārtha-Prakāśa*
4	Kauthuma and Rāṇāyanīya	*Ṣaḍviṁśa-Brāhmaṇa* considered as an appendix to *Pañcaviṁśa*). 5th *prapāṭhaka* is *Adbhuta Brāhmaṇa*	5 *prapāṭhakas*	*Sāyaṇa-Bhāṣya* titled *Vedārtha-Prakāśa*
5	Kauthuma	*Chāndogya* or *Mantra* or *Upaniṣad Brāhmaṇa*	1-2 *gṛhya* rites. Last 8 chapters (3-10) constitute *Chāndogya Upaniṣad*	
6		*Sāmavidhāna Brāhmaṇa*	3 *prakaraṇas*/ *prapāṭhakas*	*Sāyaṇa-Bhāṣya* & *Bharata-Swami-Bhāṣya*
7		*Devatādhyāya Brāhmaṇa*	3 *khaṇḍas*	*Sāyaṇa-Bhāṣya* titled *Vedārtha-Prakāśa*
8		*Saṁhitopaniṣad Brāhmaṇa*	1 *prapāṭhaka* 5 *khaṇḍas*	*Sāyaṇa-Bhāṣya*. *Dvijarāja Bhaṭṭa-Bhāṣya*
9		*Vaṁśa-Brāhmaṇa*	3 pieces	*Sāyaṇa-Bhāṣya* titled *Vedārtha-Prakāśa*

1. The contents of *Jaiminīya Brāhmaṇa* and *Pañcaviṁśa Brāhmaṇa* are similar. They differ only with regard to their style or language. The *Jaiminīya* is too long and more wordy, whilst the *Pañcaviṁśa* gives only what is strictly necessary. The author of *Pañcaviṁśa* was acquainted with the *Jaiminīya Brāhmaṇa*. Tāṇḍya, a sage, was considered the author of *Pañcaviṁśa*.[6]

6. Cf. Amalendu De's Foreword to *Pañcaviṁśa Brāhmaṇa*, tr. W. Caland.

2. *Ārṣeya Brāhmaṇa* in 3 *prapāṭhaka*s (chapters) is a quasi-Brāhmaṇa, on the whole, nothing more than an *anukramaṇikā*, a mere list of the names of *sāman*s occurring in the first two *gāna*s.
3. The *Tāṇḍya Brāhmaṇa* or *Pañcaviṁśa Brāhmaṇa* (25 books) is a mine of information about the legends and episodes, and elaborately represents the ritual of the Udgātṛ. All varieties of the *soma* sacrifices, the *ekāha, ahīna,* and *sattra* are described in it. (i) The *ekāha* has only one *sutyā* day, on which the *soma*-juice is extracted and libations made. This type of *soma* sacrifices, in which the principal ceremony is completed in a single day, is designated *ekāha,* leaving out of consideration the four preparatory days, which are required for every *soma* sacrifice. (ii) The *sattra* type lasts for more than 12 days, and sometimes for a whole year and even longer. There are seven fundamental forms (*saṁsthā*s) of the *sutyā* festival of the *soma* sacrifice, occasioned by the varying number of *śāstra*s and *stotra*s recited and sung. They are *Agniṣṭoma, Atyagniṣṭoma, Ukthya, Ṣoḍaśin, Vājapeya, Atirātra* and *Āptoryāma.* They bear the generic title *Jyotiṣṭoma.* In the description of all these types of Soma sacrifice, this Brāhmaṇa records the chants of the *Sāmaveda Saṁhitā* with all the modifications and variations of order, etc. suitable to each type. It further gives detailed directions for the sacrifices on the Sarasvatī and the Dṛśadvatī. It also mentions about the Vrātyas who lived outside the Āryan community because they either had lost their position as 'twice-born' or never attained it, and *Vrātya-stoma*s sacrifices through which the Vrātyas were reclaimed to the Aryan community.
4. The *Ṣaḍviṁśa Brāhmaṇa,* as its name implies, is an appendix to the *Pañcaviṁśa Brāhmaṇa.* It deals with the

rites of expiation and imprecation. Its last chapter ranks as a separate Brāhmaṇa, the *Adbhuta*, dealing with miracles and omens.

5. The *Chāndogya* or *Mantra* or *Upaniṣad Brāhmaṇa*, has ten *prapāṭhaka*s (chapters). The first two *prapāṭhaka*s form the *Mantra Brāhmaṇa* and contain *mantra*s for *gṛhya* rites. The last eight *prapāṭhaka*s constitute the famous *Chāndogya Upaniṣad*.
6. *Sāmavidhāna Brāhmaṇa* deals with rituals, especially employment of chants to gain all kinds of ends.
7. *Devatādhyāya Brāhmaṇa* in 3 *khaṇḍa*s deals with deities to whom *sāman*s are addressed.
8. *Saṁhitopaniṣad Brāhmaṇa* is a single *prapāṭhaka* divided into five *khaṇḍa*s. It deals with the effects of recitation, the relation of *sāman*s, and the words on which it is chanted, the *dakṣiṇā* to be given to the *ācārya*.
9. *Vaṁśa Brāhmaṇa* contains lineage of the *ṛṣi*s and their disciples through whom the learning and tradition of *Sāmaveda* came down.

We can now appreciate what a vast literature on the application and uses of musical works is inherited by us! All the *sāman*s are used in different kinds of sacrifices, and no sacrifice is complete without *sāmagāna*.

Sāmaveda Āraṇyaka

The single Āraṇyaka called *Talavakāra* belonging to *Sāmaveda* is nothing but *Jaiminīya Upaniṣad Brāhmaṇa*, which is part of the *Jaiminīya Brāhmaṇa* listed above. It is also known as *Gāyatrī Upaniṣad*. *Jaiminīya Brāhmaṇa* was published by many Western scholars in fragments, since they had not obtained the full text. However, in 1951 Raghu Vira brought out a critical and complete edition of this text (published in Nagpur).

Sāmaveda Upaniṣads

The Upaniṣads connected with Sāmaveda are,

1. *Kenopaniṣad* (or *Talavakāra Upaniṣad*)
2. *Chāndogya Upaniṣad* (last 8 *adhyāya*s of *Chāndogya* or *Mantra* or *Upaniṣad Brāhmaṇa*)
3. *Jaiminīya Upaniṣad* or *Gāyatrī Upaniṣad*

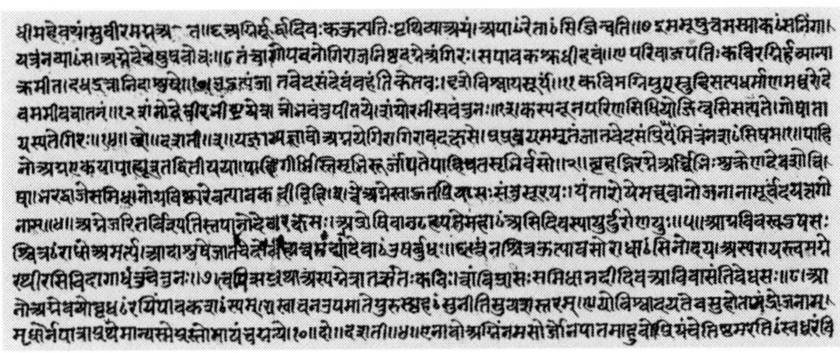

Manuscript of *Chāndogya Upaniṣad*

Chāndogya is the next biggest and the most significant collection of theological-philosophical expressions, views, doctrines and legends after *Bṛhadāraṇyakopaniṣad*. According[7] to modern critical scholarship, *Chāndogya Upaniṣad* antedates Buddhism by a number of centuries, and it is preceded perhaps only by the Upaniṣads — *Īśa* and *Aitareya.*

Sāmaveda extols the greatness of *soma* plant. This has long been a controversial word. According to some, it is *sarcostema viminalis* or *asclepias acida.* S.D. Satavalekar in his Hindi and Marathi versions of *Sāmaveda Saṁhitā* has given the real meaning and explanation of *soma. Soma* was a herb that grew with full moon, and dried with waning moon; it gave strength and vigour, but was neither toxic nor did it lead to drowsiness. It is not available anywhere in India now.

7. Cf. Introduction (1956) of Swāmi Vimalānanda in *Chāndogya Upaniṣad,* tr. Swāmi Swāhānanda, Sri Ramakrishna Math, Mylapore, Madras, 8th impression, 1996.

SĀMAVEDA – Original *śākhās*
Ṛṣi Jaimini
(1,000 as per *Caraṇavyūha*)

Saṁhitā	**Brāhmaṇa**	**Āraṇyaka**	**Upaniṣad**	**Mahāvākya**	**Śāntimantraḥ**	**Priest**
Available śākhās						
Kauthumīya (1,875 songs)		No Āraṇyaka	*Chāndogya* (8 chapters)	*tat tvam asi* (*Ch.Up.* VI.8.7)	*āpyāyantu mamāṅgāni*	Udgāta
Jaiminīya or Talavakāra (1,687 songs)	*Jaiminīya* (or *Talavakāra*)	*Talavakāra* (*Jaiminīya Upaniṣad Brāhmaṇa*) or *Gāyatrī Upaniṣad*	*Kena* (or *Talavakāra*)			
Rāṇāyanīya	*Tāṇḍya* (*Pañcaviṁśa*)					
	Ṣaḍviṁśa					
	Sāmavidhāna					
	Ārṣeya					
	Daivatādhyāya					
	Mantra					
	Saṁhitopaniṣad					
	Vaṁśa					

6

Atharvaveda

Introduction

THE importance of *Atharvaveda Saṁhitā* lies in the very fact that it is an invaluable source of knowledge of the popular belief, of the faith in numberless spirits, imps, ghosts, and demons of every kind, and of the witchcraft, so eminently important to ethnology and for the history of religion. In short, it is a very valuable store of our ancient folklore.

Atharvaveda contains materials from the *Ṛgveda*. Scholars opine that it was written down much later than the other three Vedas, perhaps around 600 BCE; although it may have been composed much earlier, say around 1000 BCE.

Veda-trayī and the Atharvaveda

There is considerable scope for dispute regarding the claim of the *Atharvaveda* to be counted as a Veda at all. With regard to the designation of the Vedas as *trayī* (triad, i.e. *Ṛgveda, Yajurveda* and *Sāmaveda*), and the eligibility of the *Atharvaveda* for inclusion among the Vedas, it is interesting to observe the divided views of the scholars on the issue.

According to one view, the *Atharvaveda*, which contains spells of all possible kinds against many diseases, enemies, etc. represented the religion of the masses, in contrast to the other Vedas relating to cosmic worship representing the religion of the classes.

Another view explains the purpose of the three Vedas and the *Atharvaveda*, to be respectively the attainment of the desired objects, and the warding off the evils. It takes the omission of the *Atharvaveda* at places where *trayī* is mentioned, as being due to want of propriety of reference, and not due to its inferiority or supposed non-Vedic character, since a large number of highly philosophical hymns occur in this Veda also, besides its sharing many hymns in common with the *Ṛgveda*.[1]

The comments of Lakshman Sarup in his *The Nighaṇṭu and The Nirukta* are worth citing here —

> For a considerable time, the *Atharvaveda* was not recognised as divine revelation. For the followers of *Atharvaveda*, it was therefore necessary to demonstrate the superiority of their own Veda to the *Ṛgveda*, the *Sāmaveda* and the *Yajurveda*. Perhaps, the most effective means employed for the achievement of this object, was to invent legends and allegorical stories, in which all the four Vedas are introduced, and in which a certain task is proposed for them. The *ṚV*, the *SV*, and the *YV*, are invariably shown to be incompetent in its performance, and it is given up as too difficult by the three Vedas in succession, being finally accomplished by the *AV*, whose superiority over the other three Vedas is thus implicitly expressed. I quote the following two stories from the *Gopatha Brāhmaṇa* in support of my statement. *tān vāg-abhyuvāca . . . aśānto nu-ayam aśva iti*.[2]

Sarup continues,

> It need hardly be said that the efforts of the followers of the *Atharvaveda* were crowned with success, for, in course of time, the *AV*, was recognised as one of the revealed scriptures. But their method of discrediting the other Vedas

1. The whole XX *kāṇḍa* is largely borrowed and adapted from the *Ṛgveda*.
2. Lakshman Sarup, *The Nighaṇṭu and The Nirukta*, p. 72, 1920, Motilal Banarsidass, 1st Indian edn., 1920-27, rpt. 2002.

> gave rise to a movement of enquiry and scepticism — a movement, the traces of which can still be discovered in isolated passages of the Āraṇyakas and the Upaniṣads. Besides the fact that the anti-Vedic ideas have been preserved in the Āraṇyakas and the Upaniṣads, which according to orthodox tradition are a part of the scriptures, indicates that the movement must have been important and widespread, so much so that even some of the Vedic scholars came under its influence, and freely gave expression to their heterodox views,[3] some of which have survived.[4]

Even in Indian literature, three Vedas and four Vedas are mentioned side by side. The literature connected with sacrifices recognises only three Vedas. Jaimini in his Mīmāṁsā-Sūtras defines only the *Ṛgveda*, the *Yajurveda*, and the *Sāmaveda*, ignoring the *Atharvaveda*, which has no place in the sacrifices. In a sacrifice, there are four kinds of priests, the Hotā, connected with the *Ṛgveda*; the Adhvaryu, connected with the *Yajurveda*; the Udgātā, connected with the *Sāmaveda*; and Brahmā, who supervises the whole sacrifice. The priest Brahmā is sometimes connected with the *Atharvaveda*. This relation is not natural; it is only an attempt at an equation.[5] It may be said that while the *Atharvaveda* represents the Indian philosophy and religion that runs parallel to the current represented by the other Vedas; it is also the earlier stage of a current that culminated in the Āgama and Tantra literature.

Rajbali Pandey writes,

> Considering its popular character, Ridgeway concludes that it is not a record of Āryan religion, but represents the beliefs of the aboriginal people.[6] This view cannot be accepted. It is

3. Say Kutsa's views.
4. Lakshman Sarup, *The Nighaṇṭu and The Nirukta*, p. 74.
5. By *Pāriśeṣa-Nyāya*.
6. *Dramas and the Dramatic Dances of non-European Races*, p. 122.

just possible that the Indo-Āryan assimilated many non-Āryan elements in their religion, but the lower strata of the Āryan community were no less interested in the lower side of the religion, than the non-Āryan populations. The *Atharvaveda* reflects the faith and rites of the common people, rather than the highly specialised religion of the priests.[7]

Cultural Value of the Atharvaveda

If by Veda we mean sacrificial literature, then *Atharvaveda* is not considered as one of the Vedas by some (say Jaimini). Nevertheless, it will ever remain one of our richest heritages representing the secular and pre-eminently intellectual aspect of our ancients. The term *atharvaṇ* was from the very beginning associated with intellectualism. The R̥gvedic seer Dīrghatamas belongs to the Atharvaṇ family. The famous philosophical hymn composed by Dīrghatamas has the two passages 'Truth is one; sages call it by various names'[8] and 'There are two birds, with fair wings, knit with bonds of union . . .'[9]. This has been the basic text for latter day Indian philosophy regarding the relation between *Brahman* and the *jīva*, and the concept occurs in this hymn. In the *Raghuvaṁśa* (I), where the King Dīlipa goes to his teacher Vasiṣṭha, to consult him on very important state matters, Kālidāsa refers to Vasiṣṭha as the repository of *Atharva*-knowledge (*Ātharvanidhi*).

There was however no conflict between the civilisation represented by the three Vedas and that represented by the *Atharvaveda*. They represent two aspects of a civilisation that is single and unitary. One can safely say that the three Vedas represent mainly the aspect of an ancient Indian civilisation dealing with the goal of man in a future life, and the *Atharvaveda*

7. Rajbali Pandey, *Hindu Samskaras*, p. 4.
8. *R̥VS* I.164.46.
9. *R̥VS* I.164.20.

represents chiefly the other aspect, dealing with the life of man in this world. The three Vedas deal with gods and sacrifices; the *Atharvaveda* deals with man, his protection from enemies, destruction of foes, kings and politics, welfare in this life, and similar other things.

Atharvaveda Saṁhitā

The *Atharvaveda* is also known as *Atharvāṅgirasa-Veda.* As the seers of *Atharvaveda Saṁhitā*, its *ṛṣis* were known as the Atharvāṅgirasa or simply the Āṅgirasa. Of these two classes of priests, the *Atharvaṇa* priests were adept in *Śānti-Puṣṭi-Karmas* — rituals related to accomplishment of peace in the family, society, for securing health, wealth, protection, and friendship. And the Āṅgirasa priests were adept in *ābhicārika* — *karmas* — performing rituals for cure of diseases (*yakṣma* — tuberculosis, *kuṣṭha* — leprosy, *śveta-kuṣṭha* — leukoderma, *jvara* — fever, *takma* — skin-disease, *kṛmi* — a kind of intestinal parasites) and destruction of wild animals, *śatru-nāśana* — destruction enemies and *śatrusenā-sammohana* — immobilising the enemy army, evil spirits (*asuras* — VI.7, *alakṣmī-nāśana*), etc.

It is also known as *Bhṛgvāṅgirasa-Veda,*[10] since Bhṛgu was Ṛṣi Aṅgirā's disciple and was instrumental in popularising *Atharvaveda*. Its other name is *Brahmaveda,*[11] since the priest is titled Brahmā.[12] Still another name is *Bhaiṣajya-Veda,* since it mostly consists of *mantras* for the cure of many diseases.

As per modern scholars as stated above, Atharvaṇa or Āṅgirasa were a class of highly intellectual priests who are reputed to be the first to have instituted the fire-worship and Soma sacrifices. They were the earliest teachers of *Brahmavidyā*. The word Atharva means *purohita,* a fire priest, and it is the oldest Indian name for 'priest' in general.

10. *etad vai bhūyiṣṭha brahma yad bhṛvāṅgirasaḥ.* – *Go.Br.* I.3.4.
11. *catvāro vā ime vedā ṛgvedo yajurvedaḥ sāmavedo brahmavedaḥ.* – *Go.Br.* II.16.
12. *Go.Br.* I.5.15.

Sage Atharvaṇa was the son of Ṛṣi Bhṛgu who was the son of Brahmā. 'Atharvaṇa' means — *na tharvati calati iti atharvaṇa* — 'the one who has no vacillation of the mind (who is steady in his vision) is called Atharvaṇa'. That which was revealed to Sage Atharvaṇa is the *Atharvaveda*.

Atharvaveda Saṁhitā Śākhās

The extant Śaunaka-Śākhā has 20 *kāṇḍa*s, 759 *kaṇḍikā*s and 5,977 *mantra*s (5,987 in Svadhyaya Mandala, Pardi edition). Śaunaka-Śākhā begins with *ye triṣaptār paryanti.* According to Patañjali's *Mahābhāṣya* and *Brāhmayajña-Tarpaṇa,* the first verse of *Atharvaveda* begins with *śan no devirabhiṣṭaye* . . . . However, this *mantra* is first *mantra* in *Paippalāda Saṁhitā,* whereas in Śaunaka-Śākhā it is the sixth *mantra* — I.1.6. It appears that the *Paippalāda Saṁhitā* was once more popular. In the Kāśmīrī recension as well as the Odisha recension of *Paippalāda Saṁhitā, śan no devirabhiṣṭaye*. . . is the first *mantra* of the *Atharvaveda.* Many hymns of *Śaunaka Saṁhitā* are quoted in *Kauśika-Sūtra* and *Vaitāna-Sūtra.* Sāyaṇa also quotes many of these in his *bhāṣya* on the *Atharva Saṁhitā* of Śaunaka-Śākhā. Maurice Bloomfield and William Dwight Whitney have made a survey of the available hymns of the Paippalāda (Kāśmīrī) recension.

Atharvaveda has many foreign words like, *kiarata, alika, viligi, tabuva, tastuva,* which are traced to be very old Chaldean words used in 4500 BCE.

Gāyatrī-mantra is believed to be the essence of the three Vedas, which means that *Atharvaveda* is excluded. According to one view, before learning the *Atharvaveda,* a *brahmacārī* must go through a second *upanayanam* ceremony. Generally, the Gāyatrī imparted to a child at Brahmopadeśa ceremony is called Tripāda-Gāyatrī — it is so called because it has three *pāda*s or quarters. Each *pāda* encompasses the essential spirit of one Veda. The *Atharvaveda* has a separate Gāyatrī, and if people belonging to other Vedas want to learn this Veda, they have to go through a second *upanayanam* to receive instruction in it. For the followers of the first three Vedas, however, there is only one Gāyatrī, and those belonging to any one of them can learn the other two Vedas without another *upanayanam*.[I]

Patañjali in his *Mahābhāṣya* has referred to nine *śākhās* of the *Atharvaveda*[13] — (i) Paippalāda, (ii) Tauda, (iii) Muṇḍa, (iv) Śaunakīya, (v) Jājala, (vi) Jalada, (vii) Brāhmaveda, (viii) Devadarśa and, (ix) Cāraṇavidya.

The *Caraṇavyūha* also furnishes a list of nine *śākhās*[14] — (i) Paippalāda, (ii) Dāntā, (iii) Pradāntā, (iv) Autā, (v) Jābālā, (vi) Śaunakā, (vii) Brahmapalāśā, (viii) Kunakhī-vedadarśī, and (ix) Cāraṇavidya.

Sāyaṇācārya accepts the existence of nine *śākhās*; however, his list is slightly different from the list of *Caraṇavyūha*. Scholars give preference to Sāyaṇa's list that is — (i) Paippalāda, (ii) Tauda, (iii) Mauda, (iv) Śaunakīya, (v) Jājala, (vi) Jalada, (vii) Brahmavada, (viii) Devadarśī, and (ix) Cāraṇavaidya.[15]

	Patañjali	**Sāyaṇa**	***Caraṇavyūha***
1	Paippalāda	Paippalāda	Paippalāda
2	Dānta	Tauda	Dāntā
3	Pradānta	Mauda	Pradāntā
4	Snāta	Jalada	Autā
5	Sautna	Jājala	Jābālā
6	Brahmadāvala	Brahmavada	Brahmapalāśā
7	Śaunaka	Śaunakīya	Śaunakā
8	Devavarśata	Devadarśī	Kunakhī-Vedadarśī
9	Cāraṇavidyā	Cāraṇavaidya	Cāraṇavidyā

13. *Ma.Bh.-Pa.Ah.* I.1.1.
14. *Ca.Vū* IV.
15. *Sā.Bh. Upodghāta.*

Of these, Śaunaka is extant. The Paippalāda-Śākhā has since been discovered, edited and published.[16]

Subject Matter of Atharvaveda

Atharvaveda is the most secular of all the four Vedas, in that, it deals with worldly matters and issues in the manner and to the extent not addressed by the other three Vedas. The definition — *iṣṭaprāptyaniṣṭa-parihārayor-alaukikam-upāyaṁ yo grantho vedayati sa vedaḥ*,[17] is validated in *Atharvaveda*. It conveys to us the knowledge of many magic formulae, since it contains *mantra*s with which one wards off misfortunes and disasters and brings about the destruction of one's enemies.

Atharvaveda is a mixture of prose and poetry. The *mantra*s of the other three Vedas also serve the same purpose as those of the *Atharvaveda*. However, what is special about *Atharvaveda* is that, it has references to some deities not mentioned in the others and has *mantra*s addressed to fierce spirits. What has come to be known as *mantrikam* (magical rites) has its source in this Veda.

Additionally, it also contains *sūkta*s that speak of lofty truths. It has Pr̥thivī-Sūkta, which glorifies this planet with all its creatures. A full hymn[18] is dedicated to the Vedic *brahmacārī*.

It is learnt from some stone inscriptions that, *Atharvaveda* had a following in Tamil country, until some centuries ago. Information about Vedic schools is provided by inscriptions found near Perani, near Eṇṇāyiram and a place near Wālājabādin the neighbourhood of Kāñcīpuram (all in Tamil Nadu). Even during the reign of the later Coḷas, the *Atharvaveda* was learnt in the Tamil country.

Incidentally, there are reportedly 18 categories among

---

16. See page no. 156 of this chapter.
17. *Tai.Br.Bh.*
18. *AV* XI.7.

brāhmaṇas in Odisha. One such category is known as *Atharvaṇikas*, which is *Atharvavedins*. Currently, *Atharvavedins* are also there in Saurashtra (in Gujarat) and Kośala (in UP),[II] though their number is small. *Atharvaveda Saṁhitā* is rarely chanted in the north, and is not heard in the south at all. Currently (in 2012) in the Kāñcī Kāmakoti Maṭh of Puri, Odisha, about 20 *brahmacārī*s are being taught the Paippalāda-Śākhā, and it is chanted everyday.

The prevalent Śaunaka-Śākhā has 20 *kāṇḍa*s (books) containing 759 *kaṇḍikā*s and 5,977 *mantra*s-verses (5,987 as per Svadhyaya Mandala, Pardi edition). The recently discovered and published Paippalāda-Śākhā also has 20 *kāṇḍa*s (books) containing 923 *kaṇḍikā*s, and 7,900 *mantra*s-verses (as per Kunja Bihari Upadhyaya, editor of *Atharvaṇaveda-Paippalāda-Saṁhitā*).

Scholars consider the last two books 19th and 20th, as *khila-kāṇḍa*, to be the later additions. The 20th book has almost entirely been taken from *Ṛgveda*. Scholars also are sceptical about book 15 (*vrātya-kāṇḍa*) from chronological point of view, and consider this to be as later addition. Thus, books 1-13 only are characteristically the most Atharvaṇic, and the rest correspond to various hymns of *Ṛgveda Saṁhitā*.

One-sixth of *Atharvaveda mantra*s are in the prose form, while the rest are in metre. About 1,200 *mantra*s of the *Atharvaveda* (1/5th) are from the *Ṛgveda*.

Of the 5,977 *mantra*s of *Atharvaveda* (Śaunaka-Śākhā), 2,696 *mantra*s are the original, envisioned by Atharvā Ṛṣi. Of the rest, 49 were by Atharvāṅgirā, 29 by Bṛhaddiva or Atharvā, 7 by Mṛgara or Atharvā, 7 by Vasiṣṭha or Atharvā, 4 by Kṛttikā or Atharvā and 7 by Bhṛgu-Ātharvaṇa. Thus, since 2,799 (2,696 + 49 + 29+ 7+ 7+ 4+ 7) *mantra*s of 220 *sūkta*s were seen by Ṛṣi Atharvā, this Veda is named after him.

The subject matter of *Atharvaveda* is divided into eight broad categories:

	Categories	Contents
1	Bhaiṣajya-Sūkta	At least 144 *sūkta*s describe the symptoms of various diseases, and names of herbs/roots/ plants for curing them.
2	Āyuṣya-Sūkta	Many *sūkta*s are prayers for long and healthy life.
3	Pauṣṭika-Sūkta	These *sūkta*s has refrence regarding agriculture, house-building and trade/ business.
4	Strīkarma-Sūkta	This category includes love, marriage, progeny and protection of progeny. It has charms / spells to neutralise the co-wife and obtain husband's love and attention.
5	Prāyaścitta-Sūkta	Hymns are there to atone for many known/ unknown wrongdoings.
6	Brahmaṇya-Sūkta	These are philosophical *sūkta*s discussing the cosmology. *Atharvaveda* is known as *Brahmaveda* because of these *sūkta*s.
7	Rājakarma-Sūkta	These hymns help the king in running the kingdom smoothly. There are *sūkta*s to defeat/destroy the enemies/opposite armies.
8	Abhicāra-Sūkta (Black-magic)	These are again charms and spells against enemies, *rākṣasas*. Although their number is insignificant, nevertheless, because of their presence, westerners name this Veda as *abhicāra-pradhāna-veda*.[19]

The proof of the pudding lies in eating it. Hence, the titles of the various *sūkta*s of the twenty *kāṇḍa*s are furnished below to give an idea about the subject matter of *Atharvaveda*. It will remove all kinds of apprehensions from the readers' minds. The name/s of the *ṛṣi*s and the number of *mantra*s in the *sūkta*s are also furnished.

19. The Buddhist and Jain monks were forbidden to devote themselves to the exorcism of the *Atharvaveda* and magic — Rajbali Pandy, *Hindu Saṁskāras*, p. 45.

Kāṇḍa I (35 Sūktas)

No. of Sūktas	Name of the Sūkta	Ṛṣis	No. of mantras
1	Medhājanana	Atharvā	4
2	Roga-upaśamana	Atharvā	4
3	Mūtra-mocana	Atharvā	9
4	Apāṁ-bheṣaja	Sindhudvīpa	4
5	Apāṁ-bheṣaja	Sindhudvīpa	4
6	Apāṁ-bheṣaja	Sindhudvīpa	4
7	Yātudhāna-nāśana	Cātana	7
8	Yātudhāna-nāśana	Cātana	4
9	Vijaya-prārthanā	Atharvā	4
10	Pāśa-vimocana	Atharvā	4
11	Nāri-sukha-prasūti	Atharvā	6
12	Yakṣmā-nāśana	Bhṛgu-Aṅgirā	4
13	Vidyut	Bhṛgu-Aṅgirā	4
14	Kulapā-kanyā	Bhṛgu-Aṅgirā	4
15	Puṣṭi-karma	Atharvā	4
16	Śatru-vādhana	Cātana	4
17	Rudhira-srāva-nivartana-Dhamanī-vandhana	Brahmā	4
18	Alakṣmī-nāśana	Draviṇodā	4
19	Śatru-nivāraṇa	Brahmā	4
20	Śatru-nivāraṇa	Atharvā	4
21	Śatru-nivāraṇa	Atharvā	4
22	Hṛdroga-kamala-nāśana	Brahmā	4
23	Śveta-kuṣṭha-nāśana	Atharvā	4
24	Śveta-kuṣṭha-nāśana	Brahmā	4
25	Jvara-nāśana	Bhṛgu-Aṅgirā	4
26	Śarma(sukha)-prāpti	Brahmā	4
27	Svastyayana	Atharvā	4

28	Rakṣoghna	Cātana	4
29	Rāṣṭra-abhivardhana, Saptnakṣayaṇa	Vasiṣṭha	6
30	Dīrghāyu-prāpti	Atharvā	4
31	Pāśa-mocana	Brahmā	4
32	Mahad-brahma	Brahmā	4
33	Āpaḥ	Śantāti	4
34	Madhuvidyā	Atharvā	5
35	Dīrghāyu-prāpti	Atharvā	4

Kāṇḍa II (36 Sūktas)

No. of Sūktas	Name of the Sūkta	Ṛṣis	No. of mantras
1	Paramadhāma	Bena	5
2	Bhuvanapati	Matṛnāmā	5
3	Āsrava-bheṣaja	Aṅgirā	6
4	Dīrghāyu-prāpti	Atharvā	6
5	Indraśaurya	Bhṛgu-Ātharvaṇa	7
6	Sapatnahāgni	Śaunaka	5
7	Śāpa-mocana	Atharvā	5
8	Kṣetriya-roganāśana	Bhṛgu-Aṅgirā	5
9	Dīrghāyu-prāpti	Dīrghāyu-prāpti	5
10	Pāśa-mocana	Bhṛgu-Aṅgirā	8
11	Śreyaḥ-prāpti	Śukra	5
12	Śatru-nāśana	Bharadvāja	8
13	Dīrghāyu-prāpti	Atharvā	5
14	Dasyu-nāśana	Cātana	6
15	Abhaya-prāpti	Brahmā	6
16	Surakṣā	Brahmā	5
17	Bala-prāpti	Brahmā	7
18	Śatru-nāśana	Cātana	5
19	Śatru-nāśana	Atharvā	5

20	Śatru-nāśana	Atharvā	5
21	Śatru-nāśana	Atharvā	5
22	Śatru-nāśana	Atharvā	5
23	Śatru-nāśana	Atharvā	5
24	Śatru-nāśana	Brahmā	8
25	Pṛṣniparṇī	Cātana	5
26	Paśu-saṁvardhana	Savitā	5
27	Śatru-parājaya	Kapiñjala	7
28	Dīrghāyu-prāpti	Śambhu	5
29	Dīrghāyuṣya	Atharvā	7
30	Kāmini-mano'bhimukhī-karaṇa	Prajāpati	5
31	Kṛmi-jaṁbhana	Kāṇva	5
32	Kṛmi-nāśana	Kāṇva	6
33	Yakṣma-vivarhaṇa	Brahmā	7
34	Paśu-gaṇa	Atharvā	5
35	Viśvakarmā	Aṅgirā	5
36	Pativedana	Pativedana	8

Kāṇḍa III (31 Sūktas)

No. of Sūktas	Name of the Sūkta	Ṛṣis	No. of Mantras
1	Śatrusenā-sammohana	Atharvā	6
2	Śatrusenā-sammohana	Atharvā	6
3	Svarāja-punaḥ-sthāpana	Atharvā	6
4	Rājā-saṁvaraṇa	Atharvā	7
5	Rājā evaṁ Rājakṛta	Atharvā	8
6	Śatru-nāśana	Jagadbīja Puruṣa	8
7	Yakṣma-nāśana	Bhṛgu-Aṅgirā	7
8	Rāṣṭra-dhāraṇa	Atharvā	6
9	Duḥkha-nāśana	Vāmadeva	6
10	Rāyaspoṣa-prāpti	Atharvā	13

11	Dīrghāyu-prāpti	Brahmā, Bhṛgu-Aṅgirā	8
12	Śālā-nirmāṇa	Brahmā	9
13	Āpo-devatā	Bhṛgu	7
14	Goṣṭha	Brahmā	6
15	Vāṇijya	Atharvā	8
16	Kalyāṇārtha-prārthanā (Bhāgya-sūktam)	Atharvā	7
17	Kṛṣi	Viśvāmitra	9
18	Vanaspati	Atharvā	6
19	Ajarkṣatra	Vasiṣṭha	8
20	Rayisaṁvardhana	Vasiṣṭha	10
21	Śānti	Vasiṣṭha	10
22	Varcaḥ-prāpti	Vasiṣṭha	6
23	Vīra-prasūti	Brahmā	6
24	Samṛddhi-prāpti	Bhṛgu	7
25	Kāmavāṇa	Bhṛgu	6
26	Dikṣu-ātmarakṣā	Atharvā	6
27	Śatru-nivāraṇa	Atharvā	6
28	Paśu-poṣaṇa	Brahmā	6
29	Avi	Uddālaka	8
30	Sāṁmanasya	Atharvā	7
31	Yakṣma-nāśana	Brahmā	11

Kāṇḍa - IV (40 Sūktas)

No. of Sūktas	Name of the Sūkta	Ṛṣis	No. of Mantras
1	Brahmavidyā	Vena	7
2	Ātmavidyā (Hiraṇyagarbha-Sūkta of *ṚV*)	Vena	8
3	Śatru-nāśana	Atharvā	7
4	Bājīkaraṇa	Atharvā	8

5	Svāpana	Brahmā	7
6	Viṣaghna	Garutmān	8
7	Viṣa-nāśana	Garutmān	7
8	Rājyābhiṣeka	Atharvāṅgirā	7
9	Āñjana	Bhṛgu	10
10	Śaṅkhamaṇi	Atharvā	7
11	Anaḍvān	Bhṛgu-Aṅgirā	12
12	Rohiṇi-vanaspati	Ṛbhu	7
13	Roga-nivāraṇa	Śantāti	7
14	Svarjyoti-prāpti	Bhṛgu	9
15	Vṛṣṭi	Atharvā	16
16	Satyānṛta-samīkṣaka	Brahmā	9
17	Apāmārga	Śukra	8
18	Apāmārga	Śukra	8
19	Apāmārga	Śukra	8
20	Piśāca-kṣayaṇa	Mātṛnāmā	9
21	Go-samūha	Brahmā	7
22	Amitra-kṣayaṇa	Vasiṣṭha or Atharvā	7
23	Pāpa-mocana	Mṛgāra	7
24	Pāpa-mocana	Mṛgāra	7
25	Pāpa-mocana	Mṛgāra	7
26	Pāpa-mocana	Mṛgāra	7
27	Pāpa-mocana	Mṛgāra	7
28	Pāpa-mocana	Mṛgāra	7
29	Pāpa-mocana	Mṛgāra	7
30	Rāṣṭradevī (Devīsūktam)	Atharvā	8
31	Senā-nirīkṣaṇa	Brahmāskanda	7
32	Senā-saṁyoyana	Brahmāskanda	7
33	Pāpa-nāśana	Brahmā	8

34	Brahmaudana	Atharvā	8
35	Mṛtyu-santaraṇa	Prajāpati	7
36	Satyaujā-Agni	Cātana	10
37	Kṛmi-nāśana	Bādarāyaṇi	12
38	Vājinīvān-ṛṣabha	Bādarāyaṇi	7
39	Sannati	Aṅgirā	10
40	Śatru-nāśana	Śukra	8

Kāṇḍa V (31 Sūktas)

No. of Sūktas	Name of the Sūkta	Ṛṣis	No. of Mantras
1	Amṛtā	Bṛhaddivo'tharvā	9
2	Bhuvana-jyeṣṭha	Bṛhaddivo'tharvā	9
3	Vijaya-prārthanā	Bṛhaddivo'tharvā	11
4	Kuṣṭhatakna-nāśana	Bhṛgu-Aṅgirā	10
5	Lākṣā	Atharvā	9
6	Brahmavidyā	Atharvā	14
7	Arāti-nāśana	Atharvā	10
8	Śatru-nāśana	Atharvā	9
9	Ātmā	Brahmā	8
10	Ātmarakṣā	Brahmā	8
11	Sampatkarma	Atharvā	11
12	Ṛtayajña	Aṅgirā	11
13	Sarpaviṣa-nāśana	Garutmān	11
14	Kṛtyā-pariharaṇa	Śukra	13
15	Rogopaśamana	Viśvāmitra	11
16	Vṛkṣa-rogaśamana	Viśvāmitra	11
17	Brahmajaya	Mayobhū	18
18	Brahmagavī	Mayobhū	15
19	Brahmagavī	Mayobhū	15
20	Śatrusenātrāsana	Brahmā	12
21	Śatrusenātrāsana	Brahmā	12
22	Takna-nāśana	Bhṛgu-Aṅgirā	14
23	Kṛmighna	Kaṇva	13

24	Brahmakarma	Atharvā	17
25	Garbhādhāna	Brahmā	13
26	Navaśālā	Brahmā	12
27	Agni	Brahmā	12
28	Dīrghāyu	Atharvā	14
29	Rakṣoghna	Cātana	15
30	Dīrghāyuṣya	Unmocana	17
31	Kṛtyā-pariharaṇa	Śukra	12

Kāṇḍa VI (142 Sūktas)

No. of Sūktas	Name of the Sūkta	Ṛṣis	No. of Mantras
1	Amṛta-pradātā	Atharvā	3
2	Jetā-Indra	Atharvā	3
3	Ātmagopana	Atharvā	3
4	Ātmagopana	Atharvā	3
5	Varcaḥ-prāpti	Atharvā	3
6	Śatru-nāśana	Atharvā	3
7	Asura-kṣayaṇa	Atharvā	3
8	Kāmātmā	Jamadagni	3
9	Kāmātmā	Jamadagni	3
10	Saṁprokṣaṇa	Śantāti	3
11	Puṁsavana	Prajāpati	3
12	Sarpaviṣanivāraṇa	Garutmān	3
13	Mṛtyuñjaya	Atharvā	3
14	Balāsanāśana	Vabhrupiṅgala	3
15	Śatru-nivāraṇa	Uddālaka	3
16	Akṣiroga-bheṣaja	Śaunaka	4
17	Garbha-dṛṁhaṇa	Atharvā	4
18	Īrṣyā-vināśana	Atharvā	3
19	Pāvamāna	Śantāti	3
20	Yakṣma-nāśana	Bhṛgu-Aṅgirā	3

21	Keśa-vardhanī	Śantāti	3
22	Bhaiṣajya	Śantāti	3
23	Apāṁbhaiṣajya	Śantāti	3
24	Apāṁbhaiṣajya	Śantāti	3
25	Manyā-vināśana	Śunaḥśepa	3
26	Pāpma-nāśana	Brahmā	3
27	Ariṣṭa-kṣayaṇa	Bhr̥gu	3
28	Ariṣṭa-kṣayaṇa	Bhr̥gu	3
29	Ariṣṭa-kṣayaṇa	Bhr̥gu	3
30	Pāpa-śamana	Uparivabhrava	3
31	Gau	Uparivabhrava	3
32	Yātudhānakṣayaṇa	Cātana	3
33	Indrastava	Jāṭikāyana	3
34	Śatru-nāśana	Cātana	5
35	Vaiśvānara	Kauśika	3
36	Vaiśvānara	Kauśika	3
37	Śāpa-nāśana	Atharvā	3
38	Varcasya	Atharvā	4
39	Varcasya	Atharvā	3
40	Abhaya	Atharvā	3
41	Dīrghāyu-prāpti	Brahmā	3
42	Paraspara-cittaikikaraṇa	Bhr̥gu-Aṅgirā	3
43	Manyu-śamana	Bhr̥gu-Aṅgirā	3
44	Roga-nāśana	Viśvāmitra	3
45	Duḥsvapna-nāśana	Aṅgirā	3
46	Duḥsvapna-nāśana	Aṅgirā, Pracetā, Yama	3
47	Dīrghāyu-prāpti	Aṅgirā, Pracetā, Yama	3
48	Svasti-vācana	Aṅgirā, Pracetā, Yama	3

49	Agni-stavana	Gārgya	3
50	Abhaya-yācana	Atharvā	3
51	Eno-nāśana	Śantāti	3
52	Bhaiṣajya	Bhāgali	3
53	Sarvato-rakṣaṇa	Bṛhaccukra	3
54	Amitra-dambhana	Brahmā	3
55	Saumanasya	Brahmā	3
56	Sarpa-rakṣaṇa	Śantāti	3
57	Jala-cikitsā	Śantāti	3
58	Yaśaḥ-prāpti	Atharvā	3
59	Oṣadhi	Atharvā	3
60	Patilābha	Atharvā	3
61	Viśvasraṣṭā	Atharvā	3
62	Pāvamāna	Atharvā	3
63	Varco-balaprāpti	Druhvaṇa	4
64	Sāṁmanasya	Atharvā	3
65	Śatru-nāśana	Atharvā	3
66	Śatru-nāśana	Atharvā	3
67	Śatru-nāśana	Atharvā	3
68	Vapana	Atharvā	3
69	Varcas-prāpti	Atharvā	3
70	Aghnyā	Kāṅkāyana	3
71	Anna	Brahmā	3
72	Vājīkaraṇa	Atharvāṅgirā	3
73	Sāṁmanasya	Atharvā	3
74	Sāṁmanasya	Atharvā	3
75	Sapatna-kṣayaṇa	Kabandha	3
76	Āyuṣya	Kabandha	4
77	Pratiṣṭhāpana	Kabandha	3
78	Dhana-prāpti	Atharvā	3
79	Ūrjā-prāpti	Atharvā	3

80	Ariṣṭa-kṣayaṇa	Atharvā	3
81	Garbhādhāna	Atharvā	3
82	Jāyā-kāmanā	Bhaga	3
83	Bhaiṣajya	Aṅgirā	4
84	Nirṛti-mocana	Aṅgirā	4
85	Yakṣma-nāśana	Atharvā	3
86	Vṛṣa-kāmanā	Atharvā	3
87	Rājña-saṁvaraṇa	Atharvā	3
88	Dhruvorājā	Atharvā	3
89	Prīti-sañjanana	Atharvā	3
90	Iṣu-niṣkāsana	Atharvā	3
91	Yakṣma-nāśana	Bhṛgu-Aṅgirā	3
92	Vājī	Atharvā	3
93	Svastyayana	Śantāti	3
94	Sāṁmanasya	Atharvāṅgirā	3
95	Kuṣṭhauṣadhi	Bhṛgu-Aṅgirā	3
96	Cikitsā	Bhṛgu-Aṅgirā	3
97	Abhibhurvīra	Atharvā	3
98	Ajarakṣatra	Atharvā	3
99	Saṅgrāmajaya	Atharvā	3
100	Viṣa-dūṣaṇa	Garutmān	3
101	Vājīkaraṇa	Atharvāṅgirā	3
102	Abhi-sāṁmanasya	Jamadagni	3
103	Śatru-nāśana	Ucchocana	3
104	Śatru-nāśana	Praśocana	3
105	Kāsa-śamana	Unmocana	3
106	Dūrvāśālā	Pramocana	3
107	Viśvajit	Śantāti	4
108	Medhā-vardhana	Śaunaka	5
109	Pippalī-bhaiṣajya	Atharvā	3
110	Dīrghāyu	Atharvā	3

111	Unmattatā-mocana	Atharvā	4
112	Pāśa-mocana	Atharvā	3
113	Pāpa-nāśana	Atharvā	3
114	Unmocana	Brahmā	3
115	Pāpa-mocana	Brahmā	3
116	Madhumadanna	Jāṭikāyana	3
117	Ānṛṇya	Kauśika	3
118	Ānṛṇya	Kauśika	3
119	Pāśa-mocana	Kauśika	3
120	Sukṛtaloka	Kauśika	3
121	Sukṛtaloka-prāpti	Kauśika	4
122	Tṛtīyanāka	Bhṛgu	5
123	Saumanasya	Bhṛgu	5
124	Nirṛtyapastaraṇa	Atharvā	3
125	Vīra-ratha	Atharvā	3
126	Dundubhi	Atharvā	3
127	Yakṣma-nāśana	Bhṛgu-Aṅgirā	3
128	Rājā	Atharvāṅgirā	4
129	Bhaga-prāpti	Atharvā	3
130	Smara	Atharvā	4
131	Smara	Atharvā	3
132	Smara	Atharvā	3
133	Mekhalā-vandhana	Agastya	5
134	Śatru-nāśana	Śukra	3
135	Bala-prāpti	Śukra	3
136	Keśa-dṛṁhaṇa	Vītahavya	3
137	Keḍa-vardhana	Vītahavya	3
138	Klīvatva	Atharvā	5
139	Saubhāgya-vardhana	Atharvā	5
140	Sumaṅgala-danta	Atharvā	3
141	Gokarṇa-lakṣyakaraṇa	Viśvāmitra	3
142	Anna-samṛddhi	Viśvāmitra	3

Kāṇḍa VII (123 Sūktas)

No. of Sūktas	Name of the Sūkta	Ṛṣis	No. of Mantras
1	Ātmā	Atharvā	2
2	Ātmā	Atharvā	1
3	Ātmā	Atharvā	1
4	Viśvaprāṇa	Atharvā	1
5	Ātmā	Atharvā	5
6	Aditi	Atharvā	2
7	Āditya-gaṇa	Atharvā	2
8	Āditya-gaṇa	Atharvā	1
9	Śatru-nāśana	Uparivabhrava	1
10	Svastidā-Pūṣā	Uparivabhrava	4
11	Sarasvatī	Śaunaka	1
12	Rāṣṭrasabhā	Śaunaka	1
13	Śatru-nāśana	Śaunaka	4
14	Savitā	Atharvā	1
15	Savitā	Atharvā	4
16	Savitā	Bhṛgu	1
17	Savitā-prārthanā	Bhṛgu	1
18	Draviṇārtha-prārthanā	Bhṛgu	4
19	Vṛṣṭi	Atharvā	2
20	Prajā	Brahmā	1
21	Anumati	Brahmā	6
22	Eko-Vibhuḥ	Brahmā	1
23	Jyoti	Brahmā	2
24	Duḥsvapna-nāśana	Yama	1
25	Savitā	Brahmā	1
26	Viṣṇu	Medhātithi	2
27	Viṣṇu	Medhātithi	8
28	Iḷā	Medhātithi	1

29	Svasti	Medhātithi	1
30	Agnāviṣṇu	Medhātithi	2
31	Añjana	Bhṛgu-Aṅgirā	1
32	Śatru-nāśana	Bhṛgu-Aṅgirā	1
33	Dīrghāyu	Brahmā	1
34	Dīrghāyu	Brahmā	1
35	Śatru-nāśana	Atharvā	1
36	Sapatnī-nāśana	Atharvā	3
37	Añjana	Atharvā	1
38	Vāsa	Atharvā	1
39	Kevalapati	Atharvā	5
40	Āpaḥ	Praskaṇva	1
41	Sarasvān	Praskaṇva	2
42	Suparṇa	Praskaṇva	2
43	Pāpa-mocana	Praskaṇva	2
44	Vāk	Praskaṇva	1
45	Indrāviṣṇu	Praskaṇva	1
46	Īrṣyā-nivāraṇa	Praskaṇva	1
47	Īrṣyā-nivāraṇa	Praskaṇva	1
48	Sinīvālī	Atharvā	3
49	Kuhū	Atharvā	2
50	Rākā	Atharvā	2
51	Devapatnī	Atharvā	2
52	Vijaya	Aṅgirā	9
53	Paripāṇa	Aṅgirā	1
54	Sāṁmanasya	Atharvā	2
55	Dīrghāyu	Brahmā	7
56	Vighna-śamana	Brahmā	1
57	Mārga-svastyāyana	Bhṛgu	2
58	Viṣa-bheṣajya	Atharvā	8
59	Sarasvatī	Vāmadeva	2

60	Anna	Kaurupati	2
61	Śāpa-mocana	Bādarāyaṇi	1
62	Ramya-gṛha	Brahmā	7
63	Tapaḥ	Atharvā	2
64	Śatru-nāśana	Kaśyapa	1
65	Durita-nāśana	Kaśyapa	1
66	Pāpa-mocana	Yama	2
67	Durita-nāśana	Śukra	3
68	Brahma	Brahmā	1
69	Ātmā	Brahmā	1
70	Sarasvatī	Śantāti	2
71	Sarasvatī	Śantāti	1
72	Sukha	Śantāti	1
73	Śatru-damana	Atharvā	5
74	Agni	Atharvā	1
75	Indra	Atharvā	2
76	Indra	Atharvā	1
77	Gharma	Atharvā	11
78	Gaṇḍamālā-cikitsā	Atharvāṅgirā	4
79	Aghnyā	Uparivabhrava	2
80	Gaṇḍamālā-cikitsā	Atharvā	4
81	Gaṇḍamālā-cikitsā	Atharvā	2
82	Śatru-nāśana	Aṅgirā	2
83	Vandha-mocana	Atharvā	2
84	Amāvāsyā	Atharvā	4
85	Pūrṇimā	Atharvā	4
86	Sūrya-Candra	Atharvā	6
87	Agni	Śaunaka	6
88	Pāśa-mocana	Śunaḥśepa	4
89	Kṣatrabhṛdagni	Bhṛgu	3
90	Ariṣṭanemi	Atharvā	1
91	Trātā Indra	Atharvā	1

92	Vyāpakadeva	Atharvā	1
93	Sarpa-viṣanāśana	Garutmān	1
94	Divya Āpaḥ	Sindhudvīpa	4
95	Śatru-balanāśana	Aṅgirā	3
96	Sutrāmā Indra	Atharvā	1
97	Sutrāmā Indra	Atharvā	1
98	Śatru-nāśana	Bhṛgu-Aṅgirā	1
99	Sāṁmanasya	Atharvā	1
100	Śatru-nāśana	Kapiñjala	3
101	Śatru-nāśana	Kapiñjala	1
102	Yajña	Atharvā	8
103	Havi	Atharvā	1
104	Vedī	Atharvā	1
105	Duḥsvapna-nāśana	Yama	1
106	Duḥsvapna-nāśana	Yama	1
107	Ātmana-Ahiṁsana	Prajāpati	1
108	Kṣatriya	Prajāpati	1
109	Gau	Prajāpati	1
110	Divya-vacana	Atharvā	1
111	Amṛtattva	Atharvā	1
112	Santaraṇa	Bhṛgu	1
113	Śatru-nāśana	Bhṛgu	2
114	Rāṣṭrabhṛta	Bādarāyaṇi	7
115	Śatru-nāśana	Bhṛgu	3
116	Ātmā	Brahmā	1
117	Pāpa-nāśana	Varuṇa	2
118	Śatru-nāśana	Bhārgava	2
119	Śatru-nāśana	Bhārgava	2
120	Pāpa-lakṣaṇa-nāśana	Atharvāṅgirā	4
121	Jvara-nāśana	Atharvāṅgirā	2
122	Śatru-nivāraṇa	Atharvāṅgirā	1
123	Varma-dhāraṇa	Atharvāṅgirā	1

Kāṇḍa VIII (15 Sūktas)

No. of Sūktas	Name of the Sūkta	Ṛṣis	No. of Mantras
1	Dīrghāyu-prāpti	Brahmā	21
2	Dīrghāyu-prāpti	Brahmā	28
3	Śatru-nāśana	Cātana	26
4	Śatru-damana	Cātana	25
5	Pratisaramaṇi	Śukra	22
6	Garbha-doṣa-nivāraṇa	Matṛnāmā	26
7	Oṣadhi-samūha	Atharvā	28
8	Śatru-parājaya	Bhṛgu-Aṅgirā	24
9	Virāṭ (philosphical *sūkta*)	Atharvā	26
10	Virāṭ (philosphical *sūkta*)	Atharvā	13
11	Virāṭ (philosphical *sūkta*)	Atharvā	10
12	Virāṭ (philosphical *sūkta*)	Atharvā	8
13	Virāṭ (philosphical *sūkta*)	Atharvā	16
14	Virāṭ (philosphical *sūkta*)	Atharvā	16
15	Virāṭ (philosphical *sūkta*)	Atharvā	4

Kāṇḍa IX (15 Sūktas)

No. of Sūktas	Name of the Sūkta	Ṛṣis	No. of Mantras
1	Madhuvidyā	Atharvā	24
2	Kāma	Atharvā	25
3	Śāḷā	Bhṛgu-Aṅgirā	31
4	Ṛṣabha	Brahmā	24

5	Pañcaudana Aja	Bhṛgu	38
6	Atithi-satkāra	Brahmā	17
7	Atithi-satkāra	Brahmā	12
8	Atithi-satkāra	Brahmā	9
9	Atithi-satkāra	Brahmā	10
10	Atithi-satkāra	Brahmā	10
11	Atithi-satkāra	Brahmā	14
12	Gau	Brahmā	26
13	Yakṣma-nivāraṇa	Bhṛgu-Aṅgirā	22
14	Ātmā	Brahmā	22
15	Ātmā	Brahmā	22

Kāṇḍa X (10 Sūktas)

No. of Sūktas	Name of the Sūkta	Ṛṣis	No. of Mantras
1	Kṛtyādūṣana	Pṛtyaṅgirasa	32
2	Brahmaprakāśana	Nārāyaṇa	33
3	Sapatnakṣayaṇa-varaṇamaṇi	Atharvā	25
4	Sarpaviṣa-dūrikaraṇa	Garutmān	26
5	Vijaya-prāpti	Sindhudvīpa 1-24, Kauśika 25-36, Brahmā 37-41, Vihavya 42-50	50
6	Maṇibandhana	Bṛhaspati	35
7	Sarvādhāra-varṇana	Atharvā, Kṣudra	44
8	Jyeṣṭha-brahma-varṇana	Kutsa	44
9	Śataudanā-gau	Atharvā	27
10	Vaśā-gau	Kaśyapa	34

Kāṇḍa XI (12 Sūktas)

No. of Sūktas	Name of the Sūkta	Ṛṣis	No. of Mantras
1	Brahmaudana	Brahmā	37
2	Rudra	Atharvā	31
3	Odana	Atharvā	31
4	Odana	Atharvā	18
5	Odana	Atharvā	7
6	Prāṇa	Vaidarbhi Bhārgava	26
7	Brahmacarya	Brahmā	26
8	Pāpamocana	Śantāti	23
9	Ucchiṣṭa-brahma	Atharvā	27
10	Adhyātma	Kaurupati	34
11	Śatru-nivāraṇa	Kāṅkāyana	26
12	Śatru-nāśaka	Bhṛgu-Aṅgirā	27

Kāṇḍa XII (11 Sūktas)

No. of Sūktas	Name of the Sūkta	Ṛṣis	No. of Mantras
1	Bhūmi/Pṛthivī	Atharvā	63
2	Yakṣma-roga-nāśana	Bhṛgu	55
3	Svargaudana	Yama	60
4	Vaśā-gau	Kaśyapa	53
5	Brahmagavī	Atharvā	6
6	Brahmagavī	Atharvā	6
7	Brahmagavī	Atharvā	16
8	Brahmagavī	Atharvā	11
9	Brahmagavī	Atharvā	8
10	Brahmagavī	Atharvā	14
11	Brahmagavī	Atharvā	12

Kāṇḍa XIII (9 Sūktas)

No. of Sūktas	Name of the Sūkta	Ṛṣis	No. of Mantras
1	Adhyātma-prakaraṇa	Brahmā	60
2	Adhyātma	Brahmā	46
3	Adhyātma	Brahmā	26
4	Adhyātma	Brahmā	13
5	Adhyātma	Brahmā	8
6	Adhyātma	Brahmā	7
7	Adhyātma	Brahmā	17
8	Adhyātma	Brahmā	6
9	Adhyātma	Brahmā	5

Kāṇḍa XIV (2 Sūktas)

No. of Sūktas	Name of the Sūkta	Ṛṣis	No. of Mantras
1	Vivāha-prakaraṇa	Sāvitri Sūryā	64
2	Vivāha-prakaraṇa	Sāvitri Sūryā	75

Kāṇḍa XV (Vrātya-Kāṇḍa)[III] (18 Sūktas)

No. of Sūktas	Name of the Sūkta	Ṛṣis	No. of Mantras
1	Adhyātma-prakaraṇa	Atharvā	8
2	Adhyātma-prakaraṇa	Atharvā	28
3	Adhyātma-prakaraṇa	Atharvā	11
4	Adhyātma-prakaraṇa	Atharvā	18
5	Adhyātma-prakaraṇa	Atharvā	16
6	Adhyātma-prakaraṇa	Atharvā	26
7	Adhyātma-prakaraṇa	Atharvā	5
8	Adhyātma-prakaraṇa	Atharvā	3
9	Adhyātma-prakaraṇa	Atharvā	3

10	Adhyātma-prakaraṇa	Atharvā	11
11	Adhyātma-prakaraṇa	Atharvā	11
12	Adhyātma-prakaraṇa	Atharvā	11
13	Adhyātma-prakaraṇa	Atharvā	14
14	Adhyātma-prakaraṇa	Atharvā	24
15	Adhyātma-prakaraṇa	Atharvā	9
16	Adhyātma-prakaraṇa	Atharvā	7
17	Adhyātma-prakaraṇa	Atharvā	10
18	Adhyātma-prakaraṇa	Atharvā	5

Kāṇḍa XVI (9 Sūktas)

No. of Sūktas	Name of the Sūkta	Ṛṣis	No. of Mantras
1	Duḥkha-mocana	Atharvā	13
2	Duḥkha-mocana	Atharvā	6
3	Duḥkha-mocana	Brahmā	6
4	Duḥkha-mocana	Brahmā	7
5	Duḥkha-mocana	Yama	10
6	Duḥkha-mocana	Yama	11
7	Duḥkha-mocana	Yama	13
8	Duḥkha-mocana	Yama	33
9	Duḥkha-mocana	Yama	4

Kāṇḍa XVII (1 Sūktas)

No. of Sūktas	Name of the Sūkta	Ṛṣis	No. of Mantras
1	Abhyudyārtha-prārthanā	Brahmā	30

Kāṇḍa XVIII (4 Sūktas)

No. of Sūktas	Name of the Sūkta	Ṛṣis	No. of Mantras
1	Pitṛmedha	Atharvā	61
2	Pitṛmedha	Atharvā	60
3	Pitṛmedha	Atharvā	73
4	Pitṛmedha	Atharvā	89

Kāṇḍa XIX (72 Sūktas)

No. of Sūktas	Name of the Sūkta	Ṛṣis	No. of Mantras
1	Yajña	Brahmā	3
2	Āpaḥ	Sindhudvīpa	5
3	Jātavedā	Atharvāṅgirā	4
4	Ākūti	Atharvāṅgirā	4
5	Jagad-Rājā	Atharvāṅgirā	1
6	Jagad-Bīja-Puruṣa (Puruṣa-Sūktam of *YV*)	Nārāyaṇa	16
7	Nakṣatra (28 *nakṣatras* addressed including Abhijit)	Gārgya	5
8	Nakṣatra	Gārgya	7
9	Śānti	Brahmā	14
10	Śānti	Brahmā	10
11	Śānti	Brahmā	6
12	Subīra	Brahmā	1
13	Ekabīra	Apratiratha	11
14	Abhaya	Atharvā	1
15	Abhaya	Atharvā	6
16	Abhaya	Atharvā	2
17	Surakṣā	Atharvā	10

18	Surakṣā	Atharvā	10
19	Śarma	Atharvā	11
20	Surakṣā	Atharvā	4
21	Chandāṁsi	Brahmā	1
22	Brahmā	Aṅgirā	21
23	Atharvāṇa	Atharvā	30
24	Rāṣṭra	Atharvā	8
25	Aśva	Gopatha	1
26	Hiraṇyadhāraṇa	Atharvā	4
27	Surakṣā	Bhṛgu-Aṅgirā	15
28	Darbhamaṇi	Brahmā	10
29	Darbhamaṇi	Brahmā	9
30	Darbhamaṇi	Brahmā	5
31	Audumbaramaṇi	Savitā	14
32	Darbha	Bhṛgu	10
33	Darbha	Bhṛgu	5
34	Jaṅgiḍamaṇi	Aṅgirā	10
35	Jaṅgiḍa	Aṅgirā	5
36	Śatavāramaṇi	Brahmā	6
37	Balaprāpti	Atharvā	4
38	Yakṣma-nāśana	Atharvā	3
39	Kuṣṭha-nāśana	Bhṛgu-Aṅgirā	10
40	Medhā	Brahmā	4
41	Rāṣṭrabala	Brahmā	1
42	Brahmayajña	Brahmā	4
43	Brahmā	Brahmā	8
44	Bhaiṣajya	Bhṛgu	10
45	Āñcana	Bhṛgu	10
46	Astṛtamaṇi	Prajāpati	7
47	Rātri	Gopatha	9
48	Rātri	Gopatha	6

49	Rātri	Gopatha, Bharadvāja	10
50	Rātri	Gopatha	7
51	Ātmā	Brahmā	2
52	Kāma	Brahmā	5
53	Kāla	Bhṛgu	10
54	Kāla	Bhṛgu	5
55	Rāyaspoṣa	Bhṛgu	6
56	Duḥsvapna-nāśana	Yama	6
57	Duḥsvapna-nāśana	Yama	5
58	Yajña	Brahmā	6
59	Yajña	Brahmā	3
60	Aṅga	Brahmā	2
61	Pūrṇa Āyu	Brahmā	1
62	Sarvapriya	Brahmā	1
63	Āyuvardhana	Brahmā	1
64	Dīrghāyu	Brahmā	4
65	Sūkta	Brahmā	1
66	Asura-kṣayaṇam	Brahmā	1
67	Dīrghāyu (*paśyema śaradaḥ śatam*)	Brahmā	8
68	Vedokta-karma	Brahmā	1
69	Āpaḥ	Brahmā	4
70	Pūrṇāyu	Brahmā	1
71	Vedamātā	Brahmā	1
72	Paramātmā	Bhṛgu-Aṅgirā, Brahmā	1

Kāṇḍa XX (143 Sūktas)

No. of Sūktas	Ṛṣis	No. of Mantras
1	Viśvāmitra, Gautama, Virūpa	3
2	Gṛtsamada or Medhātithi	4
3	Irimbiṭhi	2
4	Irimbiṭhi	2
5	Irimbiṭhi	7
6	Viśvāmitra	9
7	Sukakṣa, Viśvāmitra	4
8	Bhāradvāja, Kutsa, Viśvāmitra	3
9	Nodhā	4
10	Medhyātithi	2
11	Viśvāmitra	11
12	Vasiṣṭha, Atri	7
13	Vāmadeva, Gotama, Kutsa, Viśvāmitra	4
14	Saubhari	4
15	Gautama	6
16	Ayāsya	12
17	Kṛṣṇa, Vasiṣṭha	12
18	Medhātithi, Priyamedha	6
19	Viśvāmitra	7
20	Viśvāmitra, Gṛtsamada	7
21	Savya	11
22	Triśoka, Priyamedha	6
23	Viśvāmitra	9
24	Viśvāmitra	9
25	Gotama, Aṣṭaka	7
26	Śunaḥśepa, Madhucchandā	6
27	Gosūkti, Aśvasūkti	6
28	Gosūkti, Aśvasūkti	4

29	Gosūkti, Aśvasūkti	5
30	Varu or Sarvahari	5
31	Varu or Sarvahari	5
32	Varu or Sarvahari	3
33	Aṣṭaka	3
34	Gṛtsamada	18
35	Nodhā	9
36	Bharadvāja	11
37	Vasiṣṭha	11
38	Irimbiṭhi, Madhucchandā	6
39	Madhucchandā, Gosūkti, Aśvasūkti	5
40	Madhucchandā	3
41	Gotama	3
42	Kurustuti	3
43	Triśoka	3
44	Irimbiṭhi	3
45	Śunaḥśepa	3
46	Irimbiṭhi	2
47	Sukakṣa, Madhucchandā, Irimbiṭhi, Praskaṇva	21
48	Khila, Sārparājñi	6
49	Khila, Nodhā, Medhyātithi	7
50	Medhyātithi	3
51	Praskaṇva, Puṣṭigu	4
52	Medhyātithi	3
53	Medhyātithi	3
54	Rebha	3
55	Rebha	3
56	Gotama	6
57	Madhucchandā, Viśvāmitra, Gṛtsamada, Medhyātithi	16

58	Nr̥medha, Bharadvāja	4
59	Medhyātithi	4
60	Sutakakṣa or Sukakṣa	6
61	Gosūkti, Aśvasūkti	6
62	Saubhari, Nr̥medha, Gosūkti, Aśvasūkti	10
63	Bhuvana or Sadhana, Bharadvāja, Gotama, Parvata	9
64	Nr̥medha	6
65	Viśvamanā	3
66	Viśvamanā	2
67	Parucchepa, Gr̥tsamada	7
68	Madhucchandā	12
69	Madhucchandā	12
70	Madhucchandā	20
71	Madhucchandā	16
72	Parucchepa	3
73	Vasiṣṭha, Vasukra	6
74	Śunaḥśepa	7
75	Parucchepa	3
76	Vaśukra	8
77	Vāmadeva	8
78	Śaṁyu	3
79	Śakti or Vasiṣṭha	2
80	Śaṁyu	2
81	Puruhanmā	2
82	Vasiṣṭha	2
83	Śaṁyu	2
84	Madhucchandā	3
85	Pragātha, Medhyātithi	4
86	Viśvāmitra	1
87	Vasiṣṭha	7

88	Vāmadeva	6
89	Kṛṣṇa	11
90	Bharadvāja	3
91	Ayāsya	12
92	Priyamedha, Ayāsya, Puruhanmā	21
93	Pragātha, Devajāmi-Indramātā	8
94	Kṛṣṇa	11
95	Gṛtsamada, Suda Paijavana	4
96	Pūraṇa, Rakṣa, Brahmā , Pracetā	24
97	Kali	3
98	Śaṁyu	2
99	Medhyātithi	2
100	Nṛmedha	3
101	Medhyātithi	3
102	Viśvāmitra	3
103	Sudīti and Purumīḷha = *ṚV* VIII.71.14	3
104	Medhyātithi	4
105	Nṛmedha, Puruhanmā	5
106	Gosūkti, Aśvasūkti	3
107	Vatsa, Bṛhaddiva, Atharvā, Brahmā, Kutsa	15
108	Nṛmedha	3
109	Gotama	3
110	Sutakakṣa or Sukakṣa	3
111	Parvata	3
112	Sukakṣa	3
113	Bharga	2
114	Saubhari	2
115	Vatsa	3
116	Medhyātithi	2
117	Vasiṣṭha	3

118	Bharga, Medhyātithi	4
119	Āyu, Śruṣṭigu	2
120	Devātithi	2
121	Devātithi	2
122	Śunaḥśepa	3
123	Kutsa	2
124	Vāmadeva	6
125	Sukīrti	7
126	Indrāṇī and Vṛṣākapi	23
127	Kuntāpasūkta/Khila	14
128	Kuntāpasūkta/Khila	16
129	Kuntāpasūkta/Khila-Etaśa-Pralāpa	20
130	Kuntāpasūkta/Khila-Etaśa-Pralāpa	20
131	Kuntāpasūkta/Khila-Etaśa-Pralāpa	20
132	Kuntāpasūkta/Khila-Etaśa-Pralāpa	16
133	Kuntāpasūkta/Khila (Cryptic)	6
134	Kuntāpasūkta/Khila-Pratigara	6
135	Kuntāpasūkta/Khila-Pratirādhā, Ativāda, Devanātha	13
136	Kuntāpasūkta/Khila-Āhanasya	16
137	Śirimbiṭhi, Budha, Vāmadeva, Yayāti, Tiraścīrāṅgirasa or Dyutāna, Sukakṣa	14
138	Vatsa	3
139	Śaśakarṇa	5
140	Śaśakarṇa	5
141	Śaśakarṇa	5
142	Śaśakarṇa	6
143	Purumīḷha and Ajamīla, Vāmadeva, Medhyātithi, Medhātithi	9

Atharvaveda Bhāṣyas and English Translations

On *Atharvaveda* (Śaunaka-Śākhā), the commentary of Sāyaṇācārya (1315-1387) alone is acknowledged as the most authentic. Unfortunately, only two-thirds of it is available now. The *kāṇḍa*s on which Sāyaṇa's commentary is not available are 5, 9, 10, 12, 13, 14, 15, and 16. Besides, on 8th and 20th *kāṇḍas*, his commentary is partially available.

Jayanta Bhaṭṭa (tenth century) was a Vedic scholar, fondly remembered by Vācaspati Miśra, and later commentators. He had discussed the scriptures with many Buddhist and Jaina scholars. His *ṭīkā* titled *Nyāya-mañjarī* on the Nyāya-Sūtras is famous. His main text is *Atharvaṇa-Rakṣā,* wherein he has thrown light on the importance of the *Atharvaveda.*

ENGLISH TRANSLATION OF ATHARVAVEDA

Roth-Whitney Edition of Atharvaveda was first published in 1856. The complete translation with critical notes by Roth-William, Dwight Whitney and edited by Charles Rockwell Lanman, was published in 1905 from Cambridge. It is a product of love by three generations of Vedic scholars. W.D. Whitney was the student of Roth. Charles Rockwell Lanman was the student of W.D. Whitney.

M. Bloomfield has translated a major portion of *Atharvaveda* in his text titled *Hymns of Atharvaveda.*

A. Ludwig and J. Grill have translated *Atharvaveda* into German.

A complete English translation of *Atharvaveda Saṁhitā,* with a popular commentary of the hymns; has been authored by R.T.H. Griffith, and is published in two parts.

MODERN COMMENTARY AND TRANSLATIONS

Amongst modern commentators, Sripada Damodar Satavalekar has written a commentary on *Atharvaveda* titled

Atharvaveda kā Subodha Bhāṣya. Jayadev Sharma has published his commentary on *Atharvaveda* from Arya Sahitya Mandal, Ajmer. Devi Chand has translated the *Atharvaveda* into English with original Sanskrit Texts.

Paippalāda Saṁhitā Śākha

One manuscript of Paippalāda-Śākhā with 20 *kāṇḍa*s in Śāradā *lipi*, was discovered in Kashmir. The then Kashmir king gifted the manuscript to the famous German Indology scholar, R. Roth in 1885. In 1901, R. Roth made three photocopies of this manuscript.

Interestingly, another manuscript in Oḍiā script was discovered in Odisha by Durgamohan Bhattacharya in 1968, who edited *kāṇḍa*s 1-4 during his lifetime. A part of his comments is quoted below:

> Paippalāda-Śākhā of *Atharvaveda* was popular in ancient times in various parts of India, including south of Narmadā. It enjoyed wide recognition as a major Vedic school. Its sphere of influence extended to Gujarat, Utkal (modern Odisha state) and territories under the rule of Pāla and the Sena kings of Bengal. The output of Paippalāda-school was considerable. Testimony of Gr̥hya-Sūtras and little known Vedic commentaries of old Bengal proves *śanno devī* to be the lost but initial *mantra* of *Paippalāda-Saṁhitā*.

His edited portions (*kāṇḍa*s 1-4, out of 20 *kāṇḍa*s), titled *Atharvavedīya Paippalāda Saṁhitā* has since been published by Calcutta College, Calcutta in 1974.

Subsequently, his son Deepak Bhattacharya independently edited *kāṇḍa*s 1-15 (out of 20 *kaṇḍa*s) titled *Paippalāda Saṁhitā of the Atharvaveda* that has been published by The Asiatic Society in 1997.

Recently, Kunja Bihari Upadhyaya, from Puri, Odisha, himself a Paippalāda Śākhādhyāyī, has published (in 2009) the

Atharvaṇaveda Paippalāda Saṁhitā in its entirety of 20 *kaṇḍas*, after referring to at least four palm-leaf manuscripts. It is the result of commitment and dedication of 25 years.

Kunja Bihari Upadhyaya

Atharvaveda Brāhmaṇa

Atharvaveda has only one Brāhmaṇa, i.e. *Gopatha Brāhmaṇa*. For a long time this was considered to be attached to Śaunaka-Śākhā. However, from internal evidence, i.e. *Go.Br.Pu.* I.29[20] it becomes very clear that it is attached to Paippalāda-Śākhā. This has been confirmed by great scholars like Prajna Devi in her editorial to *Gopatha Brāhmaṇa Bhāṣyam* by Kshemakaranadas Trivedi. It has a Pūrvabhāga and an Uttarabhāga. The Pūrvabhāga has five *prapāṭhakas* containing 135 *kaṇḍikās*, while the Uttarabhāga has six *prapāṭhakas* containing 123 *kaṇḍikās*. The main subject matter is description of Śrauta *yajñas*.

Gopatha Brāhmaṇa does not have any direct connection with the Saṁhitā. It mainly glorifies the *Atharvaveda*, and the fourth priest Brahmā.

Atharvaveda Brāhmaṇa English Translation

Gopatha Brāhmaṇa was first published in 1872 by M. Bloomfield. His book is titled *The Atharvaveda and The Gopatha Brāhmaṇa* and is translated into Hindi by Suryakant Sastri.

Atharvaveda Āraṇyaka

Atharvaveda does not have any Āraṇyaka.

---

20. *śanno devīrabhiṣṭaya itthevamādhiṁ kr̥tvā atharvam-adhīyate* |
— *Go.Br.Pu.* I.29

Atharvaveda Upaniṣads

The three principal Upaniṣads — *Praśna, Muṇḍaka* and *Māṇḍūkya* belong to *Gopatha Brāhmaṇa* of the Paippalāda-Śākhā. As quoted in *Muktikopaniṣad*, of the 108 listed Upaniṣads, 31 Upaniṣads are attached to *Atharvaveda*.

The *mantra* from *Muṇḍaka*[21] is quoted by many scholars in support of their doctrine of duality. Incidentally, the idea of this verse is depicted in a Proto-Bulgarian picture in relief (seventh-eighth centuries) and reproduced on the title page of *Eighteen Principal Upaniṣads*, published by Vaidika Samshodhana Mandala, Poona.

---

21. *dvā suparṇā sayujā sakhāyā sanānaṁ vṛkṣaṁ pariṣasvajāte* |
tayoranyaḥ pippalaṁ svādvatty-anaśnan-nanyo-abhicākaśiti | |
— *Muṇ.Up.* III.1.1

Endnotes

I. 'The *upanayana saṁskāra* became compulsory somewhere towards the close of the Upaniṣadic period. There were many factors that led to it. First of all, there was the cultural factor. For any advancing civilisation, education is essential. In order to make education universal, the *upanayana* was made compulsory. Every Āryan was compelled to spend at least some years at the house of a teacher, or in some educational institution. The next but the allied factor was that, the mass of literature and learning was increasing. Different branches of learning evolved. Therefore, in order to preserve the sacred literature, the service of the entire community were conscripted by making the *upanayana* a compulsory *saṁskāra*.' — Cf. Rajbali Pandey, *Hindu Saṁskāras*, p. 123 (cf. A.S. Altekar, *Education in Ancient India*, Chapter I, pp. 11-12).

II. It is an acknowledged fact that because of the initiative and efforts made by Paramācārya of Kāñcī and Sri Jayendra Saraswati, the study of *Atharvaveda* has been revived in the south India. Students from Tamil Nadu have been sent for this purpose to Sinor in Gujarat.

III. The word Vrātya is defined by BR as 'belonging to a roving band (*vrāta*), vagrant; member of a fellowship that stood without the Brāhmanical pale.' It is further applied to the son of an uninitiated man (*Baudhāyana* I.8.16: cf. *Manu* X.190), or also to one who has let the proper time for the sacrament of initiation slip (*Manu* II.41). And the *Mahābhārata*, at V.35.46=1227, classes the Vrātya with the offscourings of society, such as incendiaries, poisoners, pimps, adulterers, abortionists, drunkards, and so on. — In The *St. Petersburg Lexicon* VI.1503, BR expresses the opinion that the praise of the Vrātya in this book is an idealisation of the pious vagrant or wandering religious mendicant. — cf. *Atharvaveda Saṁhitā*, vol. II, Book XV, p. 769, W.D. Whitney.

ATHARVAVEDA – Original *śākhās*
Ṛṣi Sumantu
(50 as per *Caraṇavyūha*)

Saṁhitā	Brāhmaṇa	Āraṇyaka	Upaniṣad	Mahāvākya	Śāntimantraḥ	Priest
Available *śākhās*						
Śaunaka (extant) 20 *kāṇḍas,* 598 *kaṇḍikās,* 5,977 *mantras*		No Āraṇyaka				Brahmā
Paippalāda (extant after revival) also *20 kāṇḍas,* 923 *kaṇḍikās,* 7,900 *mantras*	*Gopatha Brāhmaṇa*		*Muṇḍaka, Māṇḍūkya, Praśna*	*ayamātmā brahma* (*Māṇ.Up*. 2)	*bhadraṁ karṇebhiḥ*	
Dānta (extinct)						
Pradānta (extinct)						
Snāta (extinct)						
Sautna (extinct)						
Brahmadāvala (extinct)						
Devavarśata (extinct)						
Caraṇavaidyā (extinct)						

7

Commentaries on the Vedas

Necessity of Commentaries on the Vedas

THERE is a theory as to why there was a necessity to comment on the Vedas. It says that, the *ṛṣis* of the first generation were seers — *mantradraṣṭāraḥ*. However, the subsequent generations were just competent enough to interpret the Vedas. Gradually, the faculties deteriorated, and the *ācārya*s wrote Vedāṅgas (Śikṣā, Kalpa, Niruktam, Vyākaraṇa, Jyotiṣam and Chandas) to interpret the Vedas. Thereafter in subsequent years, the *ācārya*s wrote commentaries on the Vedas.

Commentaries on the Vedas

The earliest commentaries on the Saṁhitā are the Brāhmaṇas. Gradually, the problem of interpretation of the Saṁhitā became complex, and by the time of the Nirukta, several independent schools of Vedic commentaries had arisen. There was a notion among modern Sanskrit scholars that in the matter of Vedic commentaries, there was a great break in the Indian tradition. It was the belief that after Yāska (around 700 BCE), there were no such attempts to interpret the Vedas, and that the tradition of Vedic commentaries had died out until Sāyaṇa (fourteenth century) took up the work a few centuries ago. However, now an unbroken, uniform, and continuous tradition has been found, right from the Brāhmaṇa period, through Yāska (around 700 BCE), Pāṇini (around 500 BCE), pre-Sāyaṇa, Sāyaṇa (CE 1315-87), and post-Sāyaṇa commentators up to the present day. Although the force of an unbroken tradition can now be maintained, the different methods of interpretation (etymological,[1] *ādhidaivika, ādhibhautika, ādhyātmika,*[2] ritualistic,[3] spiritual,[4] etc.) reduce the value of tradition being the only repository of the authentic interpretations of the Saṁhitā.

The recent discovery of a large number of commentaries on the Vedas has proved that the tradition of Vedic interpretation in India has been always continuous and unbroken, and that Sāyaṇa had only continued this tradition. In every branch of learning, an earlier text is explained later according to the notions prevailing at such later time, and the individual opinion of the commentator gives a new colour to the ancient text in all cases of successive attempts or interpretations. Otherwise, there is no point in writing a fresh commentary. This has been so in the case of grammar, philosophy and must have been so in the matter of Vedic commentaries. This does not constitute a break in the tradition.

Traditional Commentaries on the Four Vedas

Details of the commentaries on each of the Vedas have been furnished in relevant chapters. The same is repeated here along with chronological list of commentaries for easy comparison and assimilation.

ṚGVEDA BHĀṢYAS

The commentaries on the *Ṛgveda* are those of Devaswāmi, Skandaswāmi (CE 630), his contemporaries Nārāyaṇa (CE 630) and Udgītha (CE 630), Veṇkaṭa Mādhava (CE 1050), Swāmi Ānanda Tīrtha, i.e. Madhvācārya (CE 1198-1278), Ātmānanda

1. By Yāska.
2. By Madhvācārya, founder of Dvaita School.
3. By Sāyaṇa.
4. By Aurobindo.

(CE 1250), Sāyaṇācārya (CE 1315-87), Mudgala (CE 1413), Caturveda Swāmi (end of fifteenth century). All these old *bhāṣyas* are fortunately available today. We however do not have evidence of any of these commentators having commented on all the four Vedas other than Sāyaṇācārya.

Skandaswāmi's *Bhāṣyam* is up to fourth *aṣṭaka*. The balance four *aṣṭakas* were completed by his contemporaries, Nārāyaṇa and Udgītha. Veṇkaṭa Mādhava's *Bhāṣyam* is titled *R̥gartha-dīpikā*. Swāmi Ānanda Tīrtha, i.e. Madhvācārya gave a *bhāṣyam* in verse form on the first forty *sūktas* of the first *maṇḍala* only. Ātmānanda commented on Asyavamīya-Sūkta only.

The *Bhāṣyam* of Swami Dayananda Saraswati (1824-83) and Sri Aurobindo's *The Secret of the Veda* belong to the later period, and are useful additions. Swami Dayananda Saraswati's *R̥gveda-Bhāṣya-Bhūmikā* (CE 1878) and *R̥VS-Bhāṣya* up to *Maṇḍala* VII.2.2 are available. *R̥gveda-Bhāṣya-Bhūmikā* is a prescribed text in many Indian universities. Kapali Sastry's *Siddhañjana* or *Mystic Collyrium* is a favourite with the scholars.

TRANSLATION IN INDIAN LANGUAGES

The *R̥gveda* is available in Bengali translation by Romesh Chandra Dutt, in Hindi by S.D. Satavalekar, Jayadev Sharma and Ramgovind Trivedi. There is a very fine Marathi translation with exhaustive notes done by Siddheswar Shastri Chitrav.

WESTERN TRANSLATION OF R̥GVEDA

H.H. Wilson (CE 1786-1860) translated the complete *R̥gveda* in 1850 in six parts along with *Sāyaṇa-Bhāṣya* titled *R̥gveda, English Translation*. This is the oldest and the first English translation of the *R̥gveda*. Currently this translation along with original text of the *R̥gveda*, is available in four volumes edited by Ravi Prakash Arya and K.L. Joshi, published by Saujanya Books, Delhi.

F. Max Müller (CE 1823-1900) translated the *R̥gveda* along with *Sāyaṇa-Bhāṣya* between 1849-73 in six volumes. This set is currently available in Svadhyaya Mandala, Pune. He also edited *Ṛgveda* with *pada-pāṭha.*

Ṛgveda has been translated into German by K.F. Geldner in four volumes.

R.T.H. Griffith (1826-1906) translated the *Ṛgveda* with popular commentary in two volumes titled *Hymns of Ṛgveda.*

ŚUKLA-YAJURVEDA BHĀṢYAS

The commentaries on the *Śukla-Yajurveda* are those of Śaunaka, Hariswāmi (CE 638, disciple of Skandaswāmi), Uvvaṭa (CE 1050) on *ŚYV-Mā.Saṁ.*, Gaudhara (CE 1300), Rāvaṇa (CE 1450), Mahīdhara (CE 1588) on *ŚYV-Mā.Saṁ.*, titled *Vedadīpa*, and Swami Dayananda Saraswati (1824-83) on *ŚYV-Mā.Saṁ.*

TRANSLATION IN INDIAN LANGUAGES

S.D. Satavalekar has translated *ŚYV-Mā.Saṁ.*, in Hindi.

WESTERN TRANSLATION OF ŚUKLA-YAJURVEDA

Śukla-Yajurveda was completely translated by R.T.H. Griffith (1826-1906) in 1899.

KṚṢṆA-YAJURVEDA BHĀṢYAS

Bhaṭṭa Bhāskara (eleventh century) and later Sāyaṇācārya (1315-1387) have commented on *Taittirīya Saṁhitā* of *KYV.*

WESTERN TRANSLATION

Taittirīya Saṁhitā of *KYV* was completely translated by A.B. Keith in 1914.

SĀMAVEDA BHĀṢYAS

On the *Sāmaveda*, the well-known commentaries are those of Mādhava (seventh century), Guṇaviṣṇu (thirteenth century), Bharata Swāmi (CE 1303), Mahāswāmi (around fourteenth century), and Śobhākar Bhaṭṭa (before CE 1408).

WESTERN TRANSLATION OF SĀMAVEDA

Sāmaveda was completely translated by R.T.H. Griffith (1826-1906) in 1895.

ATHARVAVEDA BHĀṢYAS

On the *Atharvaveda* (Śaunaka-Śākhā), the commentary of Sāyaṇācārya (CE 1315-1387) alone is acknowledged as the most authentic. Unfortunately, only two-thirds of it is available. The *kāṇḍas* on which Sāyaṇa's commentary is not available are 5, 9, 10, 12, 13, 14, 15, and 16. Besides, his commentary is partially available on 8th and 20th *kāṇḍas*.

TRANSLATION IN INDIAN LANGUAGES

Amongst modern commentators, Śrīpāda Dāmodar Sātavalekar has written a commentary on the *Atharvaveda* titled *Atharvaveda kā Subodha Bhāṣya*. Jayadev Sharma has published his commentary on *Atharvaveda* from Arya Sahitya Mandal, Ajmer.

WESTERN TRANSLATION OF ATHARVAVEDA

M. Bloomfield has translated a major portion of *Atharvaveda* titled *Selected Hymns of Atharvaveda* in 1897, which is part of The Sacred Books of the East (vol. 42). W.D. Whitney completely translated the *Atharvaveda Saṁhitā*, edited by Lanman, 1905. A. Ludwig and J. Grill have translated *Atharvaveda* into Germany. R.T.H. Griffith (1826-1906) has completely translated the *Atharvaveda Saṁhitā*, published in two parts.

Traditional Vedic Commentators (Chronological List)

Many secondary Vedic literatures helps us to understand several minor, yet significant details regarding the branches of the Veda. The prominent among these may be enumerated as the *Bṛhaddevatā* and several *pariśiṣṭas* and a number of texts ascribed to Śaunaka, the *Nighaṇṭu* and the *Nirukta* of Yāska, the *Ṛgveda-Sarvānukramaṇī* of Kātyāyana (not *Aṣṭādhyāyī's Vārttikakāra)* and Ṣaḍguruśiṣya's commentary *Vedārtha-Dīpikā* on it.

Śaunaka (pre-700 BCE)

Śaunaka stands first among the exponents of the Veda, if the number of his *Anukramaṇīs* and his other treatises are to be considered. Ṣaḍguruśiṣya, in his famous commentary *Vedārtha-Dīpikā* on Kātyāyana's *Ṛgveda-Sarvānukramaṇī* mentions the names of the following texts authored by Śaunaka for the preservation of the *Ṛgveda*, (i) *Ārṣānukramaṇī*, (ii) *Chando'nukramaṇī*, (iii) *Devatānukramaṇī*, (iv) *Anuvākānukramaṇī*, (v) *Sūktānukramaṇī*, (vi) *Ṛgvidhāna*, (vii) *Pādavidhāna*, (viii) *Bṛhaddevatā*, (ix) *Prātiśākhya*, and (x) *Śaunaka-Smṛti*.[5]

Additionally, the *Caraṇavyūha-Sūtra-Pariśiṣṭa*, *Śaunaka-Gṛhyasūtra*, *Śaunaka-Gṛhyapariśiṣṭa*, *Śaunaka-Śikṣā*, the fifth Āraṇyaka of the *Aitareya Āraṇyaka* are also said to be authored by Śaunaka. He also commented on the 31st chapter of *ŚYV.Mā.Saṁ.*, which is the Puruṣasūktam. Uvvaṭa did not comment on this chapter stating, *asya bhāṣya śaunako nāma ṛṣirakarot*.

Most of the Western scholars opine that Śaunaka existed between 700-300 BCE. Pt. Bhagvad Datta opines that great *ācāryas* like Śaunaka, Āśvalāyana, Kātyāyana, Pāṇini, Vyāḍi, Kautsa, etc. were contemporaries, because they refer the names of one another in their texts.[6]

The prominent among the pupils of Śaunaka are said to be Āśvalāyana, Vyāḍi and Kātyāyana, who themselves have made significant contribution to the Vedic tradition.

---

5. Cf. *Caraṇavyūha-Sūtram*, p. ii, by Umesh Chandra Sharma, Viveka Publications, Aligarh, 1978.
6. *Vaidika Vāṅmaya kā Itihāsa, Brāhmaṇa tathā Āraṇyaka Grantha*, pp. 240-43, 251. Pt. Bhagvad Datta, Delhi, 1974.

Yāska (around 700 BCE)

Yāska was the author of the earliest extant Vedic Lexicon (*Nirukta*). He preceded Pāṇini (fifth century BCE). *Nirukta* is a technical treatise on etymology, lexical category and semantics of words. Yāska has commented on around 600 Vedic *mantras* in the *Nirukta*, and has quoted profusely from the Brāhmaṇas. Yāska thus represents the culmination of the labours of long line of teachers building up the science of Vedic interpretation. Yāska refers to the threefold interpretation of the *mantras* — namely *ādhyātmika, ādhibhautika* and *ādhidaivika*. These three modes of interpreting the Vedas appear to have been well recognised in the past. Thus, the prime importance of the spiritual interpretation was maintained by scholars of deep erudition. Yāska's observation in this regard is meaningful, *yajñadavate puṣpaphale devatādhyātme vā.*

Pāṇini (around 500 BCE)

Pāṇini — fifth century BCE

Pāṇini brought together in his treatise *Aṣṭādhyāyī*, the phonetical and grammatical material relating to all the different Vedic schools (*sarva-veda-pāriṣadaṁ hīdaṁ śāstram*), a position similar to that taken up by Yāska for the *Nirukta*. Pāṇini's genius was based on synthesis; he shows a rare capacity to strike a balance between two extreme views or controversies, which had torn his predecessors into fiercely rival camps. He was always cautious and balanced, keeping his doors open for the views of differing schools. His view on leading grammatical topics like eternity of the words was like that of Yāska.

Jaimini (third century BCE)

Jaimini was an ancient sage-philosopher who may be

considered the founder of the Mīmāṁsā School. He was the disciple of Veda Vyāsa. He is most known for his great treatise *Pūrva-Mīmāṁsā-Sūtras*, a system that investigates the Vedic injunctions. The text contains 2,758 *sūtras*, in 12 chapters and contains the views of many earlier sages. It is the foundation text of the Mīmāṁsā School. The text is a commentary on the Vedas with regard to ritual practice (*karma*) and religious duty (*dharma*). Jaimini's Mīmāṁsā is considered as a ritualist's counter-movement to the mysticist Vedānta-currents of his days. His *Pūrva-Mīmāṁsā-Sūtras* was commented upon by Śabaraswāmi in the early centuries of CE, which was in turn commented upon by Kumārila Bhaṭṭa in his *Śloka-Vārttika, Tantra-Vārttika, and Ṭup-Ṭīkā,* Prabhākara Miśra in his *Bṛhatī (Nibandhana)* and Murārī in his *Tṛtīyapanthā.*

Śabaraswāmi (early centuries CE)

Śabaraswāmi dates to the early centuries CE, later than Patañjali's *Mahābhāṣya* but earlier than Vātsyāyana. Śabaraswāmi was a resident of Kashmir. His father's name was Dīptaswāmin. Śabaraswāmi is a commentator on Jaimini's *Pūrva-Mīmāṁsā-Sūtras*, which is famously known as the *Śābara-Bhāṣyam.* It has at least three commentaries — *Śloka-Vārttika* by Kumārila Bhaṭṭa, *Bṛhatī (Nibandhana)* by Prabhākara Miśra (Kumārila's disciple), and *Tṛtīyapanthā* by Murārī.

The following couplet is famous about Śabaraswāmi,

brāhmaṇyām-abhāvad varāhamihiro jyotirvidam-agraṇiḥ |
rājā bhartṛhariśca vikramanṛpaḥ kṣatrātmājayam-abhūt ||
vaiśyāyāṁ hariścandra-vaidyatilako jātaśca saṅkuḥ kṛti |
sūdrāyām-amaraḥ sadeva śabarasvāmi-dvijasyātmajaḥ ||

However, tradition says that his real name was Ādityadeva, and that he got the name Śabara for his having disguised himself in the forest fearing Jain persecution. I would like to agree with this legend.

Skandaswāmi (around CE 630)

Skandaswāmi was a resident of Valabhī, capital of Gujarat. His father's name was Bhartṛdhruva. Skandaswāmi was the *guru* of Hariswāmi,[7] the famous commentator of *Śatapatha Brāhmaṇa*. Since this commentary was written in CE 638, Skandaswāmi is attributed to the first half of seventh century, say around CE 630. Thus, he becomes a contemporary of King Harṣavardhana, poet Bāṇa, Pulakeśi II or Satyāśraya.

The oldest available commentary on *Ṛgveda Saṁhitā* is by Skandaswāmi. His commentary of *Ṛgveda* is very lucid, and ritualistic, it is therefore treated with great respect. He has furnished the details of the *ṛṣis*, *devatās* and *chandas* at the beginning of each *sūktam* and has quoted from *Anukramaṇī*s, *Nighaṇṭu*, *Niruktam* and other Vedic texts, and has presented few grammatical aspects here and there. As per Veṇkaṭa Mādhava (tenth-eleventh century), this *Ṛgveda Saṁhitā Bhāṣya* was collectively written by Skandaswāmi, and two of his contemporaries, Nārāyaṇa and Udgītha (both around CE 630).[8] Skandaswāmi commented up to fourth *aṣṭaka*, and Nārāyaṇa and Udgītha commented on the remaining four *aṣṭaka*s. This commentary is the oldest and equally authoritative, and thus influenced Sāyaṇa's commentary. Skandaswāmi's *ṭīkā* on Yāska's *Nirukta* is not available.

Ṛgveda Saṁhitā with commentary of Skandaswāmi, Udgītha, Veṇkaṭa Mādhava and Mudgalācārya has been published by VVR Institute, Hoshiarpur, and is available.

Nārāyaṇa (around CE 630)

In his *Ṛgveda Saṁhitā Bhāṣyam*, Veṇkaṭa Mādhava has written —

---

7. *vyākhyāṁ kṛtvā-adhyāpayan-māṁ śrīskandaswāmi-asti me guruḥ.*

8. *skandaswāmī nārāyaṇa udgītha iti te kramāt* |
cakruḥ sahaikam-ṛgbhāṣyaṁ padavākyārtha-gocaram ||
— Veṇkaṭa Mādhava

skandaswāmī nārāyaṇa udgītha iti te kramāt |
cakruḥ sahaikamr̥g-bhāṣyaṁ padavākyārtha-gocaram ||

It becomes evident that Nārāyaṇa had assisted Skandaswāmi in writing the *R̥gveda Saṁhitā Bhāṣyam*. Nārāyaṇa was a great Vedic scholar. His *bhakti*-text *Nārāyaṇīyam* adapted from *Śrīmad Bhāgavatam* is extremely popular in the south India. He had also written a *ṭīkā* titled *Prakriyā-Sarvasva* on the *Uṇādi-Sūtra* of Śakaṭāyana.

Udgītha (around CE 630)

As per the above *śloka* by Veṇkaṭa Mādhava, Udgītha also had assisted Skandaswāmi in writing the *R̥gveda Saṁhitā Bhāṣyam*. He had commented on the concluding part of the *Bhāṣyam*.

Kumārila Bhaṭṭa (seventh century CE)

As referred earlier, Kumārila wrote a commentary titled *Śloka-Vārttika, Tantra-Vārttika, and Ṭup-Ṭīkā* on the *Śābara-Bhāṣyam*, which itself was a commentary on Jaimini's *Pūrva-Mīmāṁsā-Sūtras*. *Śloka-Vārttika* is commentary on the 1st *pāda* of 1st *adhyāya* of *Pū.Mī.Sū.* and *Śā.Bh.* *Tantra-Vārttika* is commentary on the 2nd *pāda* of 1st *adhyāya* to 3rd *adhyāya* of *Pū.Mī.Sū.* and *Śā.Bh.*, and *Ṭup-Ṭīkā* is commentary on 4th to 12th *adhyāya* of *Pū.Mī.Sū.* and *Śā.Bh.* His *Madhyama-Ṭīkā* and *Br̥hat-Ṭīkā* are now lost works. Kumārila is credited with the revival of Hinduism in the seventh century. Neo-Hinduism appealed to the Hindus because of its simplicity.

Prabhākara Miśra (seventh century CE)

Prabhākara was a resident of Kerala, and a disciple of Kumārila. However, he surpassed Kumārila in scholarship and was titled *guru*[1] by Kumārila himself. He was also a great scholar of Nyāya. His contention is known as Prābhākara-*mata*. His commentary titled *Br̥hatī* (*Nibandhana*) is on *Śābara-Bhāṣyam*. *Br̥hatī* is still in manuscript form, except for a small fragment that has been published. *Laghvī* (or *Vivaraṇa*).

The Prābhākara-Mīmāṁsā School accepts only five *pramāṇas:*[9] *pratyakṣa, anumāna, arthāpatti, upamāna* and *śabda* as *pramāṇas.* (They do not accept *anupalabdhi* as a *pramāṇa.*) Incidentally, *śabda* as a *pramāṇa* as per Prābhākara-Mīmāṁsā School continues to this day to represent only the Veda.

Jayanta Bhaṭṭa (ninth century)

Jayanta Bhaṭṭa was a Kāśmīrī poet and philosopher of Nyāya School. He has been fondly remembered by Vācaspati Miśra, and later commentators. He had discussed the scriptures with many Buddhist and Jain scholars. His *Ṭīkā Nyāya-Mañjarī* on the *Nyāya-Sūtra* is famous. His main text is *Atharvaṇa-Rakṣā,* wherein he has thrown light on the importance of the *Atharvaveda.*

Veṇkaṭa Mādhava (tenth-eleventh century)

Veṇkaṭa Mādhava was the resident of Goman village of Coḷa State, situated on the south of Kāverī river, the current Andhra Pradesh. His father's name was Veṇkaṭācārya, who was a great scholar of *Ṛgveda.* His grandfather's name was Mādhava and mother's name was Sundarī. These details have been furnished at the end of the first chapter of his *bhāṣyam.* Śāmbaśiva Śāstrī considers him to be between CE 1050-1150. However, Laxman Sarup considers him to be of the tenth century.

Veṇkaṭa Mādhava's *Ṛgveda-Bhāṣyam* titled *Ṛgartha-Dīpikā* is very famous. It is very brief and without any grammatical explanation, but full of examples from Brāhmaṇa texts. He has been referred to in Devarāja Yajjva's (twelfth century CE) *Nighaṇṭu-Bhāṣyam.* His other works are not available.

Uvvaṭa (eleventh century)

Uvvaṭa was a resident of Anandapur, in Gujarat, and the son of Vajraṭa, who was himself a great scholar. He was in the

9. The Advaita Vedānta recognises all the six *pramāṇas* — *pratyakṣa, anumāna, arthāpatti, upamāna, anupalabdhi* and *śabda,* accepted by the Bhāṭṭa-Mīmāṁsā School, and generally agrees with it with certain modifications.

court of King Bhoja of Avantī of Malwa. Hence, his period is attributed to the eleventh century. He is known for his extensive commentary on Mādhyandina-Śākhā of *Śukla-Yajurveda*. He has also written a commentary on *Yajuḥ-Prātiśākhya*.

Besides this, he has written *Ṭīkā* on *Ṛk-Prātiśākhya, Yajuḥ-Prātiśākhya, Ṛk-Sarvānukramaṇī-Bhāṣyam*, and *Īśāvāsya Upaniṣad Bhāṣyam*. Although brief and simple, his commentary is considered authoritative.

Bhaṭṭa Bhāskara (eleventh century)

He has written *bhāṣyam* on *Taittirīya Saṁhitā* titled *Jñānayajña* as also *bhāṣyam* on *Taittirīya Āraṇyaka*.

Ṣaḍguruśiṣya (twelfth century)

He has written *Ṣaḍguruśiṣya-Bhāṣyam* on *Aitareya Brāhmaṇa*, and a commentary titled *Vedārtha-Dīpikā* on *Ṛg-Sarvānukramaṇī* of Kātyāyana (not *Aṣṭādhyāyī*'s *Vārttikakāra*), which is largely based on *Bṛhaddevatā* as its chief source.

Swāmi Ānanda Tīrtha/later Madhvācārya (CE 1198-1278)
Swāmi Ānanda Tīrtha, famously known as Madhvācārya was the propounder of both, Madhva and Gauḍiya tradition of Dvaita School. He was born in CE 1198 in Uḍipinagar in Karnataka. His mother's name was Vedavatī and *guru*'s name was Acyuta Tīrtha. He studied the Vedas and Vedānta from him, and travelled all over India popularising his contentions. His texts *Ṛgveda-Bhāṣya* and *Anubhāṣya* on *Brahma-Sūtra* is famous. Extensive research is going on in many universities on his *Ṛgveda-Bhāṣya*.

Among the ancient *ācārya*s, he was the first to formulate an *ādhyātmika* interpretation of the Vedas. However, his *Ṛgbhāṣyam* is only on the first 40 *sūkta*s of the *Ṛgveda*. He resuscitated the *adhyātma* tradition that was being sidelined by the votaries of ritualism, and attempted to explain the Vedic *mantras*, primarily at the *adhyātma* level. He tried to interpret all the terms as having their plenary significance in respect of

Lord Nārāyaṇa. He used etymology to a great purpose. He affects a harmony of all the texts, and does not relegate the *mantra* portions to the region of *karma-kāṇḍa*, as some do. He finds an inviolable principle of interpretation to demonstrate the running oneness among the passages of the various Vedic *mantras*. This can be called the *ārṣa* tradition of Vedic interpretation. It has, no doubt, some esoteric significance.

Ātmānanda (CE 1250)

Most of the commentaries on the *Ṛgveda* are ritualistic. However, Ātmānanda's commentary is of spiritual nature. His commentary is on Asyavāmīya-Sūkta only. He has referred to Skandaswāmi, Bhāskara but not to Sāyaṇa, hence is considered to be of pre-Sāyaṇa period.

Sāyaṇa (before CE 1315-1387)

There are about 50 commentators on Vedic texts. However, the credit of writing commentaries on most of the Vedic texts goes to Sāyaṇācārya. The complete *bhāṣyam* on all the four Vedas was done by Sāyaṇācārya in the fourteenth century, and not before. Sāyaṇācārya is the only authority, who has commented on all the four Vedas — their Saṁhitā, Brāhmaṇa and few Āraṇyakas. He also wrote on many other subjects. Undoubtedly, he is the undisputed authority on the Vedas.

Sāyaṇa belongs to the period of Emperor Harihara, the founder of the Vijayanagara Empire. He held the post of prime minister for 16 years (1363-79) during the 35 years of rule of Harihara's son Emperor Bukkā (1344-79). When Harihara II took over the reigns of the empire, Sāyaṇa continued in the post of the commander and minister from CE 1379 until his final departure in CE 1387. Hence, he must have been born during the early fourteenth century. His *guru* was Vidyā Tīrtha. Since he wrote the commentary, inspired by his elder brother Mādhavācārya (later Vidyāraṇya Swāmi, author of *Pañcadaśī*), his commentary is known as *Mādhavīya-Bhāṣyam*.

COMMENTARY ON SĀYAṆA'S BHĀṢYAM

Sāyaṇa had immense knowledge of grammar, Nirukta and Smṛti literature, etc. All this is evident in his *bhāṣyam*. His *bhāṣyam* is vast, full of quotations, and is accepted as authoritative. There is a lot of use of grammar in *Sāyaṇa-Bhāṣya*. Ācārya Yāska has paved the way for interpretation of the Vedas in his *Niruktam*. However, except for explanations of few *mantra*s (around 600), he has not commented on any of the Vedas as such. Sāyaṇa has used the Nirukta largely in his *bhāṣyam*, and has adopted many traditional meanings of Vedic words besides quoting Śruti, Smṛti, the Purāṇas and the *Mahābhārata* to substantiate his commentary. All commentaries by the Western researchers are based on *Sāyaṇa-Bhāṣya*.

Following are the details of his vast work:

Veda	**Saṁhitā**	**Brāhmaṇa**	**Āraṇyaka**
Ṛgveda	*Śākala Saṁhitā*	*Aitareya Brāhmaṇa*	*Aitareya Āraṇyaka*
Śukla-Yajurveda	*Kāṇva Saṁhitā*	*Śatapatha Brāhmaṇa*	
Kṛṣṇa-Yajurveda	*Taittirīya Saṁhitā*	*Taittirīya Brāhmaṇa*	*Taittirīya Āraṇyaka*
Sāmaveda	*Rāṇāyanīya Saṁhitā*	*Jaiminīya*	
		Ārṣeya	
		Tāṇḍya or *Prauḍha* or *Mahā* or *Pañcaviṁśa*	
		Ṣaḍviṁśa	
		Chāndogya or *Mantra* or *Upaniṣad*	
		Sāmavidhāna	
		Devatādhyāya	
		Saṁhitopaniṣad	
		Vaṁśa	
Atharvaveda	*Śaunaka Saṁhitā*		

A comparison of Udgītha and Skandaswāmi with Sāyaṇa shows that the latter amply draws upon the former two scholars. However, there is this difference; Udgītha and Skandaswāmi preserve the order of the words as in the Ṛk, while Sāyaṇa follows the formal prose order (*anvaya*) in interpreting the Ṛk.

A Ṛgvedic passage refers to a triad of Vedic meanings, *trayo'rthāḥ sarvavedeṣu*. Critics accuse Sāyaṇa of presenting only the ritual aspect of the Vedas while ignoring its *ādhyātmika* dimension. However, he appears to be a soft target of the critics who themselves use his *bhāṣyam* and comment. We would definitely be lost without his *bhāṣyam* on the Vedas.

Mahīdhara (late sixteenth century)

Mahīdhara was a resident of Kāśī, and was a Nāgara brāhmaṇa. He had written *Mantramahodadhi*, a tāntric text in CE 1588. From his work, he appears to have been a worshipper of Lord Narasiṁha.

His *bhāṣyam* on *Śukla-Yajurveda Mādhyandina Saṁhitā*, titled *Vedadīpa*, is extensive and widely popular. Although it appears to be influenced by Uvvaṭa's (eleventh century) commentary, it has a distinct place of its own, since it explains in a lucid manner, the completely sacrificial rituals quoting from *Niruktam*, Brāhmaṇa texts and many more Śrauta-Sūtras.

Śukla-Yajurveda Mādhyandina Saṁhitā with Uvvaṭa and Mahīdhara *Bhāṣyam* has been published by Motilal Banarsidass. *Śukla-Yajurveda Mādhyandina Saṁhitā* with *Mahīdhara-Bhāṣyam* has been edited by A. Weber.

	Commentators	**Period**	***Ṛgveda***	***Yajur-veda***	***Sāma-veda***	***Atharva-veda***
			Brāhmaṇa granthas			
1	Śaunaka	Pre-700 BCE	*Bṛhaddevatā*	*Puruṣa-sūktam* 31st Ch. of *ŚYV.Mā. Saṁ.*		

2	Yāska	Around 700 BCE (most scholars agree to this)	*Niruktam*			
3	Pāṇiṇi	around 500 BCE				
4	Śabaraswāmi	Early centuries of CE	*Sābara-Bhāṣya*			
5	Devaswāmi		*R̥gveda*			
6	Skandaswāmi (*guru* of Hariswāmi)	CE 630	*R̥gveda Saṁhitā Bhāṣya* (up to 4th *aṣṭaka*)			
7	Nārāyaṇa (author of *Nārāyaṇīyam*)	CE 630	co-authored *R̥gveda Saṁhitā Bhāṣya* (remaining four *aṣṭakas*)			
8	Udgītha	CE 630	co-authored *R̥gveda Saṁhitā Bhāṣya* (remaining four *aṣṭakas*)			
9	Hariswāmi (disciple of Skandaswāmi)	CE 638		*Śukla-Yajur-veda*		
10	Kumārila Bhaṭṭa	Seventh century	*Śloka-vārttika* on *Śābara-Bhāṣya*			
11	Prabhākara Miśra	Seventh century	*Br̥hatī* on *Śābara-Bhāṣya*			
12	Mādhava	Seventh century			*Sāma-veda*	
13	Jayanta Bhaṭṭa	Tenth century				*Athar-vana-rakṣā*

14	Veṇkaṭa Mādhava	Tenth-eleventh century	*Ṛgveda-Bhāṣyam* titled *Ṛgartha-dīpikā*			
15	Uvvaṭa	CE 1050		*Śukla-Yajurveda Mādhyandina Śākhā*		
16	Bhaṭṭa Bhāskara	Eleventh century		*Taittirīya Saṁhitā* titled *Jñāna-yajña* and *Tai. Āraṇyaka*		
17	Ṣaḍguruśiṣya	Twelfth century	*Bhāṣyam* on *Aitareya Brāhmaṇa*			
18	Ānanda Tīrtha (Madhvācārya)	CE 1198-1278	*Ṛgveda-Bhāṣya* on 1st 40 *sūktas* only			
19	Ātmānanda	CE 1250	On *Asyavāmīya-Sūkta* only			
20	Guṇaviṣṇu	Thirteenth century			*Sāma-veda*	
21	Bharata Swāmi	CE 1303			*Sāma-veda*	
22	Sāyaṇācārya	CE 1315-87	*Ṛgveda-Bhāṣya*	*Tai.Sa. Tai.Br. Tai.Ār.*	*Sāma-veda Saṁhitā/* many Brāhmaṇas	*Atharva-veda Śaunaka Saṁhitā*
23	Mahāswāmi	Fourteenth century			*Sāma-veda*	

24	Śobhakar Bhaṭṭa	CE 1408			*Sāma-veda*	
25	Mudgala	CE 1413	*Ṛgveda-Bhāṣya*			
26	Caturveda Swāmi	End fifteenth century	*Ṛgveda-Bhāṣya*			
27	Mahīdhara	CE 1588		*Śukla-Yajur-veda Mādh-yandina Saṁhitā* titled *Veda-dīpa*		
28	Dayananda Saraswati (Founder of Ārya Samāj)	1824-83	*Ṛgveda-Bhāṣya Bhūmikā* and *Ṛgveda Saṁhitā* (up to 2nd *sūktam* of 7th *maṇḍala*)	*Śukla-Yajur-veda Mādh-yandina Saṁhitā*		
29	S.D. Satavalekar (Founder of Svadhyaya Mandala)	1868-1968	*Ṛgveda* tr. in Hindi	*Śukla-Yajur-veda Mādh-yandina Saṁhitā* (Tr. in Hindi)		*Atharva-veda kā Subodha Bhāṣya* (Tr. in Hindi)
30	Sri Aurobindo	1872-1950	*The Secret of the Veda*			
31	Kapali Sastry	1886-1953	*Siddhāñjana* or "mystic collyrium"			
32	Jayadev Sharma		*Ṛgveda* in Hindi			*Atharva-veda*
33	Ramgovind Trivedi		*Ṛgveda* in Hindi			

34	Devi Chand			*Śukla-Yajur-veda* (1959)	*Sāma-veda* (1961)	*Atharva-veda*
35	Bhagadev Acharya			*Sāma-veda Jaimi-nīya Saṁhitā* (tr. into Hindi)		
36	Romesh Chandra Dutt		*R̥gveda* in Bengali			
37	Siddheswar Shastri Chitrav		*R̥gveda* tr. in Marathi			
38	Shriram Sharma (of Gāyatrī Parivār)	1911-1990	*R̥gveda* simple tr. in Hindi, Oḍiā	*Yajur-veda* simple tr. in Hindi, Oḍiā	*Sāma-veda* simple tr. in Hindi, Oḍiā	*Atharva-veda* simple tr. in Hindi, Oḍiā

Modern Commentators

According to the changing times, new light on the Vedas was thrown by Vedic savants beginning from the Brāhmaṇa texts up to Yogi Sri Aurobindo's *The Secret of the Veda*. Scholars in various branches of literature, and reformers of social thoughts in India, drew inspiration from Vedic texts (including Amartya Sen in his *The Argumentative Indian*).The Vedas, thus served as a perennial source for different schools of thought-currents in the fields of philosophy, law, art, politics, economics, culture and sociology during the first 5,000 years. Our ancestors accepted even the atheists (the Cārvākas) and accorded them a due place in the Indian philosophical systems.

Swami Dayananda Saraswati (CE 1824-1883)

Swami Dayananda is famously known as the founder of the 'Ārya Samāj'. He has written commentary on *Ṛgveda Saṁhitā* (1878) and *Śukla-Yajurveda Mādhyandina Saṁhitā*. His commentary on *Ṛgveda Saṁhitā* is up to the VII.2.2. In 1878, he wrote *Ṛgveda-Bhāṣya-Bhūmikā* to establish his opinion/contention (*siddhānta*). During his lifetime, he created a positive mass awareness about the Vedas.

In recent times, beginning from Swami Dayananda Saraswati, there have been several attempts in India at redoing Vedic commentaries. The attitude of Ārya Samāj, which claimed for the Veda a most scientific character, by seeking to establish origins of modern scientific inventions therein, was the result of a reaction to the highly critical and unjust attacks on the Vedas by the prejudiced Westerners of the early nineteenth century.

S.D. Satavalekar (1868-1968)

Sripada Damodar Satavalekar was known as 'Vedamūrti' in Maharashtra, Gujarat and Punjab. Born in 1868, he studied Sanskrit at home. He was a diploma holder from the famous J.J. School of Arts, Bombay, and flourished well as a portrait painter. In 1919, he resolved to devote his life for the propagation of Vedic knowledge and established his institution, 'Swadhyaya Mandala.' He could speak fluently in Sanskrit, Hindi, and Gujarati apart from his mother tongue Marathi. He gave us some good and critical editions of Veda Saṁhitās and many more books as his own interpretation of the Vedas. He passed away in 1968, after completing a century. His good work is still continued by Swadhyaya Mandala, Paradi, Gujarat. He has written Hindi commentaries on *Śukla-Yajurveda Mādhyandina Saṁhitā* and *Atharvaveda Saṁhitā*.

Sri Aurobindo (1872-1950)

Sri Aurobindo's interpretation of the *Ṛgveda,* published in a series of articles in his philosophical monthly *Ārya* from 1914, was a radical departure both from Sāyaṇa and the naturalistic interpretation of the nineteenth-century European scholars. He could accept neither Sāyaṇa's excessive stress on ritualism, nor the view of the Vedic *ṛṣis* as primitive barbarians drunk on *soma,* praying for rain, and scared that the sun might not rise next morning.

Sri Aurobindo's system depended on unlocking a number of symbols and myths pervading the hymns, *go* (the cows) as the light, the rivers as flows of consciousness, the Dasyus's fortresses as subconscious obstructions withholding our inner treasures, the upper and lower oceans as the two hemispheres of our being, and the various gods and goddesses as so many powers and functions of the one godhead. The battles waged by them and the *ṛṣis* become the symbols of adventure of our spiritual conquest, made possible by the infusing in us of Agni, the divine will and fire.

Ananda Coomaraswamy (1877-1947)

Ananda Coomaraswamy was a Ceylonese philosopher and a metaphysician, as well as a pioneering historian of the modern art, particularly art history and symbolism. He is described mostly as the groundbreaking theorist, who was largely responsible for introducing ancient Indian Art and Culture to the West. Coomarswamy finds the Vedas devoid of any historical content and character, and as containing an original metaphysical tradition.

Kapali Sastry (1886-1953)

Teacher, translator, commentator, essayist, and poet, T.V. Kapali Sastry was a Vedic scholar who had his early training under Gaṇapati Muni. His scholarship and spiritual *sādhanā* endeared him to Ramaṇa Maharṣi. From 1916 onwards, he was drawn to Sri Aurobindo's Yoga. Interpreting the philosophy of Ramaṇa Maharṣi and Sri Aurobindo in both English and Sanskrit became a lifelong vocation for him. Kapali Sastry has written commentary on the first *aṣṭaka* of the *R̥gveda,* inspired by the intuitive interpretation of the Vedic Hymns by Sri Aurobindo. This text titled as *Siddhāñjana* or *Mystic Collyrium* was published in 1947. Kapali Sastry's works, in both English and Sanskrit answer in detail the criticism of the spiritual interpretations of the Vedas made by several universities. They do not accept the spiritual interpretations of the Vedas, on the ground that these are opposed to the tradition, which is supposed to be the opinion of the medieval ritualists (Mīmāṁsakas) and that of Sāyaṇa.

Bhagadev Acharya

He has translated *Sāmaveda Jaiminīya Saṁhitā* into Hindi.

Devi Chand

Devi Chand has translated *Śukla-Yajurveda, Sāmaveda* and *Atharvaveda* into English. His translation is based on Swami Dayananda's (CE 1824-83) school of thought, who regarded every word of the Vedas as divine and an authority by itself (*svataḥ-pramāṇa*). It is different from the commentaries of Sāyaṇa and other traditional commentators or the Western scholars' interpretations, yet very thought-provoking. Devi Chand was the founder of DAV College, Hoshiarpur and a well-known educationist in Punjab.

Shriram Sharma (1911-1990)

Shriram Sharma, founder of 'Yugashakti Gayatri' has published all the four Veda Saṁhitās — *Ṛgveda* (*Śākala Saṁhitā*), *Śukla-Yajurveda, Sāmaveda, Atharvaveda* (*Śaunaka Saṁhitā*) with original texts, and free Hindi translation. His effort is laudable since his texts include descriptive lists of all the *ṛṣi*s of all the four Vedas, the *devatā*s and the *chandas*, which is of immense help to a fresh Vedic scholar.

Other modern commentators are Bal Gangadhar Tilak (author of *Age of the Vedas, The Orion, or Researches into the Antiquity of the Vedas*), H.D. Velanker, C.V. Vaidya, S.P. Pandit, S.B. Dikshit, Satyavrata Samasrami, Suryakanta, Lakshman Sarup (author of *The Nighaṇṭu* and *The Nirukta*), and R.N. Dandekar (founder of Vaidika Samsodhan Mandal), etc.

Western Commentators

The modern period of Vedic studies, in the early part, had two distinct schools of Vedic commentaries, represented by Roth, Benfey, Grassman, and Kaegi, on the one hand, and Pischel, Geldner, and Sieg, on the other.

The former regarded the *Ṛgveda* as predominantly an Indo-European document, so that its interpretation demanded the basis of comparative philology and comparative mythology, and consequently traditional commentators were kept in the background as of little or no help.

The other school, however, preferred the orthodox Indian tradition represented by Yāska and Sāyaṇa to the modern philological methods since, in their opinion, the Veda is pre-eminently Indian in character, and indigenous tradition would enable them to understand the spirit behind the word, linguistics being able to give them bare meaning alone. At present, due importance is attached to the traditions of ritual; internal evidence serves as a powerful tool in Vedic interpretation in several ways, e.g. ascertaining meanings of words, supplying lacunae, etc.

The modern period in the history of the Vedic studies may be said to have been inaugurated nearly two centuries ago, when H.T. Colebrooke published his monograph, *On the Vedas, or Sacred Writings of the Hindus*. The field of Vedic research has since then been so enriched by a good collection of critical editions, translations, dictionaries, grammars, bibliographies, indices, concordances, lexicons, monographs, and several other such works, besides innumerable well thought articles in research journals, that perhaps no other branch of Indology offers such a vast and varied reference material, and tools of research. Though much has already been done, there is still tremondous scope for further research in the domain of Vedic philosophy and literature.

H.H. Wilson (1786-1860)

Horace Hayman Wilson was an English Orientalist. In 1813, he established himself as a great Sanskrit scholar by translating Kālidāsa's *Meghadūtam* with a graceful, if somewhat free translation in English rhyme verse with original Sanskrit text. His other works on *Sāṁkhya-Kārikā, Viṣṇu Purāṇa* (1840), Sanskrit Dictionary and Sanskrit Grammar further establishes his commitment and scholarship. He prepared the first *Sanskrit-English Dictionary* (1819) from materials compiled by native scholars, supplemented by his own researches. This work was only superseded by the *Sanskritwörterbuch* (1853-76) of Rudolf Roth and Otto von Bohtlingk, who expressed their obligations to Wilson in the preface to their great work. In 1850, he translated the complete *Ṛgveda* along with *Sāyaṇa-Bhāṣyam* titled *Translation of the Ṛgveda Saṁhitā* published in six volumes. This is the first and the oldest English translation of *Ṛgveda*. Currently the translation along with original text of the *Ṛgveda*, is available in four volumes edited by Ravi Prakash Arya and K.L. Joshi, published by Saujanya Books, Delhi.

F. Max Müller (1823-1900)

Max Müller was born in 1823 in Prussia of the erstwhile East Germany. Between 1849 and 1873, he translated six volumes of the *Ṛgveda* along with *Sāyaṇa-Bhāṣya*. (This set is currently available with Svadhyaya Mandala.) In 1859, his *History of Ancient Sanskrit Literature* provided revolutionary information of the Vedic Literature and Culture. His *Sacred Books of the East,* written along with 20 outstanding scholars, continues to elicit praise from the Indologists and scholars of all disciplines. Published in 51 volumes of which, 49 volumes were published during his lifetime. Of these 51 volumes, he has personally translated three volumes. They are — Upaniṣads, Vedic-Sūktas and *Dhammapada* — a Buddhist text. Besides, he will always be remembered for his German translation of *Hitopadeśa* in 1844, *Meghadūtam* in 1847, *R̥g-Prātiśākhya* and his independent text — *India, What Can it Teach Us*. He edited *R̥VS* with *pada-pāṭha.*

Rudolph Roth (1821-1895)

Rudolf von Roth of Tübingen was a German Indologist and founder of Vedic philology. His book, *Zur Litteratur und Geschichte des Veda* (*On the Literature and History of the Veda,* 1846), was a ground-breaking work on Vedic scholarship and research. His chief work is the monumental *Sanskrit Wörtebuch* (*Sanskrit Dictionary,* 7 vols. Saint Petersburg, 1853-95), compiled in collaboration with Otto von Bohtlingk and published by the Saint Petersburg Academy of Sciences. He edited Yāska's *Nirukta* (1852) and, with Whitney, the *Atharvaveda* (1856-57).

A. Weber (1825-1901)

Albrecht Friedrich Weber was a German Indologist and a historian. He was a professor at Tübingen, and a contemporary of Rudolf Roth. He was a close friend of Max Müller. His most important work is his edition of *Śukla-Yajurveda* along with *Mahīdhara-Bhāṣya* (1849-59). He also wrote *History of Indian Literature*, Trubner's Oriental Series, 1878.

W.D. Whitney (1827-1894)

William Dwight Whitney was a student of R. Roth. He was an American linguist, philologist and lexicographer, was a professor of Sanskrit in Yale College (1854-94). He was assigned the responsibility of translation of *Atharvaveda* by his Professor R. Roth. *Roth-Whitney Edition of Atharvaveda* was first published in 1856-57. The complete translation with critical notes by Roth-William Dwight Whitney, and edited by Charles Rockwell Lanman, was first published in 1905, from Cambridge. It is a product of love by three generations of Vedic scholars. W.D. Whitney was the student of Prof. R. Roth. Charles Rockwell Lanman, who was a professor of Sanskrit in Harvard University, was a student of Prof. W.D. Whitney.

Julius Eggeling (1842-1918)

Hans Julius Eggeling was professor of Sanskrit at the University of Edinburgh (1875-1914). He translated and edited *Śatapatha Brāhmaṇa* of *Śukla-Yajurveda* into English in 1882 titled *The Śatapatha-Brāhmaṇa according to the Text of the Mādhyandina School* in five volumes, which is part of the monumental Sacred Books of the East, edited by Max Müller. The whole series was published by Motilal Banarsidass in 1966 and is available.

Herman Oldenberg (1854-1920)

Herman Oldenberg was a German scholar in Indology. He translated and edited two volumes of Vedic Hymns in the monumental Sacred Books of the East, edited by Max Müller.

A.A. Macdonell (1854-1930)

Arthur Anthony Macdonell was of British origin and a noted Sanskrit scholar. He was born in 1854, in Mujaffarpur of Bihar district, when his father was a colonel in the British Army serving in India. Max Müller and R. Roth were his teachers. He learnt Sanskrit from M. William.

Macdonell became famous in 1897 by writing *Vedic Mythology*. His *History of Sanskrit Literature*[10] published in 1900 is one of his immortal texts. He continued to earn fame and recognition for his texts *The Bṛhad-Devatā Attributed to Śaunaka* (1904), A *Vedic Grammar for Students* (1916), *History of Vedic Mythology, Vedic Reader,* and *Vedic Index,* all published in 1910.

M. Bloomfield (1855-1928)

Maurice Bloomfield was an American philologist and Sanskrit scholar. He translated for Max Müller's Sacred Books of the East, a major portion of *Atharvaveda* in his text titled *The Hymns of Atharvaveda* (1897). He also translated *Gopatha Brāhmaṇa* titled *Atharvaveda and Gopatha Brāhmaṇa* in 1872. His other important text is *Vedic Concordance* (1907).

10. *The History of Indian Literature* already written by Albrecht Weber in 1878.

M. Winternitz (1863-1936)

Moriz Winternitz was an eminent Austrian orientalist. He was professor of Indology and Ethnology at the German University of Prague, Czechoslovakia. He wrote *A History of Sanskrit Literature*,[11] in German titled *Geischichte der indischen Literatur*, (1907) which has since been translated into English. This is accepted as an authoritative text. Besides, he translated *Āpastamba-Sūtra* into English and published it in 1891. He has earned fame by preparing the index of Sacred Books of the East. His other important works include, *Some Problems of Indian Literature*, which is a series of talks, *Catalogue of South Indian Manuscripts Belonging to the Royal Asiatic Society of Great Britain and Ireland* (London, 1902), and *Der Mahāyāna Buddhism* (Tübingen).

A.B. Keith (1879-1944)

Arthur Berriedale Keith was a constitutional lawyer, Sanskrit scholar and an Indologist. He has written 15 texts. Some of his works are, editing of *Sāṁkhyāyana Āraṇyaka* with introduction (1905), translation of *Aitareya Āraṇyaka* with *Ṭīkā* (1909) published by Oxford, *Vedic Index* (1912), translation and editing of *Taittirīya Saṁhitā* (1914), *Indian Mythology* (1917),[12] *A History of Sāṁkhya Philosophy* (1918),[13] translation and editing of *Aitareya Brāhmaṇa* and *Kauṣītaki Brāhmaṇa* (1920), *The Religion and Philosophy of the Vedas and Upaniṣads* (1925), *A History of Sanskrit Literature* (1920),[14] *Buddhist Philosophy in India*.

---

11. *History of Sanskrit Literature* was already written by A.A. Macdonell in 1900.
12. *Vedic Mythology* by A.A. Macdonell was already published in 1897.
13. *Sāṁkhya-Kārikā* by H.H. Wilson was already available by 1913.
14. *History of Sanskrit Literature* was already written by A.A. Macdonell in 1900, and *A History of Indian Literature* by M. Winternitz in German in 1907, later translated into English in 1926.

R.T.H. Griffith (1826-1906)

Ralph Thomas Hotchkin Griffith was a scholar of Indology and is a former principal of the Banaras College. He translated *Ṛgveda* in two volumes titled *Hymns of Ṛgveda* (published in 1889). This translation followed the six-volume translation of the *Ṛgveda* by Max Müller. He has also translated *Sāmaveda* titled *Hymns of Sāmaveda* (published in 1893). His *Atharvaveda Saṁhitā* published in two parts (published in 1896). A complete English translation of *Atharvaveda Saṁhitā*, with a popular commentary of the hymns was published in two parts from Varanasi. He also translated *Śukla-Yajurveda* (published in 1899).

Some other Western Vedic commentators are, P. Peterson, Grassman, H.T. Colebrooke (1765-1837), E. Burnouf, J.G. Bühler, L. Renou, J. Muir (*Interpretation of the Veda*, Original Sanskrit Series), etc., who have made significant contribution.

Phenomenon of Oral Tradition

In the British Museum, one may see a hand-written Bible of the third and fourth century CE; and the Holy Quran of 1,300 years ago scribed beautifully. However, one would rarely find a script of 'The Vedas' of such an ancient date. The preservation of the entire text of the four Vedas, containing around 20,500 *mantras* (verses), still intact by oral transmission through the millennia is a unique phenomenon in the annals of world literature. The credit goes to the traditional brāhmaṇas of India, who could keep the texts so well preserved with the right phonetic accents and accuracy to this date.[15]

Secret of Preserving the Vedas: Vedic Chanting

Prodigious energy was expended by ancient Indian Culture; in ensuring that the Vedas were transmitted from generation

15. Cf. *The Holy Vedas*, ed. Pandit Satyakama Vidyalankara.

to generation with absolute fidelity. The Vedas are preserved intact with great care and caution until date without allowing any change in original accent. That is so because any change in the accent will change the meaning of the word. There is the science of phonetics behind it.

Memorisation of the Vedas included up to 11 forms of recitation of the same text. The texts were subsequently 'proof-read' by comparing the different recited versions. This preservation of the text without corruption, was ensured by introducing at least five modes of recitation of individual *mantras* from the *Ṛgveda*.

i. *Saṁhitā-pāṭha* (continuous recitation) is the learning/ chanting of the original Vedic text, governed by the rules of metre and rhythm.

ii. The second method is *pada-pāṭha* (word-recitation), where the *sandhis* are broken down and each word in the Saṁhitā-text is recited in its own specific accent, without *sandhi* (compound). *Pada-pāṭha* occurs after *Saṁhitā-pāṭha,* and this method gives the student the meaning of each word.

iii. The third is *krama-pāṭha* (step-recitation), where each word of the *pada-pāṭha* is recited twice, being connected both with what precedes and what follows, e.g. ab-bc-cd-de and so on. The words of every *mantra* (verse) are split, which is called *pāṭha*. The first word of every *mantra* is added to the second (ab), the second to the third (bc), the third to the fourth (cd) and so on, until each half of the particular *mantra* is completed. This *pāṭha* or method of recitation helps the student understand not only the individual words, but also how two words can be combined in recitation and what modification occurs in the *svara* in such a combination. One who studies *krama-pāṭha* is called a *kramavit*.

iv. The next process is *jaṭā-pāṭha* (mesh/woven-recitation), which is based on the *krama-pāṭha.* The first word and the second word are first recited in their original order, and then repeated in the reverse order, and then again in the original order e.g. ab-ba-ab; bc-cb-bc; cd-dc-cd and so on. Then the process is first word with the second, second with third, third with second and second with third and so on. This is called *jaṭā-pāṭha.* One who studies *jaṭā-pāṭha* is called a *jaṭā-vallabha.*

v. The most difficult of these processes is the *ghana-pāṭha,* which is recited by permutation combination of the words of each hymn. In the *ghana-pāṭha* (compact recitation), the order is ab-ba-abc-cba-abc, bc-cb-bcd-dcb-bcd and so on. One who studies *ghana-pāṭha* is called a *ghana-pāṭhi.* Even today there are about 200 *ghana-pāṭhis* in India, who can recite fluently their respective *śākhā* of the Vedas with remarkable memory. Incidentally, the *Ṛgveda* if chanted in *ghana-pāṭha* style, takes over 450 hours to chant.

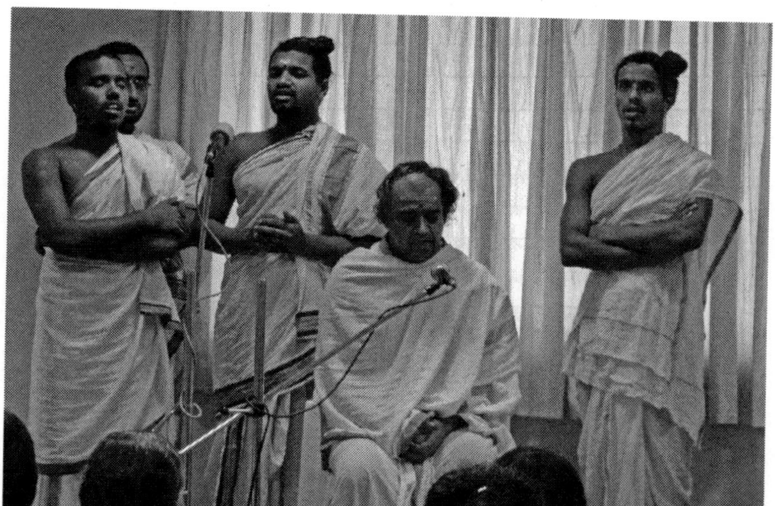

Sri Jambunatha Ghanapati chanting Veda in *ghana-pāṭha* style

The Saṁhitā-*pāṭha* and *pada-pāṭha* are called *prakṛti* (natural) *pāṭha,* while the rest are called *vikṛti* (non-natural/artificial) *pāṭha.* In *krama-pāṭha,* although the words do not occur in the natural order of abc (but as ab-bc-cd), it cannot be strictly called *vikṛti* or artificial, since there is no deliberate reversal of the words. The *vikṛti*s are eight in number,

> *jaṭā mālā śikhā rekhā dhvajo daṇḍo ratho ghanaḥ* ।
> *ityṣṭavikṛtayaḥ proktaḥ kramapūrva maharṣibhiḥ* ॥

In certain ancient edicts, notable gift-deeds, at the end of the name of some illustrious persons, there are suffixes like *kramavit, vedavit. Kramavit* means that the person is well versed in reciting the Vedas by *krama-pāṭha* method. There are many such edicts in the southern India.

Thus, the texts of the Vedas have been kept intact through all these centuries down to us. The significance of the complete measure of success achieved by this system in preserving the text from interpolation, modification, or corruption will be appreciated when we realise that in the entire text of the *Ṛgveda,* covering 1,028 *sūkta*s (hymns), or 10,552 *mantra*s or about 74,000 words, there is only one variant reading, viz. *maṁścatoḥ* for *māṁścatoḥ* in *ṚV* VII.44.3.

The reciting of the Vedas in a sonorous voice has a healing and pleasing effect on the mind and body of a person. These recitations are even today current in temples and religious orthodox houses, in the whole of India. The Vedic accent occupies a very important position in Comparative Philology, says A.A. Macdonell (1854-1930).

Written Form of Vedas

The Indologists assume that the Vedas were not written down early on, the emphasis being on very accurate oral transmission. Scholars opine that the *Ṛgveda* was composed around 1500 BCE, and was finally committed to writing at some point of time after 500 BCE.[16] It is interesting to note Maurice Bloomfield's opinion regarding written-form of the Vedas, 'I have little doubt that this oral tradition was supported at a comparatively early time by written tradition'.[17]

A.A. Macdonell opines,

> The hymns which have survived in the *R̥gveda* from the early period of Indo-Āryan invasion were almost exclusively composed by a hereditary priesthood. They were handed down in different families by memory, not by writing, which could have hardly been introduced into India before about 700 BCE. These family groups of hymns were gradually brought together until, with successive additions, they assumed the earliest collection of the *R̥gveda*. Then followed the constitution of the Saṁhitā text, which appears to have taken place about 600 BCE, at the end of the period of the Brāhmaṇas, but before the Upaniṣads, which form appendages to those works, came into existence. The creators of the Saṁhitā did not in any way alter the diction of the hymns here collected together; but only applied to the text certain rules of *sandhi* which prevailed in their time, and by which, in particular, vowels are either contracted or changed into semivowels, and 'a' is often dropped after 'e' and 'o', in such a way, as constantly to obscure the metre. Soon after this work was concluded, extraordinary precautions were taken to preserve from loss, or corruption the sacred text thus fixed. The earliest expedient of this kind was the formation of the *pada*, or 'word' text, in which all the words of the Saṁhitā text are separated, and given in their original form as unaffected by the rules of *sandhi*, and in which, most compounds and some derivatives and inflected forms are analysed. This text, which is virtually the earliest

16. The art of book-making and the knowledge of writing were known during Pāṇini's period. The words *lipikāra* and *libikāra* (*Aṣ.* III.2.21) denoted a writer and *yavanāni* (*Aṣ.* IV.1.49) a form of Greek writing.
17. *Atharvaveda* V.xix, p. 72.

> commentary on the *Ṛgveda*, was followed by other, and more complicated methods of reciting the text, and by various works called *anukramaṇīs* or 'Indexes'; which enumerate from the beginning, to the end of the *Ṛgveda*, the number of stanzas contained in each hymn, the deities, and the metres of all the stanzas of the *Ṛgveda*. Thanks to these various precautions, the text of the *Ṛgveda* has been handed down for 2,500 years with a fidelity that finds no parallel in any other literature.[18]

Elsewhere, A.A. Macdonell says,

> The hymns of the Vedas were composed many centuries before the introduction of writing into India, which can hardly have taken place much earlier than 600 BCE. They were handed down till probably long after that event by oral tradition, which has lasted down to the present day (1916). Apart from such tradition, the text of the Saṁhitā has been preserved in manuscripts, the earliest of which, owing to the adverse climatic conditions of India, were scarcely five centuries old. How soon they were first committed to writing, and whether the hymns of *Ṛgveda* were edited in the form of the Saṁhitā, and *pada* texts with the aid of writing, there seems insufficient evidence to decide; but it is almost inconceivable that voluminous prose works such as Brāhmaṇas, in particular the *Śatapatha Brāhmaṇa*, could have been composed and preserved without such aid.[19]

The Vedic knowledge was considered so precious that no perishable writing materials — birch-bark and palm-leaves — could be trusted for its preservation. Due to the ephemeral nature of the manuscript material (birch-bark or palm-leaves), surviving manuscripts rarely surpass an age of few hundred

18. Cf. *A Vedic Reader for Students*, p. xiii, by A.A. Macdonell, first published 1917, rpt. Motilal Banarsidass, 2006.
19. Cf. *A Vedic Grammar for Students*, p. 2, by A.A. Macdonell, 1916, Motilal Banarsidass, first Indian edn. 1993, rpt. 2010.

years. Paper does not appear to have been introduced into India until the Muslims made their political presence felt after the tenth century. The Vedas were written on palm-leaves and birch-barks after a long time of their oral existence.

A literary tradition set in only in the post-Vedic times, say, after the rise of Buddhism in the Maurya period, perhaps the earliest is the Kāṇva recension of the *Yajurveda* around the first century BCE. However, oral tradition continued to predominate until CE 1000. Around fourteen centuries back, commentaries on the Vedic texts appeared, perhaps because human memory began to wane.[20] There are a number of old Veda manuscripts in Nepal belonging to the Vājasaneyī tradition that are dated from eleventh century onwards. The Banaras Sanskrit University has a *R̥gveda* manuscript of the mid-fourteenth century.

Stevenson gave the text of the Rāṇāyanīya-Śākhā of *Sāmaveda* with his English translation in CE 1842.

No Vedic text was printed in India, until Max Müller (1823-1900) published his first edition of the *R̥gveda* with Sāyaṇa's commentary in CE 1874, after beginning his work in CE 1848.

Eugene Burnouf (1801-52), produced the German translation of the Kauthumīya-Śākhā of *Sāmaveda* in CE 1848.

Roth and W.D. Whitney (1827-94) edited *Atharvaveda* in 1856.

A. Weber brought in print *Vājasaneyī Saṁhitā* in CE 1852 and *Taittirīya Saṁhitā* in CE 1871.

L. Von Schroeder published critical editions of *Maitrāyaṇī Saṁhitā* in CE 1881-86, and *Kāṭhaka Saṁhitā* in CE 1900-11.

Between CE 1849 and 1944, many Western Sanskrit scholars like H.H. Wilson (1786-1860), M. Haug, B. Linder, A.C. Burnell, H. Oertal, A.F. Stenzler, D. Gaestra, Hillebrandt, Caland, R.

20. Skandaswāmi's (seventh century) commentary is the oldest available commentary.

Garbe, F. Knauer, Monier Williams (1819-99), R.T.H. Griffith (1826-1906), M. Bloomfield (1855-1928), H. Grassman, A. Ludwig, Herman Jacobi (1850-1937), H. Oldenberg (1854-1920), A.B. Keith (1879-1944), Theodore Goldstucker, etc. were the pioneers in this field of publication of Vedic texts, and they gave to the world most of the Vedic texts then available. These texts paved the way for the Indian scholars to publish the critical editions of the Vedic texts.

Ṛgveda in UNESCO's 'Memory of the World' Register[21]

The *Ṛgveda* manuscripts are of high value as unique examples of the intellectual and cultural heritage of the world. Out of the total number of 28,000 manuscripts housed at the Bhandarkar Oriental Research Institute (BORI), Pune, the 30 manuscripts of the *Ṛgveda* form a valuable part of the collection. These manuscripts evince several unique features in terms of scripts, accent marks, and support material used, among others.

F. Max Müller used one of the *Ṛgveda* manuscripts that are currently at BORI, to prepare his famous critical edition of the *Ṛgveda*, complete with translation of Sāyaṇa's commentaries. The material in this collection of *Ṛgveda* manuscripts was also used to prepare the well- known critical edition of the *Ṛgveda* by the Vaidika Samshodhana Mandala, Pune.

The *Ṛgveda* manuscripts have been selected for inscription in UNESCO's "Memory of the World" Register 2007. The National Mission for Manuscripts of the Ministry of Culture, has submitted the nomination on behalf of the BORI. The documentary heritage reflects the diversity of languages, people, and cultures in ancient India.

---

21. Cf. http://hinduism.about.com/od/scriptures/a/rigveda.htm

Period of the Vedas

Modern Indologists are of the view that *Ṛgveda* came first, that *Yajurveda* came later and so on. Traditional belief holds the Vedas to be the eternal coeval with the universe. The same arguments hold good in the matter of fixing the dates of the Brāhmaṇa, Āraṇyaka and Upaniṣads. In *Ṛgveda* itself, the *Yajurveda* and *Sāmaveda* are mentioned in a number of passages. In the Puruṣa-Sūkta (*ṚVS* X.90), there is reference to other three Vedas. However, my understanding is, fixing a probable time for the composition of the Vedas, does not reduce their greatness, or their acceptance or efficacy as a *pramāṇa*.

The scholarly understanding of the chronological framework has changed greatly in the last few years, due to truly revolutionary discoveries in archaeology. The main archaeological periods[22] are Stone Age, Bronze Age, and Iron Age. The following table roughly places the *Ṛgveda* period, which continues to be debatable with the scholars.

The Bronze Age in the Indian subcontinent began around 3300 BCE (Haṛappan 1) in the north India, with the beginning of Indus Valley Civilisation. Inhabitants of the Indus Valley, i.e. the Haṛappans developed new techniques in metallurgy and produced copper, bronze, lead, and tin.

Indus Valley Civilisation, had its mature period between 2600 to 1900 BCE. It continues into the Ṛgvedic period, which is the early part of the Vedic period. It is succeeded by the Indian Iron Age, beginning around 1300 BCE.

---

22. Names of archaeological periods vary enormously from region to region. Dating also varies considerably. The three-age system is used in many areas, referring to the pre-history periods identified by tool manufacture and use, of Stone Age, Bronze Age, and Iron Age. Since these ages are distinguished by the development of technology, naturally the dates to which they refer, vary in different parts of the world.

ROCK ART PERIOD	40,000 BCE (onwards to Historical period)[23]	
PALEOLITHIC PERIOD Mesolithic Period	**12,000 - 6,000 BCE**	
NEOLITHIC PERIOD	**(7000-3300 BCE)**	
Mehergarh I (aceramic Neolithic)	7000 - 5500 BCE	
Mehergarh II-VI (ceramic Neolithic)	5500 - 3300 BCE	
Formative Phase[24]	4,000 - 3,500 BCE	
EARLY HAṚAPPAN **EARLY BRONZE AGE**	**(3300-2600 BCE)**	
Haṛappan 1 (Ravi Phase)	3,300 - 2,800 BCE	
Haṛappan 2	2,800 - 2,600 BCE	
MATURE HAṚAPPAN **(INDUS VALLEY CIVILISATION)**	**(2600-1900 BCE)**	
Haṛappan 3A	2,600 - 2450 BCE	*Ṛgveda* Period
Haṛappan 3B	2450 - 2200 BCE	*Ṛgveda* Period
Haṛappan 3C	2200 - 1900 BCE	Ṛgveda Period Sarasvatī goes dry
LATE HAṚAPPAN (CEMETRY-H) **OCHRE-COLOURED POTTERY**	**(1900-1300 BCE)**	
Haṛappan 4	1900 - 1700 BCE	
Haṛappan 5	1700 - 1300 BCE	
FINAL PHASE Dholavīra[25]	**(1500-1400 BCE)**	

---

23. Historical periods refer to periods of human development after the development of writing. Historical records in whatever form tend to provide more political insight into the dominant nations, and hence allow categorisation according to the prevailing empires and cultures, such as Magadha Empire, Nanda Empire and Maurya Empire, etc. Naturally, these definitions of periods relate to the region of that empire and culture only.
24. Periodisation as per S.P. Gupta. (This however is the conventional chronology since Max Müller and is based on the 'Aryan Invasion Theory'.)
25. Periodisation as per S.P. Gupta. The dawn of civilisation, in G.C. Pande (ed.), *History of Science, Philosophy and Culture in Indian Civilisation*, ed. D.P. Chattopadhyaya, vol. I part I, New Delhi: Centre for Studies in Civilisations, 1999.

IRON AGE IN INDIA	(1300-272 BCE)	
Painted Grey Ware, Northern Black Polished Ware (Iron Age)	1300 - 300 BCE	Indo-Gangetic Tradition
Northern Black Polished-Ware Magadha Empire	800 - 500 BCE 684 - 424 BCE	Period of Yāska, Pāṇini and the Buddha
Nanda Empire	424 - 321 BCE	
Mauryan Period (pre-Aśoka)	321 - 272 BCE	

World Timeline

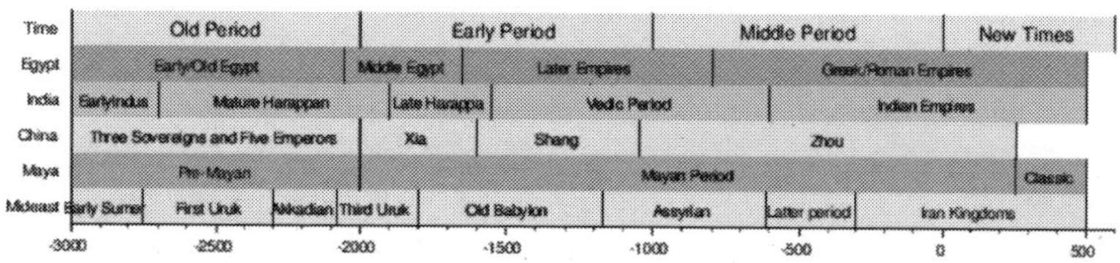

The general scholastic opinion date the Saṁhitās roughly around 2600-1900 BCE, and the circum-Vedic texts as well as the redaction of the Saṁhitās date to 1000-500 BCE, resulting in a Vedic period spanning the mid-second to mid-first millennium BCE, spanning the Late Bronze Age and the Iron Age.

Gavin Flood sums up mainstream estimates, according to which the *R̥gveda* was compiled from as early as 1500 BCE over a period of several centuries. The Vedic period reached its peak only after the composition of the *mantra* texts, with the establishment of the various *śākhā*s all over northern India that annotated the Saṁhitās with Brāhmaṇa discussions of their meaning, and reached its end in the age of the Buddha and Pāṇini and the rise of Mahājanapada period (Northern Black-Polished-Ware period). Michael Witzel gives a time span of 1500 to 500-400 BCE. Witzel makes special reference to the Near Eastern Mitanni material of the fourteenth century BCE, the only epigraphic record of Indo-Āryan contemporary to the R̥gvedic period. He gives 150 BCE (Patañjali) as a *terminus ante quem* for all the Vedic Sanskrit literature, and 1200 BCE (the early Iron Age) as *terminus post quem* for the *Atharvaveda*. As stated before, the general accepted historical chronology of the Vedas rank *Ṛgveda* as the first, followed by *Yajurveda*, *Sāmaveda* and finally the *Atharvaveda*.

Endnote

I. In the course of their studies, the students of Kumārila came across the sentence — *atratunoktan-tatrāpinoktam-itidviruktam*; this apparently meant — *atra tu noktam, tatrāpinoktam, itidviruktam* — "this has not been mentioned there, nor has it been mentioned here, thus it has been mentioned twice", an apparent absurdity. The teacher could not find a satisfactory explanation, and ultimately gave it up, and went to attend to his evening prayers. When the class assembled again, Prabhākara suggested that the sentence in question admitted of the construction — *atra tunā* (3.1) *uktaṁ, tatra apinā* (3.1) *uktam, iti dviḥ uktam*, the meaning being "what is mentioned there by means of the *nipāta 'tu'*, is again mentioned here by the *nipāta 'api'*, and thus it has been mentioned twice." Kumārila was so pleased at the ingenuity of his pupil that he thereupon conferred upon him the title *guru*.

— www.mimamsa.org/authors/prabhakara_mishra.html, accessed on 17.6.2010

Glossary

THE definitions of many of the words cited in this glossary are drawn from (i) *Vedāntasāra* of Sadānanda Yogīndra, (ii) *Vedānta-Paribhāṣā* of Dharmarāja Adhvarindra. Several secondary sources have also been referred to. These include (iii) R.K. Mission's *A Dictionary of Advaita Vedānta,* (iv) Ramakrishna Math's *Vedic Sacrifices,* (v) L. Ramamurty, *Encyclopaedia of Vedānta,* (vi) John Grimes, *A Concise Dictionary of Indian Philosophy,* (vii) Expositions of Swami Dayananda Saraswati of Ārsha Vidyā.

Abādhita : Non-contradicted, unsublated. In the epistemology of Advaita Vedānta, *pramā* — valid knowledge is that which cannot be contradicted.

Abhāva/Anupalabdhi : (lit.) absence. *Anupalabdhi* means non-cognition, non-apprehension, non-perception. By dint of this *pramāṇa, abhāva* — absence is cognised. *Abhāva* is accepted as a *pramāṇa* by the Bhāṭṭa Mīmāṁsakas and adapted by the Advaita Vedāntins.

Buddhist Schools deny the existence of *abhāva* altogether, as do the Prābhākara Mīmāṁsā and Viśiṣṭādvaita Schools. It may be noted that Advaita Vedānta recognises *abhāva* as a *bhāva-padārtha,* since as per them *abhāva* does not mean void (*śūnya*). In operating this *pramāṇa,* the object and its locus are very important. For example, we perceive the locus (*adhikaraṇa*) of a pot. When the pot is removed, from its locus, we perceive the locus (*adhikaraṇa*) of the absence (*abhāva*) of the pot (*bhūtale ghaṭo nāsti*), and not absence *per se*. The absence of an object is known due to its non-perception.

Abhicāra : Spell, magic, exorcising.

Aśvamedha : (lit.) Horse-sacrifice. It is one of the most ancient Vedic sacrifices, and can be performed only by very powerful kings or emperors to consolidate and extend their power. In this sacrifice, a horse is made to roam freely for one year, followed by the king's army. When the horse enters a foreign kingdom, its ruler could either fight against, or become an ally of the invaders. If new kingdoms were acquired this way, the horse was sacrificed as an offering. The actual sacrifice is spread over three days. If the horse gets killed, or carried away by the enemies, the sacrifice becomes nullified.

Adhikārī : An eligible/qualified person. One of the four *anubandha*s — factors of *anubandha-catuṣṭaya*. The other three are — *viṣaya, prayojanam* and *saṁbandha*. A Vedānta-*adhikārī* has to be *sādhana-catuṣṭaya-sampanna*.

Adhvaryu : One of the four classes of *ṛtviks* (the other three being Hotā, Udgātā and Brahmā) attached to *Yajurveda*. Adharyu's prescribed duties are measuring the ground, building the altar, arranging vessels, sacrificial-wood and water for the sacrifice, to fetch the animal and sacrifice it. While performing these actions, he is enjoined to repeat the hymns of the *Yajurveda*.

Adhyāya : Chapter.

Adhyayana : (lit.) means studying. In Vedic studies, it means regular practice of Vedic chanting under the guidance and supervision of a Vedic teacher.

Agnihotra : Name of a daily obligatory rite (*nitya-karma*) enjoined in the Veda to be performed by the twice-born (*dvija*s) householders, from the very day the Vedic fires are established, throughout their life. This is a fire-ritual, consisting of an oblation of cow's milk, (or gruel, or cooked rice, or curds, or ghee) offered every morning and evening into the sacred domestic sacrificial fire. In the absence of the *yajamāna*, his wife or his son or his pupil can perform this on his behalf.

Agniṣṭoma : (lit.) praise of Agni. The first of the *Somayāgas*, and is the basic model for others. A five-day Vedic fire-sacrifice requiring 16 priests. It is performed annually in spring season. The climax is reached during the *mādhyandina-savana* (extraction of the *soma*-juice, at mid-day) when the *dakṣiṇās* are also distributed.

Anadhigata : Previously unacquired, original. Otherwise not available through any other means of knowledge. Vedic statements are defined as — *abādhitam* (cannot be negated by any other means of knowledge), *anadhigatam* (not available through any of the other five means of knowledge), *arthavat phalabodhakam* (useful for the person here or hereafter, i.e. not useless statements).

Aniṣṭa : Undesirable. The Vedas contain the esoteric means for *iṣṭaprāpti* (obtaining the desired), and *aniṣṭa-parihāra* (neutralising/mitigating the undesirable).

Aṣṭādhyāyī : (lit.) of eight *adhyāyas*/chapters. An ingenious grammar-text authored by Pāṇini containing around 4,000 *sūtras*, for grammatical operations. It has eight chapters, each chapter containing four *pādas*-quarters.

Aṣṭaka : One of the two divisions/nomenclature of the *R̥gveda*. In *aṣṭaka* nomenclature, there are eight *aṣṭakas*, and each *aṣṭaka* has eight *adhyāyas* (chapters), totalling 64 *adhyāyas*, containing 2,006 or 2,024 *vargas*.

Anubandha-catuṣṭaya : The fourfold essential factors of any treatise/ philosophical works are grouped as *anubandha-catuṣṭaya*.[1] They are, (i) *viṣaya* — the subject matter, (ii) *prayojanam* — objective/purport, (iii) *adhikārī* — the eligible person for whom the work is meant, and (iv) *saṁbandha* — connection/ relation, i.e. between the text and knowledge (*pratipādaka-pratipādya-saṁbandha)*, between knowledge and *prayojanam* — (*sādhana-sādhya-saṁbandha*).

Anumānam : *Anu* = *paścāt* (along, after) + *mānam* = *jñānam* — the knowledge that takes place afterwards. Thus, *anumānam*

1. *Ve.Sā.* 5.

literally means, 'after knowledge', i.e. 'knowledge that follows other knowledge'. Inferential knowledge, that results through the instrumentation of some other knowledge (*jñāna-kāraṇaka-jñānam*). First the *liṅga* is seen, then by *liṅga* or *liṅgī* or *hetu*, the *sādhya-saṁbandha-jñānam* or *vyāpti-jñānam* takes place. This *sādhya* is known as *anumiti*. Since this knowledge takes place after *liṅga-darśana*, this is known as *anumānam*. The classic example is, *parvato vahnimān, dhūmatvāt, yathā mahānasaḥ*.

Reasoning or inference. This is achieved through the knowledge of a relationship of invariable concomitance (*vyāpti*) between what is to be proved (*sādhya*), and the mark of inference (*liṅga*), such as 'wherever there is smoke, there is fire'.

Anuṣṭubh : A kind of metre used in the *R̥gveda* having 32 (8x4 *pāda*s) syllables, with eight syllables per quarter (*pāda*).

Anuvāka/s : A section/recitation portions in the Vedas. Or a section/s in the Brāhmaṇas illustrating the *mantra*s.

Apauruṣeya/Apauruṣeyatvam : (lit.) not of human origin, a revealed text. The Mīmāṁsā rejects the view that the Veda was ever composed by anybody, and Nyāya-Vaiśeṣika ascribes its authorship to *Īśvara*. The position of Ācārya Śaṅkara about this point is midway between the two. Like the Mīmāṁsā, but unlike the Nyāya-Vaiśeṣika, he admits that the Veda is *apauruṣeya*. However, he redefines that word to make it signify not that the Veda has no author and is timeless, but that it is produced or, more properly, resuscitated at the beginning of each *kalpa*, by one that cannot interfere either with its content, or with the order of its words. In the case of works like the *Raghuvaṁśa*, the author composes it just as he likes. On the other hand, in case of the Vedas, the first promulgator of the Veda in every cycle who is *Īśvara*, repeats it anew, but precisely as it was in the other cycles (*pravāha-nityam*). The Veda is self-existent in this view also; however it is not the self-same Veda that always is, but a series of what may be described as re-issues of a timeless (*pravāha-*

nityam) edition which goes back to the beginningless time. This view is not different in substance from the Mīmāṁsā view, excepting that it finds a place for *Īśvara* in the doctrine. (Mīmāṁsā does not accept *Īśvara*.)

Apūrva : That, which did not exist before. Unforeseen consequence of an action. Unseen potency. An imperceptible/ extraordinary result produced by an action, which is fruitful in this world, or the other world, which cannot be proved through any other *pramāṇa*s than Śruti. (*pramāṇantara-aviṣayikaraṇam-apūrvatā — Ve.Sā.*)

2. As per Mīmāṁsā, the force which brings about the future effects of an action. See *Adṛṣṭa*.

Arthāpatti : *Arthāpatti* means presumption (nearest English translation, now commonly accepted). It is a valid means of knowledge — *pramāṇa* accepted by both the Mīmāṁsā and Advaita Vedānta Schools. It is an act of postulating something, to account for what apparently clashes with experience and is therefore, of the nature of hypothesis. Sometimes two rival theories are equally plausible, but appear mutually incompatible. In such cases, a presumption is to be made. *Arthāpatti* is defined as *anyathā anupapatti* — meaning 'otherwise it is not possible'. It is 'an assumption of some unperceived fact, in order to reconcile some inconsistency in perceived facts'. For instance, in the statement *pīna devadatta divā na bhuṅkte* — 'the fat Devadatta does not eat during the day', there is apparent contradiction because of two facts, (i) fat Devadatta does not eat during daytime, (ii) However, he does not lose weight. These two contradictory statements are reconciled with *arthāpatti pramāṇa* that, he must be eating during night. *Arthāpatti* is more than one-step inference. However, at the best, it remains an inference.

Arthavāda : Corroborative statement. Affirmative declaration of any purpose. Eulogistic meaning, supplemental texts which are explanatory to injunctive texts, non-essential statements.

Asura : Demons, those who delight in physical life, traditional enemies of the gods.

Atharvaveda : One of the four Vedas after compilation. It (Śaunaka-Śākhā) is about the 56 per cent the size of *Ṛgveda* (*Śākala-Śākhā*). Around 20 per cent of its content is repeated from the *Ṛgveda*. It is not used in any Vedic sacrifice, and comprises spells and charms. Currently, two of its *śākhā*s are extant — Śaunaka and Paippalāda.

Atirātra : This is also a *Somayāga* (an optional form of *Jyotiṣṭoma*) and is performed throughout the night. The Aśvins are offered *puroḍāśa*. An ewe or a ram is sacrificed unto Goddess Sarasvatī.

Ācārya : A general term for a spiritual teacher; one who instructs the knowledge of *Brahman*. A title affixed to the names of learned spiritual teachers. From the root √*car*= to go + prefix *ā* = towards; hence to approach, *Ch.Up.* VI.14.2 states – *ācāryavān puruṣo veda, tasya tāvad evaṁ ciraṁ, yāvat na vimokṣye'tha saṁpatsya iti* 'A person who has a teacher, knows'. The title *ācārya* is affixed to the names of the learned persons e.g., Śaṅkarācārya, Rāmānujācārya, Madhvācārya, Durgācārya.

Ādhibhautika : Of inanimate objects, of elements, physical, extrinsic. One of the three types of afflictions according to Sāṁkhya. *Ādhibhautika-trāpa* means 'afflictions caused by extrinsic natural influences' inflicted by other individuals, animals, birds and inanimate objects, on whom one does not have immediate control.

> *mṛga-pakṣi-manuṣyādyaiḥ piśāca-uraga-rākṣasaiḥ* ।
> *sarīsṛpādyaiśca nṛṇāṁ jāyate cādhibhautikaḥ* ॥
> — *Vi.Pu.* VI.5.7

Ādhidaivika : Cosmic, supernatural, divine, relating to deities — *adhideva*. One of the three types of afflictions according to Sāṁkhya. Cosmic/supernatural afflictions on which human have no control, e.g. — earthquake, tsunami, heavy rains, sunshine, cold-storm, etc.

śīta-vātoṣṇa-varṣā-aṁbu-vaidyutādi-samudbhavaḥ ।
tāpau dvijavara-śreṣṭhai kathyate cādhidaivikaḥ ।।
— *Vi.Pu.* VI.5.8

Ādhyātmika : One of the three types of afflictions according to Sāṁkhya. Afflictions relating to *ātmā*, the Self/person/individual. Intrinsic physical or/and mental afflictions caused to the Self, i.e. fever, body-ache, fear, anger and jealousy etc. are the *ādhyātmika* afflictions.

kāma-krodha-bhaya-dveṣa-lobha-moha-viṣādajaḥ ।
śoka-asūyā-avamāna-īrṣā-mātsaryādi-mayas-tathā ।।
mānaso'pi dvija-śreṣṭha tāpo bhavati naikadhā ।
iti evam-ādibhir-bhedais-tāpo hi-ādhyātmiko mataḥ ।।
— *Vi.Pu.* VI.5.5 and 6

Āgama :(lit.) That which has come down (traditionally), from the root √*gam* = *to go* + preposition *ā* = towards. Sacred texts. They are divided into three main branches according to the deity worshipped therein, (i) Vaiṣṇava Āgamas, which are further subdivided into Pāñcarātra and Vaikhānasa, (ii) Śaiva Āgamas that are fourfold — Kāpāla, Kālāmukha, Pāśupata and Śaiva, and (iii) Śākta Āgamas.

Āmnāya : Scripture, tradition, lineage, advice, instruction.

āmnāyasya kriyārthatvāt. ānarthakyam atad-arthānām.
— *Ja.Sū.* I.2.1

Āprī-sūktam : An *āprī-sūktam* is a particular type of ritual hymn 'consisting of invocations to a series of deified objects, (i) *idhma* or *samiddha agni*, (ii) *tanūnapāt*, (iii) *narāśaṁsā*, (iv) *iḷā*, (v) *barhi*, (vi) *divyadvāra*, (vii) *uṣāsānaktā*, (viii) *divyahotā pracetas*, (ix) the three *devīs* – *sarasvatī*, *iḷā*, *bhārati*, (x) *tvaṣṭā*, (xi) *vanaspati*, (xii) *svāhākṛti*, and said to be introductory to the animal sacrifice.' There are 10 *Āprī-sūktams* in the *Ṛgveda*.

Āraṇyaka : The Āraṇyakas are forest-books attached to the Brāhmaṇa that give philosophical interpretations to the latter, by allegorising them as well as prescribing various types of meditations (*upāsanās*) and/or symbolic worships. These are meant for ascetics/recluses who live in the forest. The famous *Bṛhadāraṇyaka* is an Āraṇyaka as well as an Upaniṣad.

Ārṣa : A *taddhita*-form derived from the word *ṛṣi*. *Ṛṣi-prayoga* means any discipline born of a *ṛṣi*.

Āstika : Orthodox (*āstika*). Name given to *darśanas* — Indian philosophical systems that accept the authority of the Vedas, The *āstika-darśanas* — are the *ṣaḍ-darśanas* — the six systems of Indian philosophy, i.e. Nyāya, Vaiśeṣika, Sāṁkhya, Yoga, Mīmāṁsā and Vedānta. Although Sāṁkhya[2] and Pūrva-Mīmāṁsā[3] do not accept the existence of *Īśvara*, nevertheless, they are considered as *āstika* systems, since they accept the Vedas as authority — *pramāṇa*.

The six *āstika-darśanas*, in fact, are of two types, (i) those which are directly based upon the Vedas (Mīmāṁsā and Vedānta), (ii) and those which are not directly based on the Vedas, but which accept their testimony, and try to show how their systems are harmonious with the Vedas (Nyāya, Vaiśeṣika, Sāṁkhya, Yoga).

Āyurveda : A treatise on medicine attributed to Dhanvantari. One of the four Upavedas attached to the *Ṛgveda*.

Iṣṭāpūrtam : The first word in this compound *iṣṭā* stands for the sacrifices offered to the gods, and the second *pūrtta* means altruistic deeds, acts of charity.

agnihotraṁ tapas-satyaṁ vedānāṁ ca-anupālanam ।
ātithyaṁ vaiśvadevaṁ ca iṣṭam-iti-abhidhīyate ॥

See *pūrta* and *dattam*.

Īśvara : Lord, Almighty, *Saguṇa Brahman*. He is *sarvajña*, *sarvaśaktimān* and *sarvavyāpī*, *abhinna-nimitta-upādāna-kāraṇa* of this *jagat*. Upaniṣad presents Him as *yato vā imāni bhūtāni*

---

2. In Sāṁkhya's 25-principle model of *sṛṣṭitattva*, *Īśvara* is not there.

3. Pūrva-Mīmāṁsā contends that performance of *karma* (rituals) creates its result; there is no need or scope of intervention by an external principle (*Īśvara*).

jāyante — *Ta.Up.* III.1. In Advaita Vedānta *Brahman* with the adjunct *māyā* is known as *Īśvara* — *māyā-avacchinna-caitanya.*

Udgātā : One of the four principal priests — *Ṛtviks* at a sacrifice, the one who chants the *Sāmaveda.*

Upamāna : Comparison or similarity is another valid means of knowledge — *sādṛśya-pramākaraṇam upamānam. Upamāna* is that *pramāṇa,* through which, an unknown object is known, with a known object based on same or comparable characteristics. *prasiddha-sādharmyāt sādhya-sādhanam-upamānam.*[4] The classic example is, a person going to the forest is told that a bison is like a cow.

Upanayana : Vedic initiation, that permits the brāhmaṇas, the kṣatriyas and the vaiśyas to study the Veda. *Upanayana* is a passport for admission into the Āryan community and its sacred literature. The theory was current that every man is born a śūdra, by performing *upanayana* he is called a *dvija* (twice-born), by studying the Vedas he becomes a *vipra,* and by knowing *Brahman,* he attains the status of a brāhmaṇa.

janmanā jāyate śūdraḥ saṁskārād dvija ucyate — etc.

Upaniṣad : Knowledge regarding the reality of *Brahman, brahma-vidyā. vedanto nāma-upaniṣat-pramāṇam* — *Ve.Sā.* 3. Concluding portions of the Vedas. Secret knowledge, mystical knowledge. *ya evaṁ veda, iti-upaniṣat* — *Mah.Up.* XXII.2.

Upāsanā : Meditation. *Ch.Up.* III.14.1 describes *upāsanā* as meditation on the *Saguṇa Brahman. Bṛ.Up.* I.5.16 states that 'by *upāsanā* one gains the world of gods — *deva.*'

Upāsanā-kāṇḍa : The Āraṇyaka portions are loosely termed as *upāsanā-kāṇḍa.*

Upavedas : There are four Upavedas attached to each of the four Vedas — (i) *Āyurveda,* the science of longevity to *Ṛgveda,* (ii) *Dhanurveda,* the discipline of archery to *Yajurveda,* (iii) *Gāndharvaveda,* the discipline of Music to *Sāmaveda,* and (iv) *Śastra-Śāstra,* discipline of arms, or *Sthāpatyaveda,* discipline of architecture to *Atharvaveda.*

4. *Ny.Sū.* I.1.6.

Upodhghāta : Introduction, preface, e.g. *Śāṅkarabhāṣya-Upodhghāta, Sāyaṇabhāṣya-Upodhghāta.*

Uttara-Mīmāṁsā : Or Vedānta, one of the six *āstika*-systems of Indian philosophy.

Ṛgveda : Or 'Hymn-Veda', or 'Veda of Praise', the most ancient sacred text consisting of 1,028 *sūkta*s — hymns (including the 11 Bālakhilya hymns) arranged in 10 *maṇḍala*s or 8 *aṣṭaka*s.

Ṛṣi : *ṛṣati jānāti iti ṛṣiḥ* — one who is a *mantra-draṣṭā,* — seer or composer of Vedic hymns.

Ṛṣikā : A female *ṛṣi*. There are 27 *ṛṣikā*s in the *Ṛgveda,* listed in the *Bṛhaddevatā* of Śaunaka.

Ṛtvik : Or *ṛtvij,* one who performs the sacrifices (*ij*) during the proper seasons (*ṛtu*), a Vedic priest. Usually the four priests are named viz. (i) Hotā — Ṛgvedic *ṛtvik,* (ii) Adhvaryu — Yajurvedic *ṛtvik,* (iii) Udgātā — Sāmavedic *ṛtvik,* (iv) and Brahmā — Atharvavedic *ṛtvik*. It is the *yajamāna*'s privilege to choose his *ṛtvik*s.

Kāṇḍas : Books.

Kaṇḍikā : Book/s. One *kāṇḍa* is divided into many *kaṇḍikā*s; as in the *Atharvaveda.*

Kalpa : Technical know-how of the Vedic rituals. *kalpyate samarthyate yāga-prayogaḥ atra* – 'that in which the practical method of *yāga* is propounded'. One of the six Vedāṅgas, — Śīkṣā, Kalpa, Vyākaraṇa, Nirukta, Chandas and Jyotiṣam. Kalpa-Sūtras are written by Āśvalāyana, Āpastamba, Baudhāyana etc.

Kalpa : Time equal to one day of Brahmā. One *kalpa* comprises four *yugas* — *Satyayuga, Tretāyuga, Dvāparayuga* and *Kaliyuga.* Current *kalpa* is *Śvetavarāha-kalpa.*

Kārikā : An independent exposition in verse-form based on a *mūlagrantha* relating to *darśana*, grammar, or a *kāvya*, e.g. (i) *Mūla-Madhyamaka-Kārikā* of Nāgārjuna, (ii) *Māṇḍūkya-Kārikā* of Gauḍapāda based on *Māṇḍūkya Upaniṣad,* (iii) *Sāṁkhya-Kārikā* based on *Sāṁkhya-Sūtra*s of Kapila.

Karma : Any action, where a free-will involved, and which creates *adṛṣṭa* — *pāpa* or *puṇya*. Action, consequence of action. In Hindu philosophy, *karma* is the law of retributive action, which brings back the individual, in this or a future life, pleasant or unpleasant situations for acts (*pāpa or puṇya*) committed.

***Karma* (types as per Veda)** : In the *karma-kāṇḍa* portion of the Veda various kinds of rituals are enumerated, (i) *vidhi* — injuncted rituals, e.g. *Agnihotra*, (ii) *pratiṣiddha* – prohibited actions, e.g. *kalañjaṁ na bhakṣet*, (iii) *kāmya-karma* is an optional rite, which is performed to fulfil any particular desire, e.g. *Putrakāmeṣṭi, Kārīri, Somayāga, Vājapeya, Rājasūya, Aśvamedha*, (iv) *nitya-karma* — daily obligatory rites, e.g. *Agnihotra*, (v) *naimittika-karma* — occasional rites as and when due are also obligatory rites, e.g. *Darśa-pūrṇamāsa*, (v) *prāyaścitta-karma* — rites for atonement of a wrong action, e.g. *Cāndrāyaṇa*.

Karma-kāṇḍa : Also known as Pūrva-Mīmāṁsā. Portion of the Veda, which inculcates the right attitude for performance of rituals and meditations for gaining *dharma*.

Khaṇḍa : Section.

Khila : Supplementary hymns.

Gṛhyasūtras : Scriptures setting down the rituals required to be performed in a home. Vedic rituals comprising domestic or life-cycle rites such as the ceremonies performed at birth, initiation, marriage, or death. 'Domestic rites', 'rites of passage', 'sacraments'. They require only one fire and one priest.

Grahaṇa : Apprehension, grasp.

Gāndharvaveda : The scripture expounding the science of music, attached to *Sāmaveda*. One of the four Upavedas.

Gāyatrī : A kind of metre used in the *Ṛgveda* having 24 (8x3 *pādas*) syllables, arranged in a triplets of eight syllables each.

Cārvāka : Or *Cāru-vāka*. Literally means sweet-tongued. The Indian Material School. Also known as Lokāyata. The philosophy of this *darśana* is — *yāvaj-jivet sukhaṁ jivet* — as long as one lives, may one live happily. It is a philosophy of hedonism. The classical authority to whom this *darśana* is traced is Bṛhaspati.

It accepts only two *puruṣārthas*, *artha* and *kāma* and rejects *dharma* and *mokṣa*. And it accepts only one *pramāṇa*, sensory perception.

Cāturmāsya : This comprises three seasonal sacrifices to be performed at four-monthly intervals, at the beginning of each of the three seasons: spring, rains, and autumn. They are Vaiśvadeva, Varuṇa-praghāsa, and Sākamedha. Sometimes one more, the Śunāsīrīya, is also added. Each of these marks the advent of a season. They are performed on the full-moon days of Phālguna or Caitra (February-March), Āṣāḍha (July), and Kārttika or Mārgaśira (November). *Puroḍāśa* and *caru* are the main offerings.

Codanā : Injunction, Mandate, Command. *Codanā-vākya*s are statements in the Veda, which are in the forms of injunctions for actions. Jaimini's second *sūtra* states — *codanā lakṣaṇārtho dharmaḥ*, meaning, '*Dharma* is that which, being desirable, is indicated by Vedic injunction.'

Chandas : 1. The Vedas. 2. Discipline of prosody and metres. One of the six Vedāṅgas, — Śīkṣā, Kalpa, Vyākaraṇa, Nirukta, Chandas and Jyotiṣa. There are many metres used in the *Ṛgveda*, list of which is given in *ṚV* X.130.4.

Jagat : The empirical world. In Advaita Vedānta, the *jagat* is visible in the shape of name and form — *vācārambhanaṁ vikāro nāmadheyam Ch.Up.* VI.1.4,5 and 6. Śaṅkara, the propounder of Advaita has presented the *jagat* as *mithyā* — *brahma satyaṁ jagat mithyā jīvo brahmaiva nāparaḥ*. Śaṅkara attributes a *vyāvahārika* reality to this *jagat*. Ontologically the *jagat* is *vyāvahārika mithyā* (*adhiṣṭhāna-ananyat* — not independently existent without *Brahman* which is ontologically *Satyam*).

Jagatī : A kind of metre used in the *Ṛgveda* having 48 syllables.

Jaimini : Author of the *Mīmāṁsā-Sūtra*, which are said to be composed in the third or second century BCE. Jaimini's purpose was to offer a systematic explanation of the Vedic rituals. For this, he elaborated upon methods of understanding the Veda, by pointing out a number of exegetical principles, which would be useful in establishing the purport of the Veda. His first *sūtra* runs as follows *athāto dharmajijñāsā* — 'Now, therefore, an enquiry into *dharma*'. He interpreted the essential meaning of the Veda to lie in its injunctive statements exhorting the performance of rituals.

Jīva : The individual Self, that transmigrates until the identity with *Brahman* is known, when further transmigration ceases. *Ve.Sa.* 13.

Jñana-kāṇḍa : The latter portion of the Vedas, which gives the knowledge of *Brahman*, also known as Uttara-Mīmāṁsā, or Upaniṣad or Vedānta.

Jyotiṣam : Discipline of astronomy. One of the six Vedāṅgas, — Śīkṣā, Kalpa, Vyākaraṇa, Nirūkta, Chandas and Jyotiṣam. A *Vaidika* must know *jyotiṣam* to arrive at the correct time to perform any Vedic ritual.

Ṭīkā : Line by line exposition of sentences and words of a *bhāṣyam*-commentary; e.g. Ānandagiri's (known as the *Ṭīkākāra) Ṭīkās on Śāṅkarabhāṣyam.* It is said nobody knows the mind of Śaṅkara better than Ānandagiri.

Ṭippaṇī : Further short notes on the *Ṭīkā*.

Tatpuruṣa : A class of compounds (*samasta-pada*), in which the last member is qualified by the first, without losing its grammatical independence. In forming the *tatpuruṣa* compound, the case endings of all members except the last are elided. For example *śāstrasya yoniḥ* — *śāstrayoniḥ* means *Brahman*.

Trayī : Threefold knowledge. The three Vedas — *Ṛgveda, Yajurveda* and *Sāmaveda* are *Vedatrayī*. The *Trayīvidyā* is especially concerned with the sacrificial procedure, which is conducted by the Hotā, Adhvaryu and the Udgātā by employing selections from the *Ṛgveda, Yajurveda* and *Sāmaveda* respectively. *Atharvaveda* is considered to be of a later origin.

Atharvaveda has no *mantra*s that can be used in a Vedic sacrifice.

Triṣṭubh : A kind of metre used in the *Ṛgveda* having 44 (11x4 *pāda*s) syllables, with eleven syllables per quarter (*pāda*).

Dakṣiṇā : 1. Priestly gift offered by the *yajamāna* (host) to the brāhmaṇas at the completion of a religious rite or sacrifice, sacrificial fee. 2. Any offering given as a gift of gratitude by a student, devotee, or individual to a teacher, *guru*, or a *mahātmā*, *sādhu*.

Darśana : From the root √*dṛś*, (lit.) looking at, viewing, perspective or point of view, and suggests that there are different ways of understanding and resolving human problems. Mādhavācārya in his *Sarva-Darśana-Saṁgraha* uses *darśana* for a system of thought.

Darśa-pūrṇamāsa : It is a *naimittika-karma* — obligatory rite (of the *iṣṭi* type), and is a basic form for many other sacrifices. It is begun on the first full moon day after the *Agnyādhāna*, and may be spread over two days. All the four principal priests participate in it.

Dattam : Protection of the weak, non-injury, charity, etc.

> *śaraṇāgata-santrāṇaṁ bhūtānāṁ cāpyahiṁsanaṁ* |
> *bahirvedi ca yad-dānaṁ dattaṁ ityabhidhīyate* ||

See *Iṣṭa* and *Pūrta*

Divya-prabandha : The divine compositions (of poems of verses). The collection of hymns of the Āḷvārs, which were composed in the Tamil language. It consists of four parts, each numbering a thousand hymns. Its main purport is devotion to the Lord. It is said to constitute the Tamil Veda, and is held by the Viśiṣṭa Advaitins to be as authoritative as the works of the *prasthāna-traya*. For this reason, Viśiṣṭa Advaita is referred to as Ubhaya-Vedānta.

Dvija : Twice born (from the root √*ja*=to be born + *dvi*=two); name for any member of the three upper *varṇa*s — brāhmaṇa, kṣatriya and vaiśya, who are eligible for Vedic initiation (*upanayana*), that permits them to study the Veda.

Dhanurveda : An Upaveda attached to *Yajurveda*, discipline of archery, a treatise derived from Viśvāmitra and Bhṛgu.

Dharmaśāstra : Code of morality. Various Dharmaśāstras are *Manu-Smṛti, Atri-Smṛti, Viṣṇu-Smṛti, Hārita-Smṛti, Yājñavalkya-Smṛti, Nārada-Smṛti, Gautama-Smṛti.*

Nāstika : Or heterodox systems in Indian philosophy are those who reject the authority/do not accept the Veda as a *pramāṇa*. The heterodox systems are, Cārvāka, Jainism and Buddhism.

Nighaṇṭu : First generation lexicon, A collection of Vedic words, numbering to 1340. *Nighaṇṭu* contains five chapters, the first three are called the Naighaṇṭuka-Kāṇḍa dealing with synonyms, the fourth Naigama-Kāṇḍa (or Aikapadika-Kāṇḍa) dealing with homonyms and the fifth the Daivata-Kāṇḍa dealing with deities. Devarāja Yajvan (twelfth century) has commented on *Nighaṇṭu*. Yāska's *Niruktam* is a commentary on the *Nighaṇṭu*. The *Nighaṇṭu* is probably not the production of a single individual, but the result of the united efforts of a whole generation, or perhaps of several generations. — Lakshman Saroop, *The Nighaṇṭu and the Nirukta*, p. 14. At one time at least 15-20 *Nighaṇṭu* were there.

Nirukta : Lexicon, science of etymology (*nirvacana-śāstra*) (Gr. *etymos*=truth, *logos*=science; science of derivation and meaning of words), authored by Yāska. It has 12 chapters, out of which 11 chapters are commentary on the five chapters of *Nighaṇṭu*. *Nirukta* contains etymology (*nirvacanam*) of 1,298 words. There are two more chapters in *Nirukta* (thus totalling 14), which are considered as *pariśiṣṭa*.

Niruḍha-paśubandha : An obligatory rite, to be performed once in six months, or once in a year. It involves the immolation of an animal, a he-goat. Indra, Agni, Sūrya and Prajāpati are the deities to be appeased. Six priests are required for this.

Nirvacanam : Utterance, pronunciation, 2. etymology of a word.

Nyāya : A system of logic. Name of one of the six *āstika* systems of

Indian philosophy, which evolved a complex system of philosophical argumentation through which it analysed both physical and meta-physical subjects. The *Nyāya-Sūtra* (containing 530 *sūtras*) is attributed to Gautama, its *vārttikakāra* is Udyotakara, and *bhāṣyakāra* is Vatsyāyana. Its most renowned method is the syllogism or *vyāpti*.

Padas : Words.

Pāṇini : The author of *Aṣṭādhyāyī*, the earliest extant standard Sanskrit grammar. The *Aṣṭādhyāyī* consists of approximately 4000 *sūtras*, and is divided into eight chapters, each of four sections. The work enumerates the technical terms used in grammar, the rules for their interpretation and application.

Paṅkti : A Vedic metre consisting of eight syllables in five *pādas* (8x5 *pādas*).

Pāriśeṣa : Remainder, remnant.

Pariśiṣṭa : (lit.) Leftover, after any classification/division.

Piśāca : Demon, ogre, imp, devil, vampire (from the root √*piś* = 'to crave for meat'). A class of demons, those whose aims and ambitions have been destroyed through immoral conduct, possibly so called either for their fondness for eating raw meat along with blood, or for their yellowish appearance. In the Vedas they are mentioned (*ŚYV* XXX.8) along with *asuras* and *rākṣasas*.

Prapāṭhaka : Chapter.

Pramāṇa : It is derived from the root √*mā* — to measure, with the prefix *pra* meaning valid. *Pramāṇa* means — *pramāyāḥ karaṇam, pramāṇam*. *Pramā* means 'knowing an object as it is'. A valid means of knowledge. Advaita Vedānta accepts six *pramāṇas*. These are — (i) *pratyakṣa* — direct or sensory perception, (ii) *anumāna* — inference, (iii) *arthāpatti* — presumption, (iv) *upamāna* — comparison, (v) *anupalabdhi* — non-cognition, and (vi) *śabda* — Śruti statements.

Pratyakṣam : Knowledge gained through direct perception a *pramāṇam*. Sense-perception. One of the six *pramāṇas*, accepted by Advaita Vedānta. According to Nyāya, *pratyakṣa* is knowledge generated by sense-object contact. Gautama has defined *pratyakṣa* as *indriyārtha-sannikarṣajanyaṁ jñānamakaṁ pratyakṣam.*

Perception is a direct means of knowledge and does not depend upon any other means of attaining knowledge. It is to be noted here that *anumāna, arthāpatti, upamāna* and *śabda,* depend upon *pratyakṣa,* the *mūla-pramāṇam.*

Pratyavāya : A concept of *pāpa,* by an act of omission — *akaraṇe pratyavāya.* This concept is not accepted by the Advaita Vedāntins.

Prayojanam : The purpose/objective. The second essential factor of *anubandha-catuṣṭaya.* The *prayojanam* of the *karmakāṇḍa* portion of the Vedas is to fulfil various desires of a large number of people. In contrast, the *prayojanam* of the *jñāna-kāṇḍa* portion (that contains the Upaniṣads) is *mokṣa* — freedom from the sense of limitation.

Puṇya : Virtuous action, kārmic good actions. Good *karma* created by good thoughts, words, actions, generated by giving, kindness and practice of *dharma.*

Purāṇa : Secondary religious literature after Śruti, Smṛti, and Itihāsa. These traditionally deal with five topics, (i) *sarga* — creation, (ii) *pratisarga* — dissolution, (iii) *vaṁśa* — lineage, (iv) *manvantarāṇi* — epochs, and (v) *vaṁśānucaritam* — the legends of future lineage.

The eighteen major Purāṇas are divided into three categories: (I) Six Vaiṣṇava-Purāṇas (i) *Viṣṇu,* (ii) *Bhāgavata,* (iii) *Padma,* (iv) *Nāradīya,* (v) *Garuḍa,* (vi) *Varāha;* (II) Six Brahma-Purāṇas, (i) *Brahma,* (ii) *Brahmavaivarta,* (iii) *Bhaviṣya* (iv) *Brahmānada,* (v) *Vāmana,* (vi) *Mārkeṇḍeya;* and (III) Six Śaiva-Purāṇas — (i) *Śiva,* (ii) *Matsya,* (iii) *Liṅga,* (iv) *Skanda,* (v) *Agni* and (vi) *Kūrma.* There are 18 Upa-Purāṇas.

Pūrta-karma : Altruistic deeds, acts of outreaching activities.

vāpī kūpa-taḍākādi devatāyatanāni ca ।
annapradānam ārāmaḥ pūrtam iti abhidhīyate ।।

See *iṣṭā-pūrta* and *dattam*

Puruṣārtha : (lit.) 'what is desired by a person'. General tendencies of human nature. This refers to the four pursuits of *artha* — securities, *kāma* — pleasure, *dharma* and *mokṣa* — liberation.

Pūrva-Mīmāṁsā : Or Mīmāṁsā. One of the six *āstika*-systems of Indian philosophy. (lit.) enquiry/investigation and correct interpretation of the Vedas. The Veda is described as a Mīmāṁsā-Śāstra, since both portions of the Veda require analysis. However, the term is often used to refer to the earlier section of the Vedas, and is accepted as a shortened term for the Pūrva-Mīmāṁsā *darśana*. Interestingly, Pūrva-Mīmāṁsā does not accept *Īśvara*.

Bṛhaddevatā : Authored by Śaunaka is an index of the 'many gods', a much more extensive work than any other *anukramaṇīs*. It contains about 1,200 *śloka*s in *anuṣṭubh*, occasionally interspersed with *triṣṭubh*s. It is divided into eight *adhyāya*s corresponding to the eight *aṣṭaka*s of the *Ṛgveda*. Following the order of the *Ṛgveda*, its main object is to state the deity for each verse. A peculiarity of this work is that it refers to a number of supplementary hymns (*khila*s) which do not form part of the canonical text of the *Ṛgveda*.

Bṛhatī : A kind of metre used in the *Ṛgveda* having 36 (9x4 *pāda*s) syllables, with nine syllables per quarter (*pāda*).

Bahuvrīhi : (lit.) possessing much rice; name of an attributive/ adjectival compound (*samasta-pada*) that consists of two or more nouns in apposition to each other, but refers to another word/substantive outside the compound — the final compound member. Examples are (i) *Pitāmbaraḥ*, referring to Kṛṣṇa, (ii) *Mahābāhuḥ* — one whose arm is mighty, say Arjuna or Lord Rāma.

Bālakhilya : Thumb-size deities born out of Brahmā's hair, 60,000 in number.

Brahmā : *Saguṇa Brahman*, Caturmukha Brahmā, creator of this *jagat*.

Brahmā : One of the four principal Vedic Priests — *ṛtvik*s (other three being Hotā, Adhvaryu and Udgātā). The Brahmā is supposed to be the most learned and is supposed to supervise the other three *ṛtvik*s in any sacrifice and correct mistakes, if any.

Brāhmaṇa : A specific portion of each of the four Vedas, containing is explanatory treatise on the *mantras*, for the performance of sacrificial rites, rules for the use of *mantra*s-hymns and explanation and illustrations of them.

Bhāṣya : A commentary on the *mūlagrantha*. An elaboration of the cryptic or aphoristic statements of the original text, and the meaning of the words contained therein.

sūtrārtho varṇyate yatra vākyeiḥ sūtrānusāribhiḥ |
svapadāni ca varṇyante bhāṣyaṁ bhāṣyavido viduḥ ||[5]

Bhāṣyakāra : Commentator (from the root √*kṛ* — to do + *bhāṣya*=commentary). The most well-known *bhāṣyakāra*s are Śabarswāmi for *Mīmāṁsā-Sūtras*, Śaṅkara for Advaita Vedānta, Rāmānuja for Viśiṣṭādvaita, and Madhvācārya for Dvaita, Durgācārya for *Nirukta*.

Patañjali is called *mahābhāṣyakāra*. Next earliest commentary in *Mahābhāṣya* style was seen after around 300 years by Śabarswāmi who followed Patañjali's style, was seen again after 500 years in Śaṅkara.

Bhūḥ : The earth, the material world.

Bhuvaḥ : The mid-region.

Maṇḍala : Books — The *Ṛgveda* has two types of division/ nomenclature — *maṇḍala* system and *aṣṭaka* system. As per the *maṇḍala* system, *Ṛgveda* is divided into 10 *maṇḍalas* containing 1,028 *sūkta*s — Hymns (inclusive of the 11 *bālakhilya* Hymns).

Mahābhārata : One of the two great epics of India. Originally titled *Jaya*, then *Bhārata*. Consists of 106,000 *śloka*s-couplets divided into 12 books (*parva*s) describing the ancient history of India up to the time of appearance of Kṛṣṇa, 5,000 years ago. It is the longest poem in the world containing legendary and philosophical material worked into and around a central

5. Cf. Introduction to commentary on *Mahābhāṣya*.

heroic narrative, which portrays the struggle between two Bhārata families: the Kauravas and the Pāṇḍavas. Written by Vyāsa, it existed in various forms for well over 2,000 years and is called the fifth Veda. Its most famous text is the *Bhagavad-Gītā*.

Mantra : (lit.) a tool for the mind. Sacred sound. In the Vedic tradition, a sound from the Vedas, repeated either orally or mentally and used as an aid in bringing concentration to the mind. The most well-known *mantra* is *oṁ*. Chanting *mantra* is one of the most common forms of *sādhanā* (spiritual practice).

Manu : Father of the human race, identified with Prajāpati. However, the name Manu is especially applied to 14 successive mythical progenitors and sovereigns of the earth. The first Manu was Svayaṁbhu Manu. The 7th Manu, known as Vaivasvat Manu is regarded the ancestor of the present race of humans.

Mīmāṁsā : See Pūrva-Mīmāṁsā.

Mīmāṁsaka : A follower of the Pūrva-Mīmāṁsā, say Kumārila Bhaṭṭa, and Prabhākara Miśra.

Yāga : Vedic fire-ritual/sacrifice.

Yajamāna : The sacrificer. The chief person in a sacrifice. The *puṇya/apūrva* result of the sacrifice goes to him. The performing priest/s receive *dakṣiṇā* for their services rendered.

Yajña : Religious offering or ritual, sacrifice.

Yajurveda : One of the four Vedas, where the collection of the *mantras* are in prose-form. *Yajurveda* has two divisions — *Śukla-Yajurveda*, and, *Kṛṣṇa-Yajurveda* — Its subject matter is liturgy, rituals, sacrifices and how to perform the same.

Yajus : A sacrificial prayer or formula, the body of sacred *mantras* in prose chanted at Vedic fire-sacrifice.

Yama : Twin, one of a pair. Also name of the god of death. He is the son of Vivasvat (the Sun) and Saraṇyu, the daughter of Tvaṣṭṛ. His twin sister is Yamī.

Yāska : The earliest lexicographer, author of *Nirukta* (commentary on the difficult Vedic words contained in the lists called *Nighaṇṭu*). Yāska lived before Pāṇini.

Yoga : One of the six *āstika* (orthodox) Indian philosophical systems. Also known as 'Sa-īśvara Sāṁkhya'. Codified by Patañjali in his *Yogasūtra* containing 194 *sūtras*.

Yūpa : An octagonal wooden post, to which the animal to be sacrificed is tied.

Vaṁśa-maṇḍala : Family-books. *Maṇḍala*s II-VII of the *R̥gveda* are termed as *vaṁśa-maṇḍala* by the Western scholars, since all the *sūkta*s contained therein are seen by a particular *r̥ṣi* and/ or his descendants.

Vaiśeṣika : One of the six *āstika* systems of Indian philosophy, which maintains that the creation originated through the combination of minute 'atoms' — *aṇu*. The word *Vaiśeṣika* is derived from *viśeṣa*, which means 'difference' or 'peculiarity'. This school suggests that diversity rather than unity, is the essence of creation. Kaṇāda is said to have written the *Vaiśeṣika-Sūtra*, that contains 570 *sūtra*s.

Vājapeya : This is performed by one, desiring for unlimited dominion. This *yāga* has many special features. The number 17 is all-important. For instance, 17 animals are sacrificed, 17 objects are distributed as fees, and it lasts for 17 days. A chariot race in which the *yajamāna* also takes part, and is always helped to win, is another interesting feature of this sacrifice.

Vedāṅga : Texts auxillary to the Vedas, which assist in explaining the meaning of the Vedas. There are six of them — Śikṣā (pronunciation), Kalpa (liturgy), Chandas (prosody), Jyotiṣam (astronomy), Vyākaraṇam (grammar), Niruktam (lexicon).

> *chandaḥ pādau vedasya, hastau kalpo'tha paṭhyate* ǀ
> *jyotiṣam-ayanaṁ cakṣuḥ niruktam srotram ucyate* ǀǀ
> *sikṣaṁ ghrānaṁ tu vedasya mukhaṁ vyākaraṇaṁ smr̥tam* ǀ
> *tasmāt sāṅgam-adhiṣṭyaiva brahmaloke mahīyate* ǀǀ
> — *Pā.Si.* 41-42.

Patañjali says *brāhmaṇo niskāraṇaṁ ṣadaṅga vedo adhyeta* —

A brāhmaṇa should study the Vedas along with the six limbs even without any purpose (i.e. to maintain them for posterity).

Vedānta : (lit.) concluding portions of the Veda. Known as Upaniṣad. Vedāntins consider this as the essence of the Vedas. Name of *darśana* that is directed to the analysis of the Upaniṣads. According to *Ve.Sā*. 'Vedānta is a valid means of knowledge, the *Śārīraka-Sūtras* and other books that help in the elucidation of its meaning'.

Vedas : (lit.) knowledge. Collections of scriptures, which were envisioned/channelled by the *ṛṣis*. From the root √*vid* – to know, (lit.) knowledge. This vast body of literature has been compiled into four books – *Ṛk, Yajus, Sāma* and *Atharva*. Each of them further divided into four portions/sections — (i) Saṁhitā, (ii) Brāhmaṇa, (iii) Āraṇyaka, (iv) Upaniṣad. (*Atharvaveda* does not have Āraṇyaka).

Viṣaya : The subject matter. The second essential factor of *anubandha-catuṣṭaya*. In Vedānta, the subject matter is *mokṣa* — freedom, whereas in the Vedas, the subject matter is all the other three pursuits — *dharma, artha* and *kāma*.

Vyākaraṇam : Grammar, one of the six *Vedāṅga*s — limbs of the Vedas.

Vyutpatti : Etymological meaning; of *śuśruṣā* is *śrotum icchā* — desire to listen (to the *śāstra*).

Rājasūya : It is a very elaborate *yāga* extending over two years, and comprising a number of *iṣṭis*, and Soma sacrifices. It can be performed only by very powerful kings or emperors, as it involves a heavy fee of 240,000 cows to the priests. The *abhiṣecanīya* rite involving *abhiṣeka* (sprinkling of sacred water) of the *yajamāna* king is considered to be its objective.

Rākṣasas : Demons, evil-minded beings, who do not perform *yajña*, and partake the discarded objects of the *yajña*.

Ruḍhi : Conventional/popular meaning; e.g. *śuśruṣā* means *śrotum icchā* — a desire to listen. Popular meaning is to serve the *guru*/elders.

Lipikāra/Libikāra : A scribe.

Śabda-pramāṇa : *Śabda* is an independent and valid means of knowledge, a *pramāṇa* accepted by all the six *āstika* systems of Indian philosophy. *Śabda*, to all intents and purposes remains an external *pramāṇa*. Hence it requires *śraddhā*.

Śākhā : Recension, branch.

Śāstra : Sacred scriptures.

Śatapatha : A 100 paths, a 100 chapters.

Śikṣā : The discipline of pronunciation of Vedic texts and *sandhiḥ*. Śikṣā is one of the six *Vedāṅgas*.

Śrauta : Vedic.

Śrauta-Sūtras : Śrauta-Sūtras provide systematic instructions about various sacrifices. They are functional manuals for the priests, and give the *modus operandi* of various rites in detail. Of these extant works, the following are considered as ancient and authoritative. Āpastamba, Āśvalāyana, Baudhāyana, Bhāradvāja, Kātyāyana, and Satyāśāḍha Śrauta-Sūtras.

Śruti : Derived from the root √*śru* — to hear, literally what is heard. Scriptures or revelations whose origin cannot be traced to any mortal being. It is the source of knowledge in matters transcending sensory perceptions (*atīndriya-viṣaya*). The Vedas are referred to as Śruti. *Śabda-pramāṇa* indicates the authority of intuition that was regarded as embodied in the Vedic texts, the Śrutis. Indian philosophers lay down certain conditions before a reference is made to a revealed text. They are: (i) the revealed truth should be extra-empirical (*anadhigata*), (ii) it should not be contradicted by other *pramāṇa* (*abādhita*), (iii) the reason should foreshadow what revelation states.

In view of the majority of Indian philosophical systems, reason by itself is incapable of discerning the whole truth. It may often lead to two or more plausible conclusions, and without the aid of revelation, it is impossible to avoid sceptism.

Saṁbandha : Connection — the relation between the text and the purpose (*prayojanam*). The second essential factor of *anubandha-catuṣṭaya*.

(i) Śāstra & Subject Matter = *Pratipādaka-pratipādya*

(ii) Subject matter & Knowledge = *Sādhana-Sādhya* or *pramāṇa prameya*.

Saṁhitā : The Saṁhitā portion contains the *mantras*. The *mantras* are hymns, prayers. These Saṁhitā are five — *Ṛk*, *Śukla-Yajus*, *Kṛṣṇa-Yajus*, *Sāma* and *Atharva*.

Saṁvāda-Sūktam : Dialogue-hymns. There are 20 dialogue hymns in the *Ṛgveda*. The seed/idea of a drama is said to have been taken from one of the dialogue-hymns — i.e. Kālidāsa's *Vikramorvaśīyam* is said to have been written, the source being *Purūravā-Urvaśī-Saṁvāda RV* X.95.

Sāṁkhya : One of the six *āstika*-systems of Indian philosophy that posits that *pradhāna/prakṛti* is the creator of this *jagat*. Does not accept *Īśvara*.

Sāman : A text or verse from the *Sāmaveda*.

Sāmaveda : 'Veda of Chants', one of the four Vedas. It contains a number of hymns, mostly borrowed from the *Ṛgveda*. These set to tune, are chanted by the Sāmavedic priest Udgātā at Soma sacrifices.

Saptarṣi : The seven great *ṛṣis*. The list of *saptarṣis* differs in the Vedic texts. The earliest list is in *Ja.Br.* II.218-221 listing — Vasiṣṭha, Bharadvāja, Jamadagni, Gotama, Atri, Viśvamitra and Agastya. The next list is in *Bṛ.Up* II.2.6 listing — Gautama, Bharadvāja, Viśvāmitra, Jamadagni, Vasiṣṭha, Kaśyapa and Atri. The *Go.Br.* I.2.8 lists — Vasiṣṭha, Viśvāmitra, Jamadagni, Gautama, Bharadvāja, Guṅgu, Agastya and Kaśyapa.

The list of *saptarṣis* also differs for each *manvantara*. The listed are *saptarṣis* for the current seventh *manvantara*, i.e. *Śveta-Varāha-Kalpa* are — Gautama, Bharadvāja, Viśvāmitra, Jamadagni, Vasistha, Kaśyapa and Atri (as listed in *Go.Br.* I.2.8).

Smṛti : (lit.) 'what is remembered'. From the root √smṛ – to remember. Its authority is traced, directly or indirectly, to Śruti or revelation. *Bhagavd-Gītā*, various Dharmaśāstras and all the 18 Purāṇas are Smṛti literature.

Soma : Name of a medicinal plant and its juice used in the earliest Vedic sacrifices as offering and inspiration. Probably *sarcostema viminalis* or *asclepias acida.*

Sūkta : Literally *su-uktam,* meaning well-said, Ṛgvedic hymn/s. There are 1,028 *sūktas* in the *Ṛgveda.*

Sūtra : Aphorism. Derived from the root √*siv* — to sew, and literally means a thread. According to tradition, a *sūtra* should enjoy the following characteristics,

> *alpākṣaram asandigdhaṁ sāravad-viśvatomukham* ।
> *astobham-anavadyaṁ ca sūtraṁ sūtravido viduḥ* ।।

(i) *alpākṣaram* — composed of minimum number of letters, (ii) *asandigdham* — free from doubts, clear, (iii) *sāravat* — endowed with meaning, (iv) *viśvatomukham* — universally applicable, (v) *astobham* — free from embellishment, (vi) *anavadyam* — free from grammatical error.

This definition is from *Skanda Purāṇa* and has been cited by Madhva in his *Madhvāddhṛtam.* I.1.1.

Svataḥ-prāmāṇyam : Self-validity, intrinsic validity. In this, a means of knowledge is said to be completely capable of revealing those objects, which fall within its scope without requiring the corroboration by any other means of knowledge for verification. *Svataḥ-prāmāṇyam* is attributed to Śruti-*pramāṇa,* although all other five *prāmāṇa* are also *svataḥ-pramāṇa.*

Hotā : One of the four principal priests (other three are Adhvaryu, Udgātā and Brahmā) at a sacrifice who recites the hymns of the *Ṛgveda.*

Select Bibliography

Primary Sources

Agrawala, Vasudeva Sharan, *The Cultural Heritage of India,* vol. I, Chapter 16, Yāska and Pāṇini, The Ramakrishna Mission, Institute of Culture, Calcutta, 2nd edn. (Revised and Enlarged) rpt. 2003.

Aurobindo, Sri, *Hymns to the Mystic Fire,* Sri Aurobindo Ashram, Pondicherry, 1970.

Aurobindo, Sri, *The Life Divine,* Sri Aurobindo Ashram, Pondicherry, 1970.

Aurobindo, Sri, *The Secret of the Veda,* Sri Aurobindo Ashram, Pondicherry, 1st edn. 1956, 5th Impression 2005.

Bali, Saraswati, *Sayana's Upodhghata to the Taittirīya Saṁhitā and The Ṛgveda Saṁhitā,* Pratibha Prakashan, Delhi.

Basham, A., *The Wonder That was India,* 3rd rev. edn. 1967, Fortieth Impression 2003, Rupa & Co., New Delhi.

Bhate, Saroja, *Pāṇini,* Sahitya Akademi, New Delhi, 2002.

Bhise, Usha R., *The Khila-Sūktas of the Ṛgveda. A Study,* BORI, Poona, 1995.

Bloomfield, M., Sacred Books of the East, vol. 42 *Hymns of the Atharvaveda,* rpt. Motilal Banarsidass, Delhi, 2008.

Bronkhorst, Johannes, *From Pāṇini to Patañjali: The Search for Linearity,* BORI, Pune, 2004.

Cardona, George, *Pāṇini, His Works and its Traditions,* vol. I, 2nd edn., Revised and Enlarged, Motilal Banarsidass, Delhi, 1997.

Chand, Devi, *The Samaveda* (tr.) 1961, edn. 2004, Munshiram Manoharlal, New Delhi.

Chand, Devi, *The Yajurveda* (tr.) 1964, edn. 2004, Munshiram Manoharlal, New Delhi.

Chand, Devi, *The Atharvaveda* (tr.) 1982, Munshiram Manoharlal, New Delhi.

Chauhan, D.V., *Understanding Ṛgveda*, 1985, BORI, Poona.

Danino, Michel & Sujata Nahar, *The Invasion that Never Was*, 2nd edn., Revised and Enlarged 2001, The Mother's Institute of Research, Delhi and Mira Aditi, Mysore.

Danino, Michel, *The Lost River: On the Trail of the Sarasvati*, Penguin Books India, 2010.

Danino, Michel, *Indian Culture and India's Future*, D.K. Printworld (P) Ltd., New Delhi, first published in India, 2011.

Eggeling, Julius, Sacred Books of the East, vol. 12: *The Śatapatha Brāhmaṇa*, 1882, rpt., Motilal Banarsidass, Delhi, 2008.

Feuerstein, George, Subhash Kak and David Frawley, *In Search of the Cradle of Civilisation*, Quest Books, Wheraton, USA, 1995, Indian Edition, Motilal Banarsidass, Delhi, Revised and rpt. 2008.

Frawley, David, *Gods, Sages and Kings: Vedic Secrets of Ancient Civilisation*, Motilal Banarsidass, Delhi, Indian Edition, rpt., 2003.

Griffith, Ralph T.H. (tr.), *The Hymns of Ṛgveda*, 2 vols., Low Price Editions, Delhi, 1995.

Griffith, Ralph T.H. (tr.), *The Hymns of the Atharvaveda*, Republished Munshiram Manoharlal, New Delhi, 2002.

Jagannathan, Sakuntala, *Hinduism: An Introduction*, Vakils, Feffer and Simons Pvt. Ltd., Mumbai, 2005.

Kantikar, V.P. and W. Owen Cole, *Hinduism*, Hodder Education, London, 2003.

Kak, Subhash, *The Astronomical Code of the Ṛgveda*, Aditya Prakashan, New Delhi, 1994.

Kapoor, Kapil, & Avadhesh Kumar Singh (eds.), *Indian Knowledge Systems*, vols. 1 and 2, D.K. Printworld, New Delhi, 2005.

Kashyap, R.L., *In Search of the Ṛgveda, First 121 Sūktas*, Sri Aurobindo Kapali Sastry Institute of Vedic Culture, Bangalore, 2003.

Kashyap, R.L. (ed.), *Ṛgveda Mantra Saṁhita*, Sri Aurobindo Kapali Sastry Institute of Vedic Culture, Bangalore, 2003.

Keith, A.B., *A History of Sanskrit Literature*, Oxford 1928, Motilal Banarsidass, Delhi, rpt. 1993, 2010.

Keith, A.B., *The Religion and Philosophy of the Vedas and Upanisads*.

Krishna, Chaitanya, *A Profile of Indian Culture*, Clarion Books, Delhi, 2nd edn., 1987.

Macdonell, A.A. & A.B. Keith, *Vedic Index of Names and Subjects*, 2 vols., 1912, Motilal Banarsidass, Delhi, rpt. 1958-2007.

Macdonell, A.A., *A Vedic Reader for Students*, First Published: England, 1917, Motilal Banarsidass, rpt. 2006.

———, *A Vedic Grammar for Students*, First Indian Edition: Delhi 1993, Motilal Banarsidass rpt. 2010.

Macdonell, A.A., *A History of Sanskrit Literature*, Motilal Banarsidass, Delhi.

Müller, F. Max, *India: What It Can Teach Us?*, Vishv Books, New Delhi.

Müller, F. Max and H. Oldenberg, *Vedic Hymns*, Sacred Books of the East, vol. 46, Motilal Banarsidass, Delhi, rpt., 2008.

Müller, F. Max and H. Oldenberg, *Vedic Hymns*, vols. 32 & 46, Sacred Books of the East, vol. 32: rpt., Motilal Banarsidass, Delhi, 2008.

Pandey, Rajbali, *Hindu Samskaras*, Motilal Banarsidass, Delhi, 2nd Revised edn., 1969, rpt., 1998.

Peterson, Peter, *Hymns from the Ṛgveda*, BORI, Poona, 1974.

———, *A Second Selection of Hymns from the Ṛgveda*, BORI, Poona, 1972.

Reddy, V. Manmohan, *Interpretations of Vedas: Swami Dayananda and Sri Aurobindo*. The Mother's Integral School, Hyderabad, First edn. 2007.

Saraswati, Chandrashekharendra Swami, *Hindu Dharma: The Universal Way of Life*, Bharatiya Vidya Bhavan, Mumbai, Fourth edn., 2000.

Saraswati, Atmaprajnananda Swamini, *Daśaśānti*, Arsha Vidya Vikas Kendra, Bhubaneswar, 2008.

Saraswati, Atmaprajnananda Swamini, *Rūpasiddhi*, Arsha Vidya Vikas Kendra, Bhubaneswar, 2008.

Saraswati, Atmaprajnananda Swamini, *Ṛṣikās of the Ṛgveda*, D.K. Printworld, New Delhi, 2012.

Saraswati, Atmaprajnananda Swamini, *Vision of Vedānta as Reflected in Taittirīyopaniṣad with Special Reference to Śāṅkara-Bhāṣya*, Ph.D Thesis, forthcoming.

Sarup, Lakshman, *The Nighantu and The Nirukta*, 1st Indian edn., 1920-27, Motilal Banarsidass, Delhi, rpt., 2002.

Schmidt, Hanns-Peter, *Some Womens' Rites and Rights in the Veda*, BORI, Poona, 1987.

Shende, N.J., *The Religion and Philosophy of the Athavaveda*, BORI, Poona, 1952 edn., rpt., 1985.

Srinivasacharya, K.S. *An Introduction to the Vedas*, The Alliance Company, Madras, First Impression 1999.

Talageri, Shrikant G., *The Ṛgveda: A Historical Analysis*, Aditya Prakashan, New Delhi, First Publication 2000.

Tilak, B.G., *The Orion, or Researches into the Antiquity of the Vedas*, Tilak Brothers, Poona, 1893.

Waterstone, Richard, *India: The Cultural Companion*, Duncan Baird Publishers, London, 2002.

Whitney, William Dwight (tr.), *Atharvaveda Saṁhitā*, 2 vols., Motilal Banarsidass, Delhi, rpt., 2001.

Winternitz, M., S. Ketkar (tr.), A *History of Indian Literature (1927-33)*, 2 vols., Munshiram Manoharlal, New Delhi, 3rd edn., 1991.

Secondary Sources

http://en.wikipedia.org/wiki/Bronze_Age_India

http://en.wikipedia.org/wiki/ List_of_archaeological_periods

http://wikipedia.org/wiki/Iron_Age_India

www.astrojyoti.com

http://en.wikipedia.org/wiki/Sruti

http://en.wikipedia.org.wiki/Saptarshi

http://en.wikipedia.org/wiki/Periodization of the Indus Valley Civilization

http://en.wikipedia.org.wiki/Brahmanas

www.advaita-vedanta.org – Advaita-I A Brief Introduction to Purva-Mimamsa-3 (The Eternity of All Words)

www.advaita-vedanta.org – Advaita-I A Brief Introduction to Purva-Mimamsa-4 (In Defense of the Vedas)

www.advaita-vedanta.org – Advaita-I A Brief Introduction to Purva-Mimamsa-8 (Miscellaneous Topics, Conclusion)

www.mimamsa.org/authors/prabhakara mishra

http://hinduism.about.com/od/scriptures/a/ rigveda.htm

http://vishalagarwal.voiceofdharma.com/ uttamapatala.html

Index